77
ONE-WEEKEND
WOODWORKING
PROJECTS

77
ONE-WEEKEND
WOODWORKING
PROJECTS

PERCY W. BLANDFORD

TAB BOOKS
Blue Ridge Summit, PA

FIRST EDITION
EIGHTH PRINTING

© 1987 by **TAB Books**.
TAB Books is a division of McGraw-Hill, Inc.

Library of Congress Cataloging-in-Publication Data

Blandford, Percy W.
    77 one-weekend woodworking projects.

    Includes index.
    1. Furniture making—Amateurs' manuals.   2. Woodwork—
Amateurs' manuals.   I. Title.   II. Title: Seventy seven
one-weekend woodworking projects.
TT195.B586   1987   684'.08   87-1963
ISBN 0-8306-0774-9
ISBN 0-8306-2774-X (pbk.)

TAB Books offers software for sale. For information and a catalog, please contact
TAB Software Department, Blue Ridge Summit, PA 17294-0850.

Contents

Introduction

Amateur woodworkers are always looking for projects on which to exercise their skill. Usually they have most time to devote to the hobby at weekends, so projects that can be completed in one weekend have special appeal, and that is what this book is all about.

Of course, one person's capacity for work differs from another's. There is also the question of available time. One person might want to work during all his waking time, while another will regard a few hours as the extent of his weekend work. Available equipment will also affect what can be produced in a given time. With the same skill, much more can be done in a shop equipped with many power tools than with just a few hand tools and a table as a bench.

It is difficult to compromise in planning projects. No one is an average craftsman, so this book is an attempt to provide something for everyone, although the time available has been assumed to be about twelve hours. There are some pieces of furniture that would take a skilled woodworker with plenty of hand and power tools all this time

to make to a high standard. Beginning woodworkers with little equipment might need several weekends to achieve the same results, even if they had the skill. They would be better advised to choose one of the many simple projects, which should be easy to make in a weekend with only the most basic tool kit. As more tools are acquired and more skill gained through practice, they should be able to move on to more skilled work.

In any case, it is assumed that the necessary materials are ready. You cannot allow visits to the lumber yard and hardware store as part of the constructional time. Plan ahead, so you will not be held up for a part. Try to visualize every step and know what you will have to do. You might spend odd times during the week sharpening edge tools.

The book is divided into chapters to provide convenient groupings, but some of the projects have many applications in and out of the home. Do not assume, for instance, that the only items applicable to the bedroom are in Chapter 7. Some projects described in other chapters might be of use in your bedroom, while some bedroom furniture could find a place in other rooms.

All projects have dimensioned drawings and materials lists. Most things could be made to other sizes. If you cut your own wood, work to the given sections, if possible. If you buy wood already planed, it may be sold as the size before planing and will actually be undersize. In many cases that will not matter, but you will have to allow for 1 inch being only 7/8 inch, or whatever the size, when marking out joints or assemblies. If a part has to provide strength, it would be unwise to make it with a section much smaller than specified.

Unless marked otherwise, all sizes are in inches. Widths and thicknesses specified are actual sizes, but lengths mostly allow a little extra for cutting.

Some plywood now available is in metric thicknesses. As a guide: 6 mm is just under 1/4 inch, 8 mm can be regarded as 5/16 inch, 9 mm is about 3/8 inch, 12 mm is just under 1/2 inch.

Have many pleasant woodworking weekends.

Chapter 1

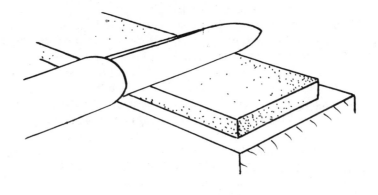

Overview

This is not a book on woodworking techniques. The aim is not to show you how to use your tools or how to make joints, but to give you ideas for things to make. However, we all learn as we tackle new projects and no woodworking enthusiast can ever say that he knows it all or that his manual dexterity with tools has reached perfection. We increase our knowledge and skill with every piece of woodwork we complete.

The author assumes that the reader has some tools and has acquired enough skill to use them efficiently. The tool kit need not be extensive and the shop might be no more than a bench in the corner of the garage. It is possible to make most projects described in this book entirely with hand tools. Power tools are always worth having, mainly because they take the hard work out of some tasks and because they can produce mechanical accuracy on such routine tasks as cutting wood to size or leveling surfaces. For the more detailed work of marking and fitting parts together, hand work with a little skill might be better and more

satisfying. To use power tools for just about every operation usually calls for modified designs, which result in look-alike mass-production furniture. The projects described in this book are individual pieces of craftsmanship; choose the best methods to suit the tools and equipment you have.

If you want to make something in a weekend or in a few hours at some other time, you should know what you intend to do and have everything ready. Success in making things from wood, however, is largely due to your attitude. Your approach to the job in hand has a considerable bearing on its success. Aim to do a good job and not necessarily a quick one. Tackle each stage to the best of your ability. Some parts of the job may be less interesting than others, but give them the attention they deserve. Speed will come, but the unsatisfactory result of rushing your work—a gap in a joint or some other visible error—will always be there. You will look at it later and feel dissatisfied, and even if it is not obvious to other observers, it can be frustrating and lessen your pride in the work.

Much of the joy of weekend working is anticipation. Approach the task with the intention of making something that you will be proud to describe as all your own work.

PREPARATION

The difference between an expert woodworker and a beginner is not just the expert's skill with tools, but quite often his approach to the job. He is able to visualize the many steps needed from start to finish. He knows the move after the next and the one after that every time. He knows what tools and equipment are needed for every stage. He has all the material ready, including such things as pins and screws of the right lengths. He plans the sequence of jobs, so everything is ready at the right time and he is not held up waiting for a part, or for a sub-assembly that needs time for glue to set.

When you decide on a project, consider all the materials needed. Get them and check sizes. Some sizes might not be quite the same as specified, and this will probably not matter—so long as you allow for the differences when marking out. You might have to make the final surface smooth with hand planing, which will reduce thicknesses enough to affect the fit of joints. Do not assume that any sizes of wood will fit their descriptions. Do not, for instance, cut slots to fit 1/2-inch plywood, which you intend to get later. Some plywood thicknesses are metric and what you are offered could be 12mm, which is marginally thinner.

There is also the problem of matching woods. One of the beauties of wood as a natural product is its variations, but if you have to get a small piece to make up the quantity you bought earlier and it has a different appearance, you might have difficulty in disguising it in a piece of furniture.

Make sure you have suitable screws, nails, pins, bolts, or other fasteners. Buying just the quantity you need for a particular project might be justified if you do not expect to make anything else, but if many other things are to be tackled, it is cheaper and more convenient to buy larger quantities so you build up a stock of the many small items you can expect to use fairly frequently. It is surprising how often you reach for a few 3/4-inch pins or 6-gauge by 1-inch screws, or something similar. You would be frustrated if you made it a policy to only buy the bare quantity that seemed to be adequate for a particular project.

Tackle work systematically. Prepare all wood to width and thickness. Sort it into parts. You might be able to use a piece with a knot on one side (or something else that spoils the appearance of one surface) internally or with its other side outwards. Mark the pieces for the places they will occupy. Avoid the ends of boards as they come from the supplier. If shakes or other flaws are going to open, particularly if the furniture will be in central heating conditions, they will do so at the original ends. Cut off and scrap a few inches.

There is a great temptation to rush into making the easiest parts first. That might not matter, but think through the work you have to do. There might have to be some pieces glued to make up width or some parts that have to be joined before they are built into something else. Although modern glues set fairly quickly, you still have to wait several hours before doing further work on glued parts. It would be better to do the glued work first, then it will be setting while you are working on other parts.

You can save time and ensure accurate matching of parts if you do as much marking out as possible in the early stages. There are often four legs and four or more rails that have to match each other. There might be some pieces where only certain spacings have to be the same and other sections of them are different. So far as you can, group parts together and use a try square and pencil or knife across all of them (Fig. 1-1) so there is no doubt about matching measurements. Errors might not then matter. Suppose rail positions on four legs are meant to be 3 inches from their bottoms and you inadvertently mark them 3 1/4 inches. If they are all the same it is unlikely to affect the finished table.

If there is machining to be done, it will save time and effort to do all of one process on all parts at one time, so far as design considerations allow. All rabbets could be cut at one time. It would be

Fig. 1-1. Where parts have to be the same they should be marked together.

better to mark and drill all dowel holes at one operation than to set up drilling arrangements several times. The same reasoning applies to hand work. Suppose there are several mortises. They should be drilled or cut with a router and all chopping out and squaring ends done to every mortise, rather than plan the work in steps tied to other operations.

Think about the final treatment. Whether you apply paint, polish, or varnish, the quality will depend on the conditions of the wood surfaces. Machine planing will probably have to be followed by hand planing and sanding. At what stage will you do these things? Many projects are framed. You cannot get at their inner surfaces easily once you have started assembly, so legs, rails, and other parts of a carcase are better finished to the sanding stage before they are put together, either just the inside surfaces or all round. Make sure there is nothing on the bench top that could mark a sanded surface. A nail or even a piece of grit can cause damage. A hand brush is an important bench tool.

An important part of the overall time taken to complete a project is the initial think-through of the stages involved. Do this thoroughly. Besides the overall time-saving involved, even the most complicated job looks easier when you break it down into stages, each of which you feel are within your capabilities and the capacity of your tools and equipment. You can be proud of what others look at and regard as a very ambitious project, yet you know all the stages involved were quite simple.

If you want to see through a project from the bare materials to completion within two days, you might have to arrange that all gluing will be done by the evening of the first day, then joints will be strong enough for further work on the second day. It is usually possible to plan the work stages to permit this.

ACCURACY

It is important that parts that should be the same size really are. Mark out similar things together, as previously suggested. Having marked and made the parts accurately, you should then assemble them. Even when parts are the correct size it is possible to put them together in a twisted or unsymmetrical manner. Your otherwise good workmanship can be spoiled by unsuccessful assembly.

In many cases, what you are making will have most of the parts and their assembly at 90 degrees. If you make good use of your squares, you have gone some way towards getting satisfactory results. Similarly, when using a power tool, never work freehand if there is a means of setting the tool squarely. This applies to table saws and to drilling. Holes for dowels that are slightly out of square due to freehand drilling can affect the shape of the final assembly. Use the drill on a stand or through a guide.

If you are making something large that has to be square, it is no use checking, for instance, with a 12-inch square when the parts extend 36 inches. What seems accurate at 12 inches might be significantly out at the greater distance. For larger parts it is wiser to check squareness geometrically or make yourself a large plywood square (see "Large Square," Chapter 12).

Many assemblies have opposite sides with square corners in both directions. It is possible to get such an assembly twisted if you do not put the parts together symmetrically. This is particularly so with legs and rails, but it can happen when some parts are flat boards. If there is time, it is often best to first assemble two opposite sides and let their glue set before joining them with the parts the other way. Squaring is then done in two stages and there is less risk of upsetting previous squaring while working on a further stage.

If you are making something like a stool or table that has rails joined to legs, it is usually best to first make up the long sides, because it is easier to get them true while flat on the bench. There is less risk of error the short way.

Besides using a square, compare diagonals (Fig. 1-2A) that will be the same if the assembly is accurate. A strip of scrap wood with pencil marks on the edges might be more convenient than a tape rule. Check that the assembly is flat. Sight across from a reasonable distance away (Fig. 1-2B). If near and far sides are not parallel, you have a twist to remove. Usually, you have to spring it too far the other way, so it comes back flat. You might have to leave it under a weight while the glue sets. Put together the matching parts for the other side. Check them in the same way and check that the two assemblies match when brought together. You might leave one over the other under a weight while the glue sets.

When you assemble the parts the other way, again measure diagonals at the sides (Fig. 1-2C), and do the other checks just mentioned. Make sure the assembly is standing on a level surface. Sight across the parts just assembled. Near and far rails should be parallel at lower levels as well as at the top. If they are not, you have twists to rectify.

Check squareness of the top by comparing diagonals (Fig. 1-2D). Sight from above. The lower rails should be parallel with the top rails if there is no twist. At this stage, errors tend to compound themselves. A twist one way might affect another direction and you might have to check more than once each way.

Finally, stand back and look at the assembly from as many directions as possible. You will soon see if one leg looks misaligned in relation to another or if there is some other error that could be put right before the glue has hardened. It is a good idea to leave the assembly with a board over the top and a weight on that.

In some assemblies there are parts that are not

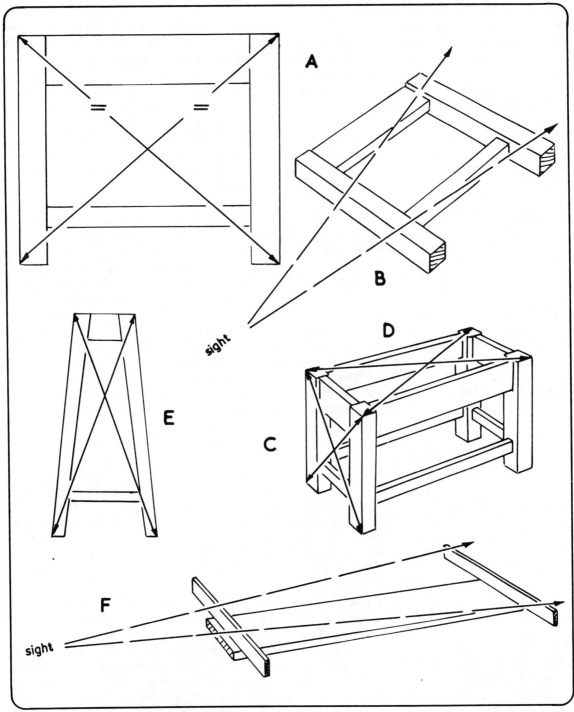

Fig. 1-2. Squareness and symmetry of an assembly too large for your try square can be checked in all directions by comparing diagonals (A-E). Twist of a board is checked by sighting over strips (F).

5

the same at opposite sides, but you can usually find points where you can measure diagonals. It is best to find diagonals as long as possible; the larger the distances compared, the greater the degree of accuracy, although in some assemblies you have to settle for the diagonals of internal parts. Any diagonal check is better than none or than testing with a square that is too short.

Not every assembly has to be square with parallel sides. Diagonals can be used for testing if the assembly is tapered but has a symmetrical outline (Fig. 1-2E). Check twist by sighting in the same way as with a parallel assembly.

Another possible cause of error in an assembly could be twisted boards. If you make up a carcase partly with rails and partly with wider pieces, there is no way you can get everything true if a board is twisted. A board that was planed true when bought or prepared might warp or twist if not used for several weeks.

A traditional craftsman says a board is "in winding" if it is twisted. You might not be able to see much twist if you sight along a 6-inch board, so put two parallel strips across near the ends and sight over them (Fig. 1-2F). These "winding strips" exaggerate any twist and you can see what corrections you will have to make.

SHARPENING

Many occasional woodworkers try to press on with cutting tools that are no longer sharp, when they would do better work if they allowed time for sharpening more frequently. They might even gain time overall due to the more efficient performance of the tools. This particularly applies to chisels, knives, and plane irons.

Skill in sharpening is easy to acquire. There are two stages: grinding and honing. Edge tools do not have to be ground very often and you might prefer to pay someone else to do your grinding. However, power grinders with wheels about 6 inches in diameter are common, although not ideal for woodworking tools. Be careful of overheating. If tool steel is heated beyond its tempering temperature it will be softened. If blue or other color appears at the cutting edge during grinding, you

have softened the steel in the area that is colored. You can remove the color, but that does not restore hardness. Have a container of water nearby and frequently dip the tip of the tool into it, so it does not get too hot.

This brings the problem of returning the tool to the stone at the same angle each time. There are jigs for grinding, but you can probably manage with your hand. If you hold with your finger or knuckle against the tool rest (Fig. 1-3A) and return to the same position each time, that should be sufficient.

You will spend more time honing using an oil or water stone. For the best cutting edge do this in two stages, starting with a medium-grit stone and finishing on a fine one. For frequent touching-up you only use the fine one. The medium grit will usually be man-made, such as Carborundum, and the fine one natural, such as Arkansas.

You can see if an edge needs honing by looking at it towards a light, which will be reflected from the shiny rounded edge. You must sharpen until that is removed.

Use thin oil or water. They do not mix, so always use the same lubricant on a stone. Do not use a stone dry because this will cause rapid and uneven wear.

Hold and control the plane iron or chisel with one hand, and with the fingers of the other hand apply pressure near the edge. Try to use all of the stone (Fig. 1-3B) to keep wear on its surface even and to achieve quick sharpening.

Wipe off oil and examine the edge. If the shine has gone, feel the flat side towards the edge. If the edge has been rubbed down fully, there will be a tiny particle of steel known as a "wire edge" clinging to it and it will feel rough. To remove it, rub the tool with a circular motion flat on the stone (Fig. 1-3C). Finally, slice across the edge of a piece of scrap wood.

If that honing has been on the medium stone, repeat on the fine one. Not many rubs are needed because you only have to remove the coarse scratches and replace them with fine ones. Make sure none of the grit-laden oil from the first stone gets transferred to the fine stone, because that

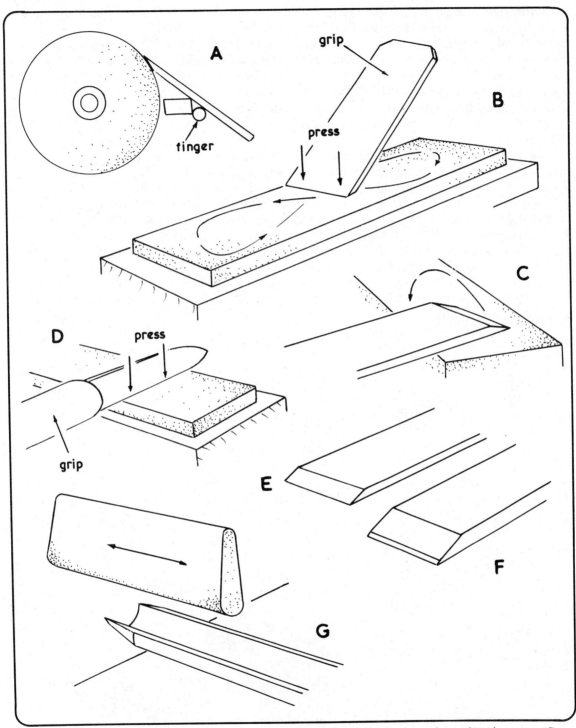

Fig. 1-3. A cutting edge might have to be ground (A), then honed (B-F). A slip stone has to be used inside a gouge (G).

would interfere with producing a fine edge.

Sharpening a knife is very similar. One hand on the handle controls the angle and the fingers of the other hand apply pressure to the blade (Fig. 1-3D). You will have to follow any curve in the edge. After many rubs on one side, do the same on the second side. Continue until you can feel a wire edge, then remove that by slicing across scrap wood. Use both stones for the finest edge.

The actual cutting angles vary. An axe must have a more obtuse angle than a razor or the edge would shatter at the first cut. Angle for wood-cutting tools might vary in similar ways, with those for hardwoods preferably slightly more obtuse than those for softwoods. In practice, however, an average angle can be used. With most sharpening you only have to follow existing angles. If it is a thin chisel or plane iron, the honing bevel and grinding bevel can be the same (Fig. 1-3E). With thicker tools, less time is needed each time on an oilstone if the grinding bevel is longer and there is a second honing bevel (Fig. 1-3F).

With knives, you can sharpen to quite a fine angle if the blades will only be used for marking out wood. For general purposes they will have to be slightly more obtuse if they are not to dull too quickly.

For gouges and other curved tools you need a rounded oilstone called a "slip stone," with a cross-section curve less than the tool it is to sharpen. The outside can be sharpened on an ordinary stone with a rolling action, but for the inside the slip stone is used like a file (Fig. 1-3G). If the gouge has its bevel inside, most of the work will be done with a slip stone and you only remove the wire edge on a flat stone. In that case it helps to have a fairly coarse slip stone for quick action inside, followed by a fine one. If you are a carver, you will need slip stones of special sections for some tools.

Chapter 2

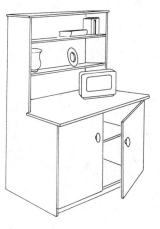

Domestic Aids

There are many things that are useful around the home, yet they may have no specific place. Sometimes you feel the need for a particular item that would make life easier, yet there is no standard piece of furniture, appliance, or accessory that will do the job. It is then that your skill as a woodworker can come into its own as you make something exactly suitable for a purpose, whether it has to operate in a certain way or exactly fit a space.

Many such items are described elsewhere in the book, but some that do not readily fit under other chapter headings are described here. Whether your present skill is limited or advanced, you can get a lot of satisfaction out of making wooden items that will add to the comfort and convenience of you and your family.

CASSETTE RACK

Audio cassettes in their cases tend to be tossed around and left in odd places, so you might not be able to find the one you want. A rack to hold a number of cassettes is easy to make (Fig. 2-1).

It could be any length and you could make more than one or put a double row on one base. The finished rack and its contents can stand on a shelf or be put in a drawer, with the name on the cases easily read and the one you want lifted out. The racks can be lifted by their ends.

A common size of a cassette case is 15mm by 70mm by 110mm. For the purpose of making the rack you can assume that a cassette will slide into a groove 3/4 inch wide and the overall length will fit into 4 3/8 inches. However, check the sizes of your own cassettes.

How you space the grooves in the sides depends on the type of wood. A softwood or open-grained hardwood might not be strong enough in its short grain between the slots for the grooves to be cut very close without a risk of the wood breaking. The drawing (Fig. 2-2A) shows the gaps about the same widths as the grooves, which would suit almost any wood. With a close-grained hardwood you could get in more cassettes by reducing the gaps.

Fig. 2-1. A cassette rack holds audio cassettes so you can read the labels.

1. Cut the wood for the sides and mark out the slots. They are shown at 75 degrees. This is not critical and you can experiment with a cassette to see which angle you prefer. However, do not tilt too much or you will make weak corners to the slots.

2. Cut the grooves to half the thickness of the wood (Fig. 2-2B). Smooth the insides of the grooves and take off the sharpness of the upper corners.

3. Cut the ends and round their upper corners to half thickness (Fig. 2-2C).

4. Make the two ends (Fig. 2-2D). They

could fit between the sides and be held to them with glue and pins, or they could be notched in. The important thing is their length, as this controls

Materials List for Cassette Rack
(Length as required)

2 sides	3/4	×	1 1/2
2 ends	1/2	×	1 1/2
1 base	1/2	×	5 3/4

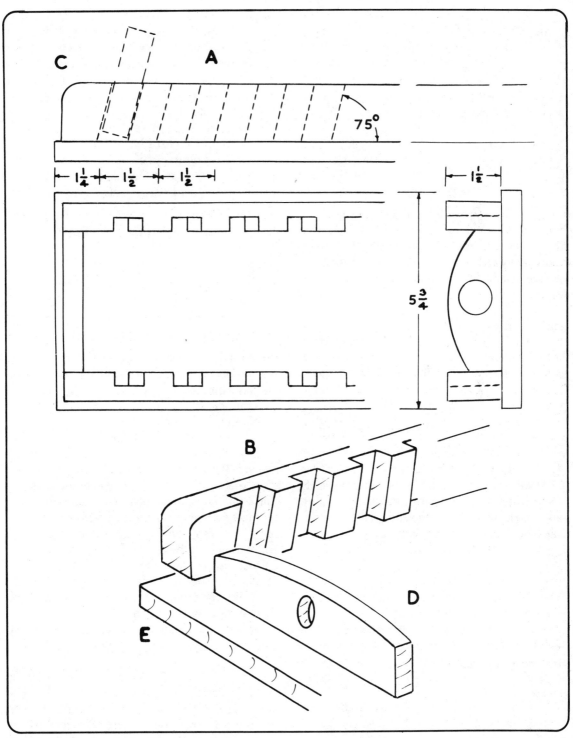

Fig. 2-2. Construction details of the cassette rack.

the fit of the cassettes. Try a cassette in a pair of grooves. Allow an easy fit, then cut the lengths of the ends to suit. Round the top edges and drill finger holes for lifting. Round the top and the hole edges.

5. Make the bottom to extend up to 1/4 inch outside the other parts (Fig. 2-2E). Glue and pin it to them.

6. There is no need for a high-gloss finish, but one or two coats of varnish will seal the wood.

WOOD MAT

In earlier days, when mud and dirt came up to the house door something outside was needed for the first wiping of footwear before passing through the doorway to a fabric mat. In more recent days the outside mat might have been a metal scraper mat, but before that it was a pattern of strips of wood.

Such a mat still has uses. Shoes dirty from the garden can be wiped on it. If the ground is wet, the mat forms a dry place to stand either outdoors or in the laundry or garage. It can be used in the kitchen or elsewhere when an extra few inches of height are needed. Another use would be under plant pots, allowing water to drain through.

If the mat is to be used for scuffing mud off shoes, it should be made of hardwood, preferably with a non-splintering grain. If it is to be a plant stand it could be softwood. The size shown (Fig. 2-3A) suits a door mat, but for other purposes the shape could be altered. So it stands without tipping, fit battens flush with the ends of the top strips. Gaps are shown 1/2 inch wide. They should not be much wider, or someone could trip in them.

1. Decide on the number and sizes of strips. See that they are straight. Cut them all to the same length with square ends.

2. Make the battens to go underneath, slightly too long at first. Mark on the end ones the spacing of the top strips. Mark on the outer top strips the positions of the battens, spaced equally (Fig. 2-3B).

3. In the simplest construction the parts could be nailed, but it will be better to use a waterproof glue and screw from below so no metal

shows on the top—preferably with two screws at each outer crossing to prevent twisting—although single screws may be sufficient at the other places.

4. One way to get even gaps is to use a strip 1/2 inch wide as a spacer. Start attaching the battens to the first top strip, then use the spacer to get the position of the next top strip, and so on across the mat. Check squareness as you progress and cut off any surplus ends of battens at the far side.

5. Take off sharpness of edges and corners. It will be best to leave the mat as bare wood, so it can be scrubbed occasionally.

Materials List for Wood Mat

6 strips	1	×	2	×	25
4 battens	1	×	1	×	15

TELEVISION TURNTABLE

Which is the best seat for viewing television? If you want to view from a different position, can you turn the set? A turntable under the set makes it easy to alter the screen to face any way you want it, with a minimum of trouble.

This turntable (Fig. 2-4) consists of a board under the set, joined to a base with a "lazy susan" bearing. These turntable bearings turn smoothly on a circle of balls and are obtainable in several sizes. You could use a 4-inch bearing for a small set, but for most table models a 6-inch size will be more suitable. Sizes shown (Fig. 2-5) will serve as a guide and will have to be adapted to suit your set. The base could be square, octagonal, or round, but should be wider than the top.

Solid wood may be used, either a cheap wood stained, or a hardwood to match other furniture. Veneered particleboard is also suitable. Not much will show when the set is in position.

1. Make the top (Fig. 2-5A) to fit under the television case. It need not extend to the full length of the case, but if there are feet it should be taken past them and drilled so they go through and the two surfaces are in contact. Otherwise, the turnta-

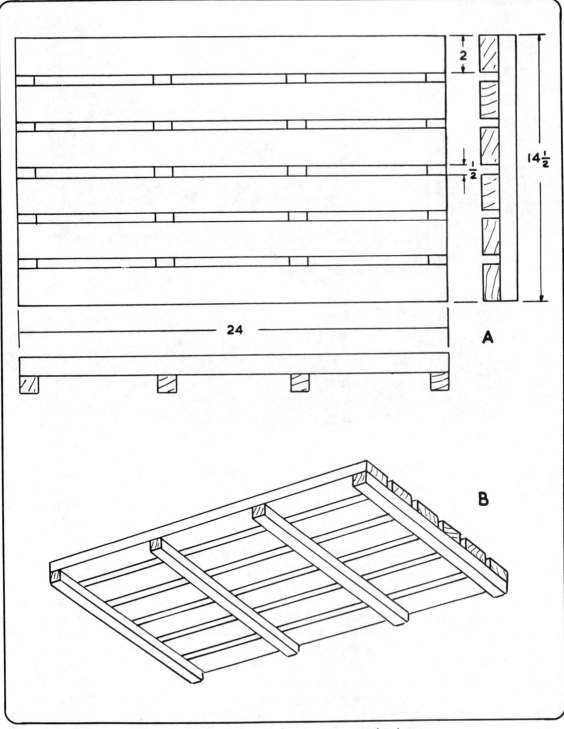

Fig. 2-3. A wood mat made from strips can be used to stand on or as a support for plants.

Fig. 2-4. A turntable allows a television set to be moved for the best viewing position.

ble top might bend after a time if the weight is taken only at the ends under the feet.

2. Make the base (Fig. 2-5B). Shape it if you wish.

3. Mark the centers of both parts and draw on the outlines of the lazy susan bearing (Fig. 2-5C). The largest ones are round, but others are square. The shape does not affect the method of fitting.

4. The turntable can be allowed to turn a full circle, but in most circumstances you will want to limit the movement. This can be done with projecting dowels. Two dowels can extend down from the top (Fig. 2-5D and E). On the same circle are four dowels projecting up from the base (Fig. 2-5F, G, H). On the turntable shown the pitch circle for the dowel positions is 5-inch radius. The top

dowels are on the centerline. The bottom dowels are shown at 45 degrees, to give a movement just under 90 degrees, but you can space them to allow whatever movement you require. Measure the thickness of the lazy susan bearing and have the dowels project enough to hit each other, but not so far as to rub on the other part (Fig. 2-6).

5. The usual lazy susan bearing does not come apart, so it is impossible to drive screws through it into the wood both ways. Instead, wood screws are driven upwards into the top, but self-tapping screws, or screws into already-threaded holes, are driven through the base into the bearing plate. One plate has small holes for the self-tapping screws or threaded holes. Position that plate on the base and mark through for small pilot holes to give you the positions on the other side,

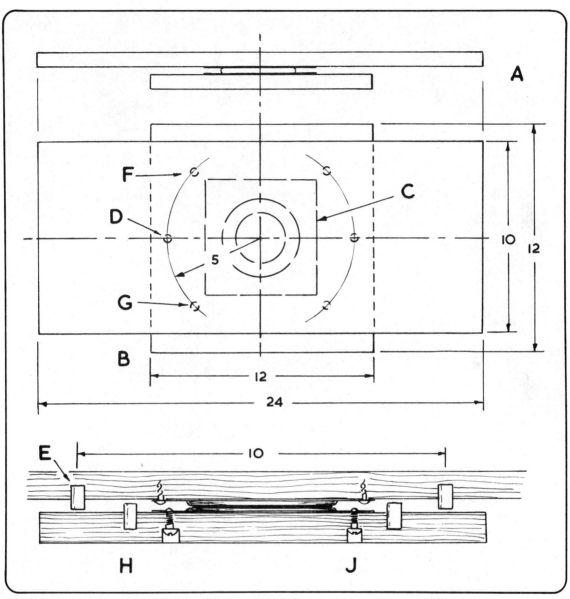

Fig. 2-5. Suggested sizes for the parts of a television turntable.

where you can enlarge the holes to suit the screws (6-gauge self-tapping should suit a 6-inch bearing plate). Counterbore so the screw heads are below the surface and their ends enter the plate far enough (Fig. 2-5J), but not so far as to touch the other plate.

6. If you have made a trial assembly of the base, remove the screws and position the lazy su-

san bearing on the underside of the top. Drill for wood screws (6-gauge should suit a 6-inch bearing plate). Screw the bearing permanently to the top board.

7. Finish the wood with polish or varnish.

8. Put a little oil on the balls in the bearing. Put the base in place and attach it with the self-tapping screws.

Fig. 2-6. The turntable parts are joined with a lazy susan bearing. Dowels limit movement.

9. If there are no feet under the television case to locate it in holes in the turntable top, glue cloth or thin rubber all over or only at the corners of the wood. Similar material under the base will prevent that slipping and prevent damage to a polished table top.

```
┌─────────────────────────────────────┐
│                                       │
│            Materials List for         │
│          Television Turntable         │
│                                       │
│                                       │
│      1 top      3/4 × 10 × 25         │
│      1 base     3/4 × 12 × 12         │
│                                       │
│      1 lazy susan bearing—6-inch size │
│                                       │
└─────────────────────────────────────┘
```

BULLETIN BOARD

Somewhere to pin up reminders, recipes, notes, and other temporary pieces of information can be of use in a kitchen, garage, or child's bedroom, as well as in a club or similar places. The board could simply be a piece of plywood, but most plywood is too hard for pins to be pushed in easily. A better material is softboard, of the type used for some kinds of insulation. If left with edges exposed it is liable to crumble, so it is better framed. This bulletin board (Fig. 2-7) has a wooden outline similar to a picture frame. It could be left at that, but a shelf is easily added at the bottom to take pins, felt pens and other small things. Another shelf can go at the top to carry ornaments.

Softboard about 3/8 inch thick is suitable, but any reasonable thickness can be used. Some softboard is stiff as it is, but if you have doubts about

Fig. 2-7. The framed bulletin board has a shelf above it.

the finished board being rigid enough, it can be backed with hardboard or thin plywood (Fig. 2-8A).

The size can be made to suit needs and the available wall space. The drawing (Fig. 2-8B) suggests sections of materials and proportions. The frame is a unit; the shelves can be added when the frame is made or can be attached later. Any wood can be used. The light brown color of the softboard can be changed with paint, which will soak in—do not expect to put on a gloss finish. The frame may then be finished in any way you wish. A black frame around a green board looks efficient and encourages neat displays.

1. Prepare frame material. Cut rabbets to suit the board with about 3/8-inch overlap (Fig. 2-8C). The front may be molded, if you wish, or it could be rounded or beveled towards the board.

2. Miter the corners. There should be little strain on these joints and their security will be helped by nails or screws through the framed board into the rabbets. It should be sufficient to glue the miters and drive fine nails both ways (Fig. 2-8D).

3. Fit in the softboard, with its hardboard backing. Delay final fixing until after any painting or staining has been done, then use a few screws from the back.

4. Shelves have to project enough to be useful, but in some places too much could be a nuisance, due to the risk of knocking. The suggested width is 3 inches. The bottom shelf can be screwed under the frame. A strip at the front prevents things

falling off (Fig. 2-8E). Round all edges and corners. The top shelf may be made in the same way, but a strip upwards provides backing for items being displayed (Fig. 2-8F). It could be straight across or decorated with curves.

MIRROR KEY RACK

If keys are hung on a row of hooks, they are not very beautiful and they are obvious to people who may not have authority to use them. If the keys are hung in a shallow cabinet they are protected, but a plain door may look a little better than the exposed rack. Instead of a door there could be a framed picture or a mirror. The rack then acquires a new use, and the fact that it holds keys as well is much less obvious. Anyone looking in the mirror to tidy his or her hair will probably not realize what is behind the reflection, particularly if there are no handles or fasteners.

Sizes will depend on how many keys you wish to hang, but the front should also be a reasonable size. If there is a picture you want to use, that will determine size. A mirror will probably have to be cut to suit your frame, but it should still be a suitable size to use (Fig. 2-9). The sizes shown (Fig. 2-10A) were provided as a guide to construction.

Almost any wood can be used, but a close-grained hardwood will look most attractive. If you will fit a mirror, get it first because its thickness controls the depth of the rabbet and it is easier to fit a frame to the glass than trim glass to fit a frame. If you want to display a picture or photograph, get thin glass to match and cut a piece of hardboard to go behind it.

1. Cut the rabbets in the frame material. It might be easier to start with wider wood and cut it to size after working the rabbets and the chamfer on the front. Make the rabbet in the back to suit the plywood (Fig. 2-10B). For the front you must allow for the thickness of the mirror and a piece of card behind it, or for the picture and its glass and backing. In both cases there will be fillets nailed in (Fig. 2-10C).

2. Make the two frames with mitered corners. You could strengthen the miters with thin

Materials List for Bulletin Board		
2 frames	7/8 ×	1 × 25
2 frames	7/8 ×	1 × 19
1 board	18 × 24 × 3/8 softboard	
1 board	18 × 24 × 1/8 hardboard	
2 shelves	3/8 ×	3 × 19
1 strip	3/8 × 1/2 × 19	
1 strip	3/8 ×	2 × 19

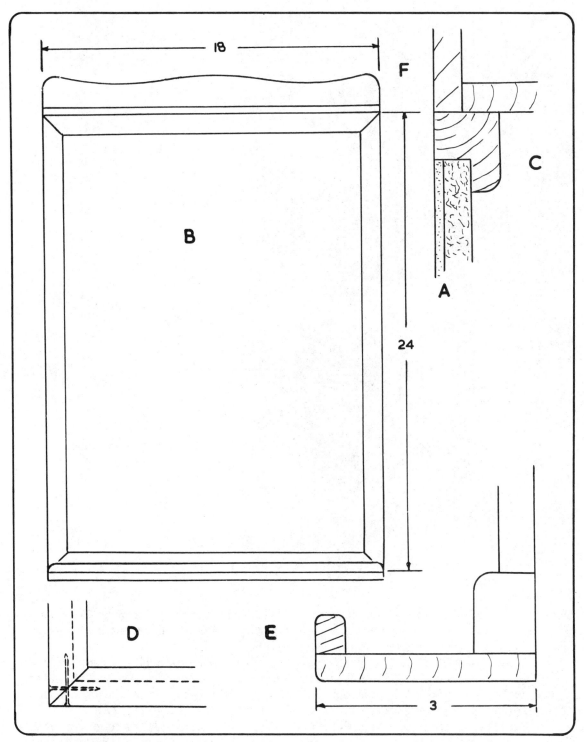

Fig. 2-8. Sizes and construction details of the bulletin board.

19

Fig. 2-9. This key rack has a mirror front to hide the keys.

nails each way, but 1/4-inch dowels are suggested (Fig. 2-10D). Make them overlength and plane them off when the glue has set. Check that the two frames are the same size.

3. Glue and pin the plywood into the back (Fig. 2-10E). Drill for the key hooks, but do not fit them yet. Also drill for two screws into the wall.

4. Cut a piece of card to go behind the mirror and make fillets thick enough to come level

with the inner surfaces of the frame. They can overlap at the corners or be mitered, if you wish (Fig. 2-10F).

5. Cut recesses for hinges. For the size rack shown, two 1 1/2-inch hinges should be satisfactory. Let them in to give only a slight clearance when the rack is closed (Fig. 2-10G).

6. At the other side fit a spring or magnetic catch inside. If you want to keep the rack as secret

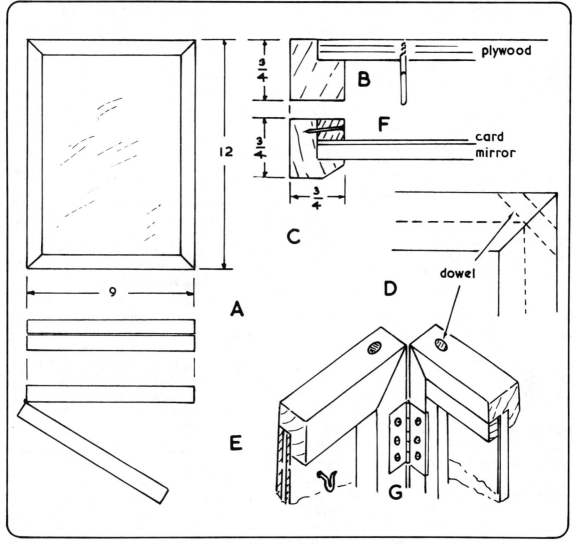

Fig. 2-10. Hooks for keys are in the back panel and the mirror is in the hinged door.

as possible, do not fit a handle. The door is easily opened with a finger grip at the side.

7. Remove the mirror, hinges, and catch, then finish the wood. There could be a different finish for the key panel—green is appropriate. Even if the wood is given a light finish it is worthwhile painting the inside of the mirror recess black to reduce unwanted reflections around the edges.

8. Reassemble the rack with mirror or picture, hinges, catch and key hooks, then mount it in position.

Materials List for Mirror Key Ring

4 frames	3/4 × 3/4 × 13
4 frames	3/4 × 3/4 × 10
2 fillets	3/8 × 3/8 × 12
2 fillets	3/8 × 3/8 × 9
1 key panel	9 × 12 × 1/4 plywood

PORTABLE UMBRELLA STAND

A large umbrella stand or one that is part of an-other piece of furniture is valuable, but a stand of light construction may be used in a hallway or porch—then if you need it elsewhere it can be picked up, with its contents if necessary, and carried easily to a new position.

This stand (Fig. 2-11) is intended for use with umbrellas and canes, but it could also hold fishing poles, golf clubs, and other long and narrow games equipment. Sizes might have to be modified to suit special contents, but those shown (Fig. 2-12A) will suit most uses in your home.

An attractive hardwood is advisable, but choose straightgrained pieces for the fairly slender legs so there is little risk of warping. The joints could be all mortises and tenons if you wish, but the instructions and drawings show dowels.

1. Mark out the four legs together. They are the same and the markings should be on two adjoining faces (Fig. 2-13A). The tops of the legs extend above the rails. These are prominent and should be decorated. Allow for the design you prefer.

2. The simplest top has the end squared, then chamfers cut all around (Fig. 2-13B). Alternatively there could be rounding (Fig. 2-13C). You could round the tops completely. Tapering in a shallow cone to a central point (Fig. 2-13D) looks attractive if cut neatly. There could be added finials or knobs. Tall ones would be inappropriate, but a shallow broad design (Fig. 2-13E) could be used.

3. Make the rails both ways. See that the ends are square and lengths match.

4. Mark the rails and legs for dowels. Two 5/16-inch or 3/8-inch dowels in each joint should be sufficient. To provide sufficient glue area in the legs, drill the holes to meet and miter the dowel ends (Fig. 2-13F).

5. Put strips inside the bottom rails (Fig. 2-13G) to support the plywood bottom (Fig. 2-12B).

6. Make the division (Fig. 2-12C) a suitable depth to fit over the plywood bottom when that has been fitted.

7. Make the handle to fit between the top rails (Fig. 2-13H). Well round the edges of the curved top and the hand hole.

8. Mark and drill for dowel joints in the division and handle (Fig. 2-13J).

9. Shape the tops of the legs, if this has not been done already. Take the sharpness off the lower ends to prevent splintering on a rough floor or marking floor covering. The upper edges of all rails could be rounded slightly. In any case, take the sharpness off all edges and sand the parts before assembly.

10. Join the legs with the short rails. Check squareness and that the assemblies match as a pair.

11. Cut the plywood bottom. Notch its corners to fit around the legs. It may be left slightly oversize for trimming to a close fit during assembly.

12. Join the end assemblies with the long rails. At the same time fit the handle between the top rails and the plywood bottom and division between the bottom rails.

13. The plywood will keep the lower parts square, but check squareness at the top and sight from above to see that there is no twist.

14. Finish in any way you wish, but if you expect the stand to hold wet things, exterior or boat varnish is advisable.

Materials List for Portable Umbrella Stand	
4 legs	1 × 1 × 26
2 rails	5/8 × 2 1/2 × 15
2 rails	5/8 × 2 1/2 × 9
2 rails	5/8 × 3 × 15
2 rails	5/8 × 3 × 9
1 division	5/8 × 2 1/2 × 9
1 handle	5/8 × 4 × 9
2 bottom strips	1/2 × 1/2 × 15
2 bottom strips	1/2 × 1/2 × 9
1 bottom	9 × 15 × 1/4 plywood

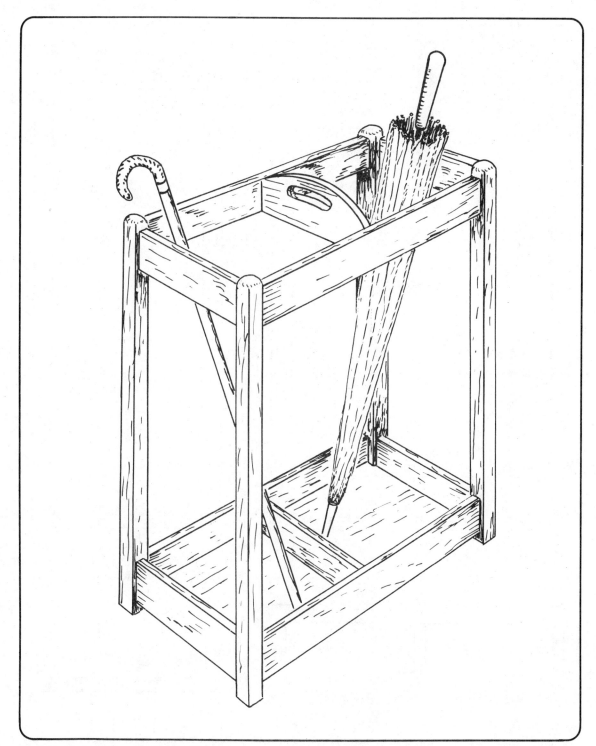

Fig. 2-11. The portable umbrella stand has two compartments and a central lifting handle.

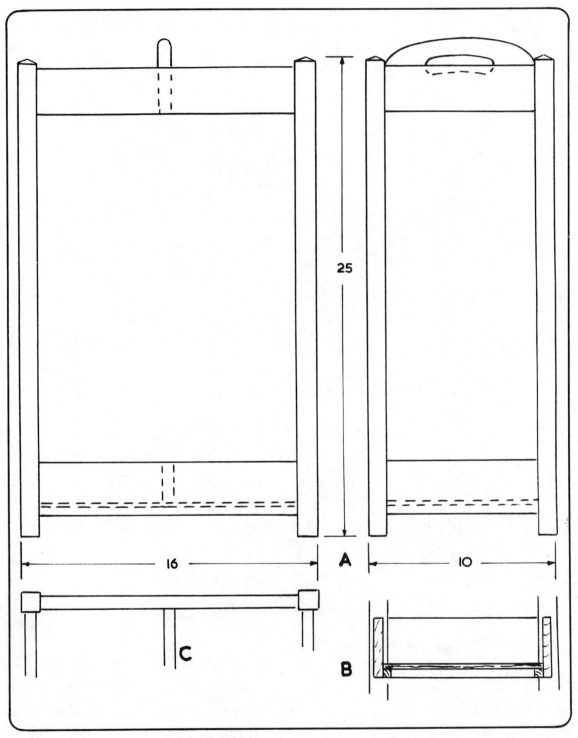

Fig. 2-12. Main sizes of the portable umbrella stand.

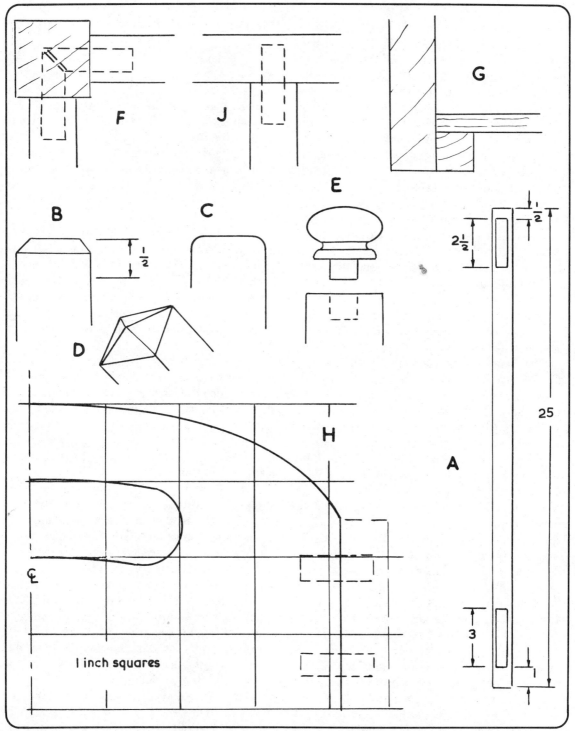

Fig. 2-13. Construction details and the handle shape for a portable umbrella stand.

MUSIC CENTER

With the assortment of electronic music equipment in the home, it is convenient to have a stand that will take such things as television set, video unit and cassettes, records, tape recorder, or radio. The most convenient material to make such a unit is veneered particleboard, obtainable in several widths, so you can measure the equipment you want to accommodate and build around it.

The music center illustrated (Fig. 2-14) has an open top with raised ends to prevent things sliding off. That will hold a television set or other items you are using. Underneath there is space for the largest records to stand on edge, with video cassettes on a shelf and a large space below. One shelf is arranged to slide forward so the video or record player on it can be brought out without lifting. The whole music center is on casters, so it can be moved about.

The final sizes will have to be arranged to suit your equipment, but those shown (Fig. 2-15A) will provide a starting point.

The veneered particleboard should be obtained with its surfaces and edges already covered, but you will need some strip matching veneer to put on cut edges. Casters should be obtained before starting work, so their depth can be allowed for.

There are several possible ways of making joints between the panels. You could use dowels everywhere (Fig. 2-15B). The bottom can be screwed upwards because the screw heads will not show, but screws with their heads on the surface would be unsuitable elsewhere. You could counterbore the screws and glue in matching plastic plugs (Fig. 2-15C). Another way is to use strips of 1/2-inch-square wood under the shelf and top, with screws driven both ways (Fig. 2-15D). If you arrange a shelf to slide, the parts providing the movement will have to be screwed in any case.

If the music center is to be without casters and to be used fairly permanently against a wall, the back could be a piece of hardboard screwed on. If it will be moved about and the back will be seen, however, it would be better to use plywood and fit it inside. That can be done by putting 1/2-inch-

square strips around (Fig. 2-15E) the outer panels, then cut the shelves back to this line.

1. Make the two sides (Fig. 2-15F) and mark on the positions of other parts. Veneer the top edges.

2. Make the division (Fig. 2-15G) with matching positions on both surfaces. Cut it to width to clear the back.

3. The bottom overlaps the sides (Fig. 2-15H) by 1/4 inch. Veneer the ends. Mark the top to match this and come between the sides. Mark on both where the division will come. Mark and cut the narrow shelf to match.

4. These parts can be assembled using any of the joining methods suggested. It should be satisfactory to have dowels or screws within 1 inch of back and front edge, then others at about 3-inch intervals. Use glue between the surfaces, regardless of the joints used. Measure diagonals and make sure the assembly stands square and without twist.

5. Cut the back plywood to size. Put wood strips around inside (Fig. 2-15E) the sides, top, and bottom, cutting away at the division and shelf. The strips may be held with glue and screws or nails. You can put the back in temporarily to hold the assembly square if you want to leave the job before finishing, but it is easier to fit the sliding shelf if it is left out until later.

6. Make and fit two 3/4-inch-square wood strips to support the sliding shelf (Fig. 2-15J).

7. Make the shelf to slide on these strips (Fig. 2-15K). Because its ends will show when pulled out, veneer them, but make the shelf size so it will slide easily without excessive play.

8. Make sliding assemblies 3 inches long to screw under the rear of the shelf (Fig. 2-15L). Glue wood together so they have enough clearance to slide easily on the supporting strips. Drill for three screws upwards into the underside of the shelf.

9. Try the action of the shelf. Wax on the wood will improve sliding.

10. Decide how far you want the shelf to slide forward and fit stops (Fig. 2-15M) on the supporting strips. It would be unwise to bring the shelf too

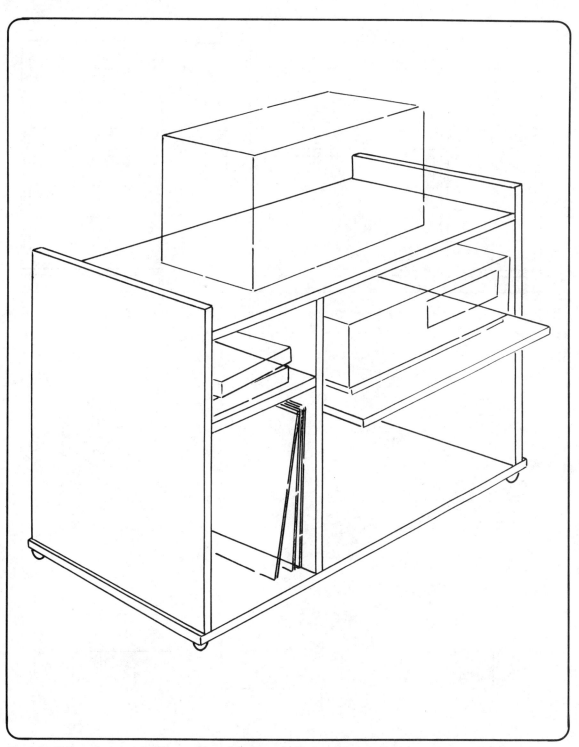

Fig. 2-14. This music center provides accommodation for television, video, and other electronic music equipment.

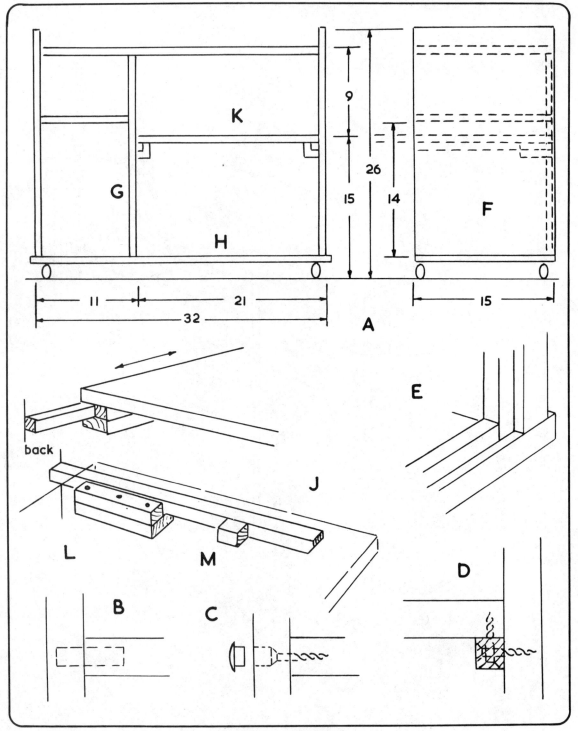

Fig. 2-15. Sizes and details of the music center, including a sliding shelf.

28

far forward, but up to half of it extended should be satisfactory.

11. With plastic veneer no finishing treatment is necessary. Treat wood veneer with stain and varnish or polish. The back plywood may be stained and varnished. That is most conveniently done before it is finally fitted. Fix it with screws or nails to the strips. Add the casters.

Materials List for Music Center
Veneered particleboard

2 sides	3/4 × 15 × 25
1 bottom	3/4 × 15 × 33
1 top	3/4 × 15 × 31
1 division	3/4 × 15 × 23
1 shelf	3/4 × 11 × 15
1 shelf	3/4 × 15 × 21

Wood

1 back	1/4 × 25 × 33
2 back frames	1/2 × 1/2 × 25
2 back frames	1/2 × 1/2 × 33
2 shelf supports	3/4 × 3/4 × 15
2 shelf guides	3/4 × 3/4 × 3
2 shelf guides	3/4 × 1 1/2 × 3

WALL UNIT

An arrangement that includes adjustable shelves, a worktop, and storage underneath would take much longer than a weekend to make out of solid wood, but if veneered particleboard is used, preparation and construction are simplified. This wall unit (Fig. 2-16) is made almost entirely of veneered particleboard, with many of the parts used in stock widths, so very little veneering of cut edges will be required. Sizes could be varied to suit your requirements or space, but a working height of about 30 inches and a total height of 60 inches will give reasonable proportions and will suit users with normal reach. The back of the cupboard is closed with hardboard, but the shelves are open.

Much of the construction is very similar to the music center and the instructions for that should be read. Where parts meet you can use dowels at all positions (Fig. 2-15B). Where screw heads would not show there could be simple screwing, but an alternative to dowels is to counterbore screws and cover the heads with matching plastic plugs (Fig. 2-15C). Some parts could be joined with wood strips underneath, screwed both ways (Fig. 2-15D).

Check the available standard widths of particleboard already veneered on surfaces and edges. Some sizes may be modified to use boards without cutting to width. You will also need strip veneer to cover some cut edges.

1. It helps to make a rod of the total height. This can be any piece of spare wood, possibly 1 inch by 2 inch. On it mark the positions of all the horizontal parts (Fig. 2-17A). Try this in the location the unit will be placed in to see if positions of parts will suit your needs.

2. Each side is made by joining a 9-inch piece to a 12-inch piece (Fig. 2-17B). Use glue and dowels at about 4-inch spacing, and clamp to make a close, inconspicuous joint.

3. Use the rod to mark the heights of the parts that will join the sides. The top, the worktop, and the bottom are the important parts that will keep the assembly in shape.

4. The two upper shelves could be attached permanently to the sides, but a method of adjusting their heights is shown. Holes in the sides (Fig. 2-18A) take short pieces of 3/8-inch or 1/2-inch dowel rod (Fig. 2-19A). If you wish to use this method, mark and drill holes 1 1/2 inches in from each edge of the sides. Space them to suit the probable heights you will want, but having them 2 inches apart vertically to within 6 inches of top and bottom of the space should suit most needs.

5. The bottom (Fig. 2-18B) fits between and level with edges of the sides and there is a plinth, or kick rail, below (Fig. 2-18C). Cut these to size and dowel them together, or use a screwed wood strip inside.

6. The rear part of the worktop fits between the sides (Fig. 2-18D), so should be the same length

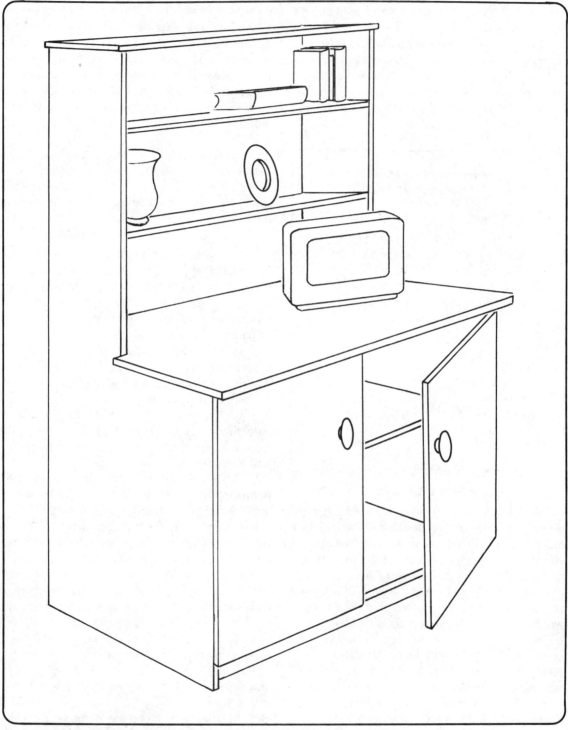

Fig. 2-16. A wall unit with several uses.

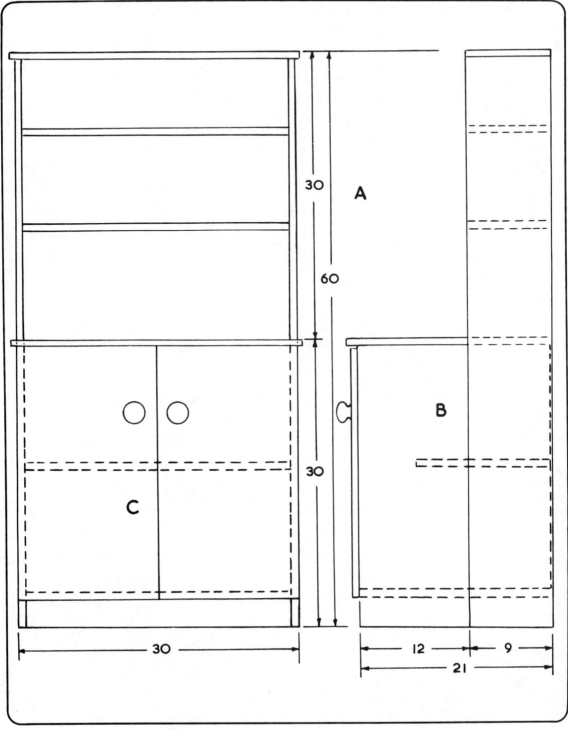

Fig. 2-17. Suggested sizes for the wall unit.

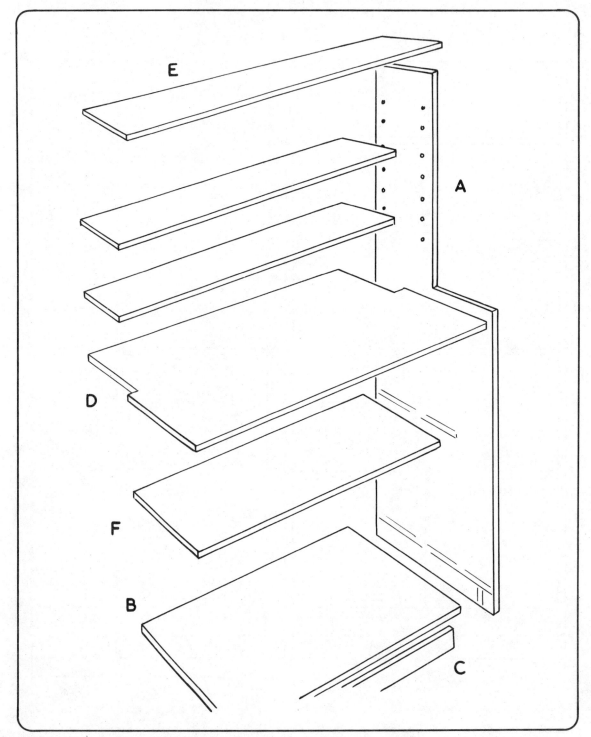

Fig. 2-18. *The wall unit parts, including adjustable shelves.*

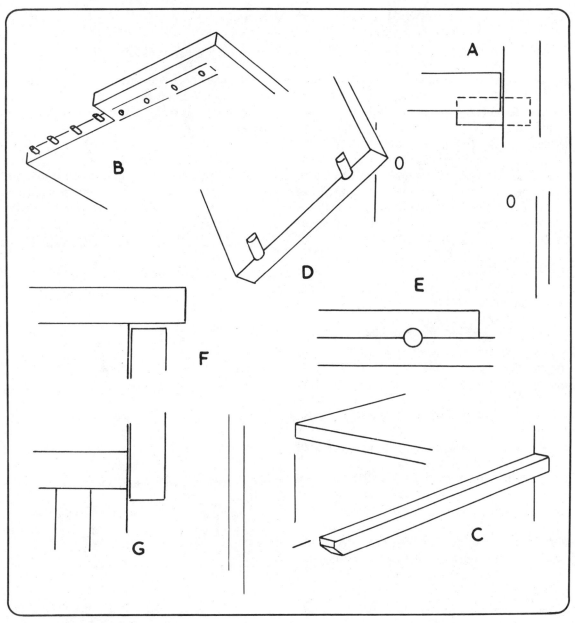

Fig. 2-19. Details of the wall unit parts.

as the bottom, but the forward part should over-hang the sides by 1/2 inch (Fig. 2-19B).

7. The top (Fig. 2-18E) also overhangs the sides and should be the same overall length as the worktop. Veneer the cut edges of the overhang-ing parts.

8. In the simplest construction a hardboard back for the cupboard could be nailed or screwed on. It is better, however, to let in a plywood or hardboard back, particularly if the unit is to be used as a room divider, or in another position away from a wall. So the back can be let in, fix strips inside

the area enclosed by the worktop, bottom and sides. They can be fitted now or after assembly (Fig. 2-15E).

9. Prepare the two sides and the three horizontal parts for joining, and have the back ready to fit in. Assemble these parts. If the back is put in temporarily, it will hold the unit square. In any case, check squareness by comparing diagonals and see that there is no twist.

10. The inside shelf (Fig. 2-18F) rests on wood strips (Fig. 2-19C) screwed to the sides. Of course, there could be more than one shelf, but leaving them loose allows them to be lifted out for changes or cleaning. Do not make shelves the full depth or they will obstruct the view inside.

11. The upper shelves have half holes (Fig. 2-19D) that fit over the dowels so when the weight of a shelf is on the dowels they cannot come out, but if you lift the shelf, the dowels can be moved to another position.

12. The half holes can be drilled by clamping the shelf end to a piece of scrap particleboard, then locating the center of the drill bit on the meeting line (Fig. 2-19E). Any drill bit could be used, but a Forstner bit will make holes without the deeper center penetration due to the spur of other bits. Cut sufficient pieces of dowel rods squarely across their ends, and only just short enough to fit in with minimum clearance.

13. Make the two doors (Fig. 2-17C). They overlap the sides. Their tops come under the projecting edge of the worktop (Fig. 2-19F), but at the bottom they can overhang (Fig. 2-19G).

14. Hinge the doors to the sides. There could be decorative hinges on their edges and the sur-

faces of the sides, or you could put thin hinges between the doors and the side edges.

15. Arrange two knobs or handles at a suitable height to be reached.

16. The doors will close against the bottom. You could also put a short strip behind them as a stop under the worktop, but if you fit spring or magnetic catches there, they would also act as stops.

17. Stain and varnish the back, if you wish, before nailing or screwing it in place. If the unit is covered with plastic veneer, it will not need any finishing treatment, but finish wood veneer with stain and polish.

Materials List for Wall Unit
Veneered particleboard

2 sides	3/4 × 9 × 60
2 sides	3/4 × 12 × 30
1 bottom	3/4 × 21 × 30
1 worktop	3/4 × 24 × 32
1 top	3/4 × 9 × 32
2 shelves	3/4 × 9 × 30
1 shelf	3/4 × 18 × 30

Wood

1 back	30 × 30 × 1/8 hardboard or 1/4 plywood
4 back strips	1/2 × 1/2 × 30
2 shelf supports	3/4 × 3/4 × 18

Chapter 3

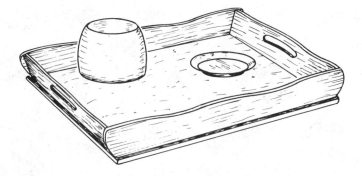

Kitchen and Dining Room

We all spend a considerable time either preparing meals or eating them. There is plenty of scope for making wooden articles that can be used anywhere that food has to be dealt with. Anything that makes work easier, improves the appearance of a table, looks good in itself and is probably something other people do not have, will be welcome.

Individually-produced examples of kitchen equipment can be made to suit your exact requirements. Accessories for the dining room can be made to look good as well as be efficient and useful. There are things described elsewhere in this book that might find uses in a kitchen or dining room, but some specifically for these places are described here. They will probably suggest others that you can design yourself.

In general, wood is safe with food—many of our ancestors used wood extensively for eating and food preparation. For direct contact with food, avoid resinous wood and any with an odor. Items that are just holders or carriers for food enclosed in other containers can be finished in any way. If you want to seal wood that will be touching food,

vegetable oil (as used for cooking) will make a safe and attractive finish.

HOT PADS

It is often difficult to know what to do with small pieces of hardboard or thin plywood. A set of hot pads or table mats can be made from oddments and used under vases or pots of plants as well as on a dining table. Ordinary 1/8-inch hardboard has good heat insulation and may be used without treatment. A stand for a set of pads can be made mostly of the same material. If that is given a gloss finish, it will contrast nicely with the duller natural surface of the pads.

Various numbers and sizes of pads are possible, and you can design your own to suit your needs or the available materials. The set shown (Fig. 3-1) has six mats 5 inches square and two mats 6 inches by 8 inches, all fitting into a stand (Fig. 3-2A).

Although the parts are simple, it is important that they are accurately made and square, with the

Fig. 3-1. Two sizes of hot pads in a stand.

same bevels on all corners, so the set matches when put together. An error will be very obvious among the other pieces.

1. Decide on the numbers and sizes, then mark out and cut the pads at the same time. With a table saw, sizes can be kept the same by using the fence. Frequently check squareness of corners.

2. Edges might need planing, but with a fine saw you can probably go straight into sanding.

3. With this set there are 40 corners to be cut off to matching bevels (Fig. 3-2B). Tedious marking out and sawing can be avoided if you make a simple jig from scrap wood (Fig. 3-2C). This goes over the edge of the bench like a bench hook. A corner of a pad or other part is pushed into the guides which automatically regulate the amount

of corner projecting, then that is cut off with a fine back saw running alongside the guide (Fig. 3-2D).

4. The important parts are the guides at 45 degrees, which are mounted with their edges level with the edge of a baseboard. Use a square corner of hardboard marked with the bevel to set the guides so the bevel line comes over the baseboard edge (Fig. 3-2E). The guides should be slightly thicker than the hardboard. Sizes of other parts are not critical. Put a strip with a straight edge over the guides to hold down the hardboard you are cutting. Mount the baseboard on another piece that extends a little for the saw teeth to drop on, instead of marking the bench. Put a block underneath to press against the edge of the bench. The jig is shown for righthanded cutting, but if you put the block under the other end you can use it

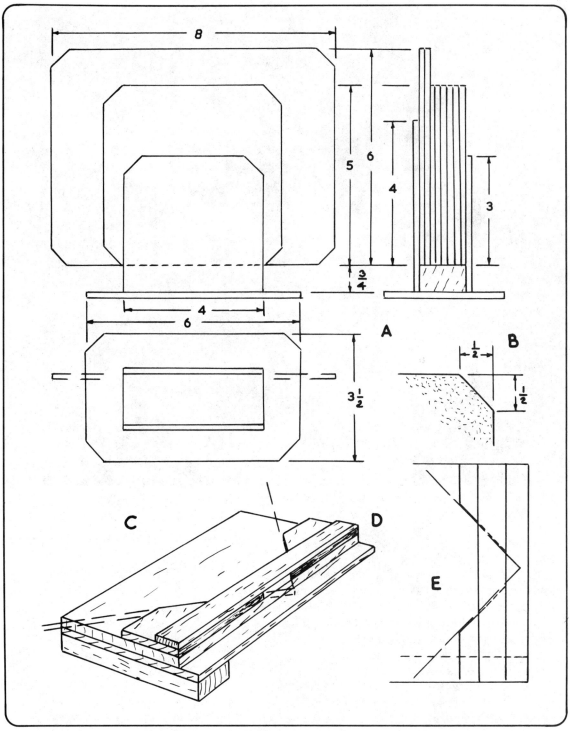

Fig. 3-2. Sizes for hot pads (A, B) and a jig for cutting their corners (C-E).

Fig. 3-3. The jig for cutting hot pad corners mounted in a vise.

lefthanded. If the block is fitted centrally, the jig may be gripped in a vise (Fig. 3-3).

5. Cut all the corners of all pads. Sand the edges and angles, being careful to avoid uneven pressure and distorted shapes.

6. Make a block of wood to go under the stacked pads (Fig. 3-4A). Its width must be the same as the combined thickness of all the pads.

7. Make the back (Fig. 3-4B) and front (Fig. 3-4C) of the stand, with the top corners cut to the standard bevels. Try clamping them to the wood block and test the fit of the pads. Adjust the width of the wood, if necessary.

Materials List for Hot Pads
(all hardboard, unless marked)

6 pieces	5	×	5	
2 pieces	6	×	8	
1 piece	4	×	5	
1 piece	4	×	4	
1 piece	4	×	6	
1 piece	3/4	×	1 1/2 × 5 wood	

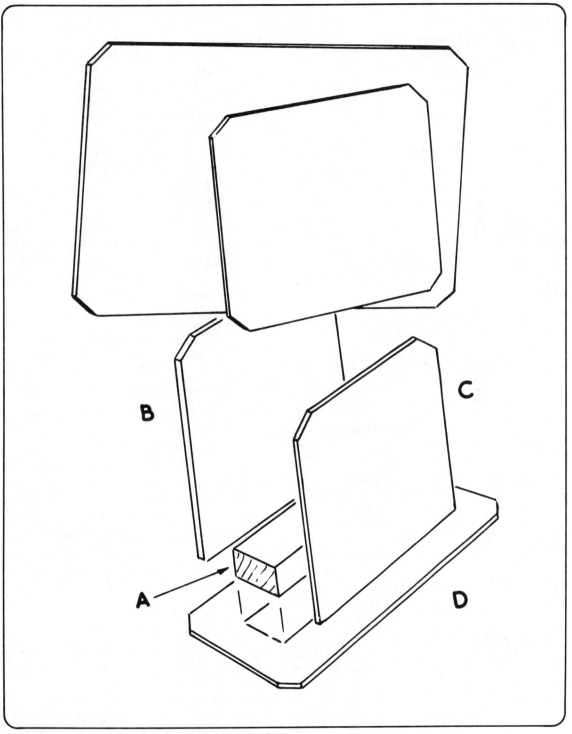

Fig. 3-4. The parts that make the hot pads and their stand.

8. Glue and pin or screw the back and front to the wood block.

9. Make the bottom of the stand (Fig. 3-4D) and attach it to the wood.

10. That completes construction, but the stand could be varnished and might be decorated with a decal on the front. The bottom could have cloth glued on to prevent slipping.

PLATE EASEL

Decorated plates may be hung on the wall, stood on a shelf or kept in a glass-fronted cabinet. If you have a single commemorative plate, or one you just like the look of, it could be mounted on its own easel or stand to put on a table or desk where it can be admired. You can change the plate if you want variety or want to select a plate to suit an occasion.

The stand has to match the plate, but there is considerable tolerance, and plates larger or smaller than the one originally intended can usually be fitted in.

This stand (Fig. 3-5) is designed to suit a plate about 10 inches diameter and 1 inch deep, which is a common size for decorated plates. It is intended to open 45 to 60 degrees for this size plate (Fig. 3-6A), but the exact angle is unimportant and adjustment will allow a plate of another size to be held.

There are two identical parts hinged on their rear edges. The plate rests against two flat surfaces on each part and is retained at the bottom by lips (Fig. 3-6B). For a plate 1 inch (or less) deep, there needs to be about 1 1/4 inches from the flat surfaces (Fig. 3-6C) to allow for the angle and the thickness of the wood. If yours is a much deeper plate, this distance will have to be increased.

The stand could be made of 1/4-inch plywood, preferably of mahogany or similar wood, for the sake of appearance and strength at the lips. Solid wood could be used, but it should be cut with the grain following the slope of the plate for maximum strength at the lips.

1. Draw the outline on grid of 1-inch squares on paper or on one piece of wood (Fig. 3-6D).

Make sure the rear and bottom edges are straight and square to each other, so the easel will open and stand level.

2. The best way to cut the shapes is to fretsaw them, using a hand or power fretsaw. Alternatively, the shapes can be worked by drilling and/or careful cuts with chisel, gouge and file, or Surform tool. The two pieces can be cut together, if they are nailed through the waste parts.

3. Leave the rear and bottom edges square. Some of the other edges could be left square or be rounded. Edges that will be in contact with the rim of the plate should be well rounded, including all the edges that show at the front. This means from the bottom edge, all around the lip, and up to the flat bearing surface on each piece. The edges of the cut-out will look better rounded. In any case, make sure all saw marks are removed.

4. There will be little load on the hinges, so they can be quite light: 1 inch long, held with 1/4-inch screws (Fig. 3-6E).

5. Try the assembled easel with its plate. If it is satisfactory, stain and varnish the wood. Because most plates are a light color, it will usually look best if the wood is given a dark stain.

Materials List for Plate Easel

2 pieces   7 × 8 × 1/4

MAGNETIC CHEESEBOARD

This is a leaf-shaped cheeseboard where the knife fits into a groove in the leaf stem handle (Fig. 3-7). It is held there by a magnet gripping the blade. A simpler board could be made without provision for the knife, if you wish.

Any wood can be used, but because the board should not be polished or varnished, softwood (because of its porosity) is not suggested. A light-colored hardwood looks hygienic, but a darker wood shows up attractively on a light-colored table cloth. Cutting will be done on the board, so a close-grained wood is preferable. The completed

Fig. 3-5. This plate easel folds and will form a stand for a decorative plate.

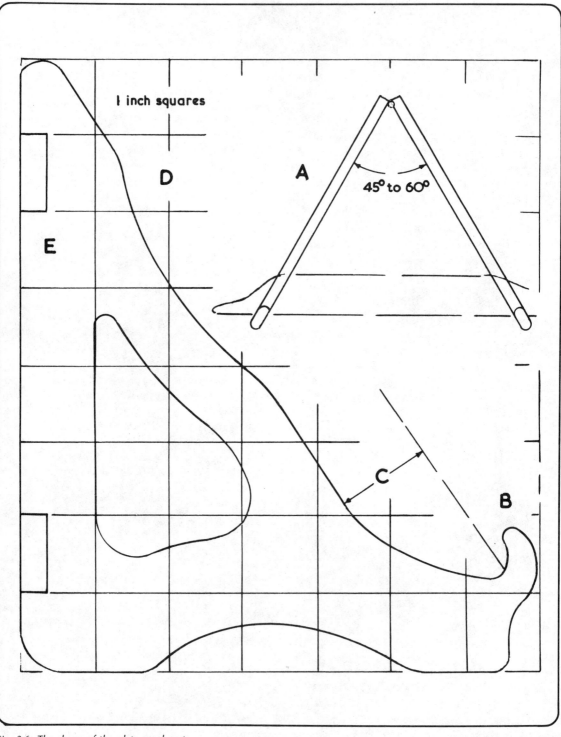

I inch squares

D

A

45° to 60°

E

C

B

Fig. 3-6. The shape of the plate easel parts.

42

Fig. 3-7. This cheeseboard is shaped like a leaf and has a magnet to grip the blade of the knife, which has its handle fitting into a groove.

cheeseboard may be left untreated, but rubbing it with vegetable cooking oil will emphasize the grain markings, allow safe contact with food, and prevent the wood from absorbing water when it is washed.

1. The board could be cut from one piece of wood 8 inches wide, but to reduce the risk of warping it might be better made of two or three pieces glued to make up the width—preferably with the curves of end grain in opposite directions.

2. The knife will have to be provided with a shaped handle, so you may have to obtain an unhandled knife or remove the handle from an existing one. Most suitable knives have tangs about 1 inch long and that suits a wood handle you can make. Obtain the knife and a small round magnet. A magnet diameter of 3/8 or 1/2 inch and a depth

of 1/4 inch would be suitable. Some stainless steels are non-magnetic; make sure this is not the case with the knife you use.

3. Draw and cut the outline of the board (Fig. 3-8A).

4. Cut the profile of the knife handle (Fig. 3-8B). Drive the knife tang into an undersize hole in the handle (Fig. 3-8C). It could be coated with epoxy glue for extra security. Round the handle, if you wish.

5. Draw around the handle on the board handle, with the knife handle end extending a short way. Allow about 1/16 inch each side of the knife handle for the width of the slot.

6. Cut the slot in the board for the knife handle. Its depth (Fig. 3-8D) should allow the blade to rest flat on the surface of the board. The ends of the groove are flared open slightly. This, with

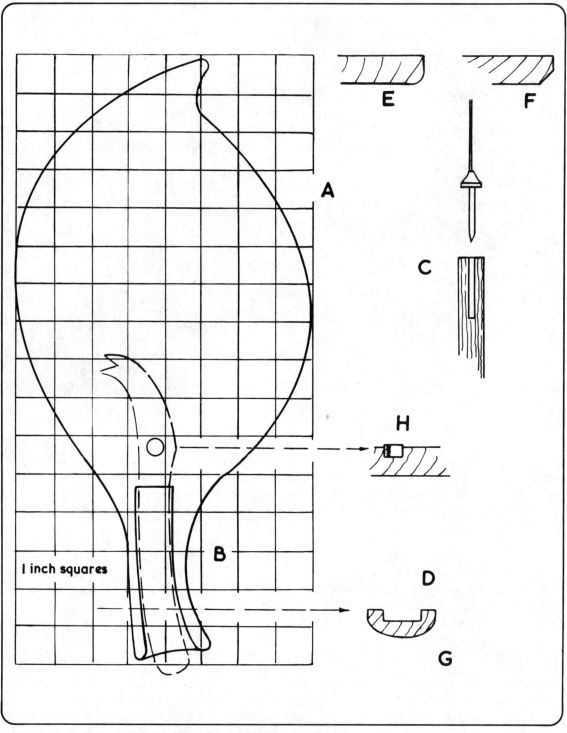

I inch squares

A

C

E

F

H

B

D

G

Fig. 3-8. Shape and details of the magnetic cheeseboard.

the slight overhang of the handle end, makes it easy to remove and replace the knife.

7. The main part of the board could be left with square edges, but it looks better if the underside is rounded (Fig. 3-8E) or beveled (Fig. 3-8F). At the handle end thoroughly round underneath (Fig. 3-8G), so fingers can be slipped under for picking up.

8. Drill for the magnet and secure it with epoxy glue so its top is slightly above the wood surface (Fig. 3-8H).

9. Sand all over. The knife handle may be varnished. Treat the board with vegetable oil, preferably by immersing and draining.

Materials List for Magnetic Cheeseboard

1 piece	3/ 4 × 8 × 16
1 piece	1/2 × 1 1/4 × 6

TABLE LAZY SUSAN

A dish on a turntable makes a good centerpiece on a dining table, possibly during the main course, or at the end of the meal when people are relaxing, but still wish to help themselves to nuts, candy, and other tidbits. For some meals there are large rotating platforms carrying many dishes, but for most of us just one dish, probably of the type divided into segments, is more practical.

If you have a particular dish that will always be used, the lazy Susan can be made to suit it, but it is possible to make such a stand to suit a variety of plates or dishes. The use of a lathe allows you to make a stand to match the dish, or you can use an octagonal or hexagonal outline to make an attractive stand.

There are many variations, from two simple discs to turned designs with molded edges and the top forming a dish itself. The important part is a lazy susan bearing, which consists of two linked plates with a ball race to give smooth turning. These bearings can be bought in sizes from 3 inches upwards. For a single dish or plate of average size, 3-inch or 4-inch bearings will be suitable.

1. For the simplest lazy Susan, make two identical discs about the size of the base of the dish and join them with the bearing (Fig. 3-9A). The method of fitting the bearing is described in the instruction for the television turntable (Fig. 2-5).

2. Without a lathe the discs could be sawn and the outlines smoothed, but it will be easier to get an accurate outline if you use a hexagon or octagon. A regular hexagon is drawn by stepping off the radius around the circumference of a circle, then joining these points (Fig. 3-9B). An octagon is drawn from a square. Measure half a diagonal from the corners along each side and join those points (Fig. 3-9C).

3. To prevent the dish from slipping, cloth may be glued to the wood. You could also glue abrasive paper to the wood with its grit side outwards. Fine abrasive paper sold as "wet and dry" is particularly suitable because the grit is very securely bonded. Both surfaces could be treated so the lazy Susan can be turned over.

4. You can turn the top to fit the dish. If there is a recess the wood can be turned to fit (Fig. 3-9D). If the bottom is deeper, there can be a recess in the wood (Fig. 3-9E). If the bottom of the dish is flat, the wood can be turned with a lip (Fig. 3-9F). When the dish is larger than its support the edge of the wood is not very obvious, but if it is larger and lipped, the outside can be curved (Fig. 3-9G) or molded.

5. One way of retaining a round dish on an octagonal or hexagonal stand is to use dowels. Make the stand large enough for you to position four or three small dowels near the points (Fig. 3-9H). Round their tops and let them stand high enough to retain the dish (Fig. 3-9J).

6. The base does not have to be as large as the stand, whatever the shapes. It can be set in about 1 inch all around without affecting stability. Use wood screws upwards in the bearing and self-tapping screws through the base (Fig. 3-9K). Covering the base with cloth will hide the screw heads and prevent slipping.

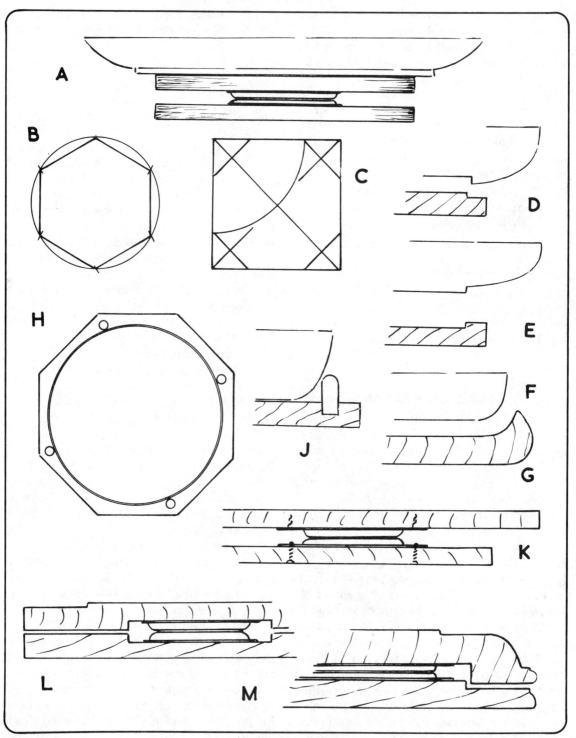

Fig. 3-9. The table lazy Susan can be turned on a lathe or sawn octagonal, and the bearing fitted to the surfaces or let in.

Fig. 3-10. This lazy Susan has the turned top overhanging the bearing and base and is designed to fit a particular dish.

7. Lazy Susan bearings are about 3/8 inch thick, so if you make the simplest assembly using 3/8-inch plywood the total height is 1 1/8 inch. The height can be reduced by letting the bearing into one or both pieces (Fig. 3-9L). Except for a small amount of clearance, you can almost eliminate the bearing thickness.

8. An interesting and attractive lathe project hides the bearing by letting it in and making the top part to overhang the base (Fig. 3-10). When assembled and cloth on the bottom hides the screw heads, your guests will be unable to see how you arranged rotation of your lazy Susan (Fig. 3-9M). The top surface can be made to suit a particular dish or left flat and made non-slip to take any plate.

DEEP TRAY

For many purposes a shallow tray is satisfactory, but if you need to carry piled-up dishes, bottles, glasses, or any other fairly high load, it is safer to have a tray with deep sides. This tray (Fig. 3-11A) has upright sides 3 inches deep to hold the contents secure, but appearance is improved by sloping ends pierced with hand holes. Top edges are shaped all around. Corners are made with shallow dadoes and screws, which are not hidden. Round-head brass or plated screws may be regarded as decoration.

Although the bottom appears solid, it is plywood in a frame, with the joint lines covered by the tray ends and sides (Fig. 3-11B). The plywood

47

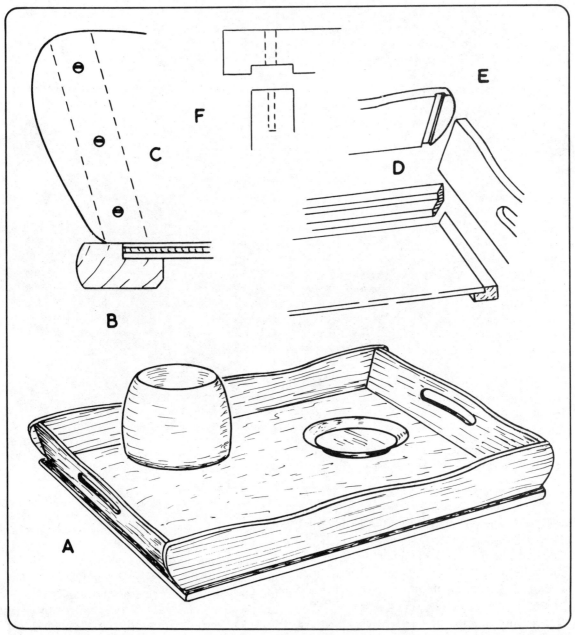

Fig. 3-11. A deep tray (A) will carry more than a shallow one. Base is framed plywood (B) and corners are notched (C-F).

panel could be left with its normal surface exposed, or it might be veneered or covered with Formica. A pictorial place mat could be glued to the plywood. Untreated plywood might be covered with a loose place mat that could be removed for clean-

ing. If ready-veneered plywood or place mats are used, the tray size will have to be adjusted to suit. The size given should be satisfactory for general purposes (Fig. 3-12A).

Any wood can be used. All solid parts are 5/8

inch thick. Softwood may match pine furniture, but a stronger tray will be made from a good hardwood that is finished with polish, varnish, or lacquer.

1. Prepare all the wood to width and thickness.

2. Make a full-size drawing of an end (Fig. 3-12B) to suit the actual sections of the wood to be used. The angle shown is 15 degrees, but this is not important so long as you maintain the same angle throughout.

3. Prepare the bottom first, as the need to

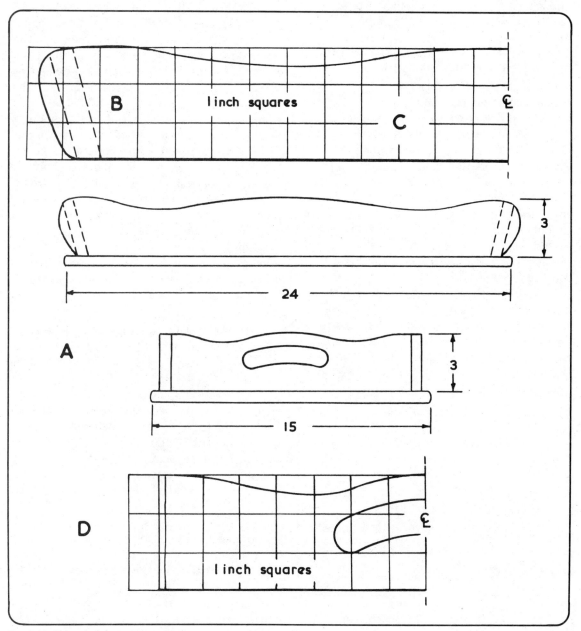

Fig. 3-12. Shapes of deep tray parts.

cover its joints will settle the final sizes of the sides and ends. Cut sufficient strips with rabbets to suit the plywood (Fig. 3-11B).

4. Miter the corners.

5. Assemble the plywood and its frame. The glue can be augmented by light pins driven down through the plywood close enough to its edges for the heads to be hidden when the other parts are fitted.

6. Mark and cut the dadoes before shaping the sides. Put them in positions that will allow the ends to cover the plywood joints (Fig. 3-11E). The dadoes can be quite shallow (Fig. 3-11F), because strength will be provided by the screws.

7. Mark and shape the outlines of the sides (Fig. 3-12C). See that each side is symmetrical and the opposite sides match. Round the exposed edges.

8. The ends are cut squarely (Fig. 3-12D). Bevel the bottom edges. Cut the hand holes by drilling at the ends and sawing away the waste. Round the edges to make a comfortable grip. Cut the shaped top edges and round them to match the top edges of the sides.

9. Join the sides to the ends with glue and screws (Fig. 3-11C). Position this assembly over the bottom and mark the locations of screws to be driven upwards. Their number will depend on the intended loads, but if glue is also used, 6- or 8-gauge screws 1 1/4 inch long and about 5 inches apart should be satisfactory.

Materials List for Deep Tray

2 bottom sides	5/8 × 1 1/4 × 25
2 bottom ends	5/8 × 1 1/4 × 16
1 bottom panel	14 × 23 × 1/4 plywood
2 sides	5/8 × 3 × 26
2 ends	5/8 × 3 × 15

---

10. Finish the tray with polish, varnish, or paint. Strips of cloth glued under the bottom frame—all around or just at the corners—will prevent slipping or marking a polished table top.

KNIFE BOX

A deep tray with a central handle is traditionally called a knife box, but it can have many other uses. Although it was, and still could be, used for cutlery, it might be used around the home for cleaning materials, in the garden for small tools and packets of seeds, or in the shop or elsewhere for carrying tools. This box (Fig. 3-13) is a size that will suit many purposes (Fig. 3-14A), but dimensions can be altered to suit your needs without affecting constructional methods.

The wood chosen depends on use. For cutlery it would best be an attractive hardwood given a clear finish. For garden use it could be any wood, including exterior-grade plywood, given a painted finish. In the shop it might be any wood, possibly without any finish applied.

Construction can range from simple nailed joints to notched or dovetailed corners. Dovetails give a quality appearance under a clear finish.

1. Mark out the pair of ends (Fig. 3-14B). The slopes are drawn at 15 degrees, but the exact angle is unimportant, providing the box is symmetrical.

2. Mark out the wood for the division/handle (Fig. 3-14C). In the simplest construction ends could be nailed to it, but it is better to notch into dado slots (Fig. 3-14D).

3. Make the handle hole by drilling the ends and sawing away the waste. Shape the outside of the wood and round all edges that the lifting hand will touch.

4. Make the two sides (Fig. 3-14E) slightly too long. Bevel the edges to match the angle of the ends.

5. The ends could be notched over the sides (Fig. 3-14F), then thin nails driven both ways to make strong corners. If the nails are set below the surface and covered with stopping, they will be inconspicuous under any finish.

Fig. 3-13. A deep box with a central handle can be used for cutlery, but there are other uses. This is one made of oak and the bottom is covered with cloth.

6. If dovetails are used, their cutting is straightforward (Fig. 3-14G), except their angles should be related to the sides of the wood and not tilted to the angle of the side, which would not be as strong due to the shortening of the grain at one side of each tail.

7. Assemble these parts. Check squareness. If necessary, level the lower edges.

8. Make the bottom (Fig. 3-14H) so it extends about 1/2 inch all around. Screw and glue it to the other parts.

Materials List for Knife Box

2 ends	1/2 × 3	× 10
2 sides	1/2 × 3 1/2	× 15
1 division	1/2 × 6	× 15
1 bottom	1/2 × 9	× 16

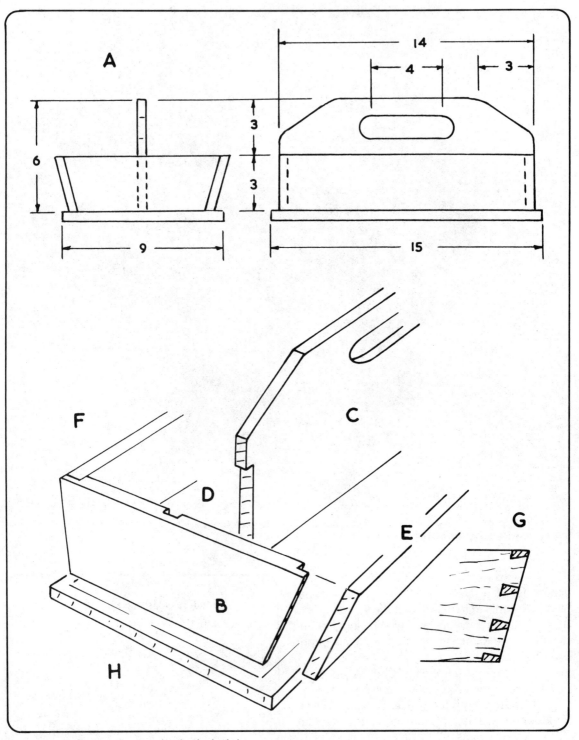

Fig. 3-14. Sizes and construction details of a knife box.

FRENCH CUTLERY CARRIER

Cutlery may be kept in a fitted box or cabinet, or go into compartments in a drawer, or be in a sectioned tray. This carrier offers another solution. The idea is from France. The cutlery goes vertically into the four sections of a box with a central handle (Fig. 3-15). The sizes suggested (Fig. 3-16A) will easily carry the knives, forks, and spoons for six place settings.

The design can have other applications if sizes are adapted. Four bottles or drink cans could go into compartments of suitable size. Milk cartons might be carried safely. There could be mixed loads if you settle on what may be fitted in, so the carrier could bring home the milk, be taken out to get drinks and then used for cutlery.

For the sizes shown all the wood could be 1/2 inch thick. It could be softwood, but it would have a rich appearance for use with the best cutlery if it is made of mahogany or other hardwood with a dark finish. A moderate gloss would be appropriate.

Although it is possible to fit the partitions into dadoes in the sides and use dovetails at the corners—if you want to give the carrier a cabinet finish, for most purposes it will be adequate to use glue and fine nails sunk below the surface at all joints. The following instructions assume that will be the method used, but an enthusiast can easily adapt the design to cut joints.

1. The key part is the central division that extends up to form the handle (Figs. 3-17A and 3-18A). The division the other way (Figs. 3-17B and 3-18B) should be the same width and its grain upright. Cut deep halved slots in these pieces to make push-fit joints.

2. For the handle there is a curved top and a hole large enough for two or three fingers (Fig. 3-18C). Round the edges of the hole and the exterior parts that will be held.

3. The outside pieces are joined to the two divisions and to each other (Fig. 3-17C). There could be two short pieces and two long pieces overlapping them at each level, but if they overlap in turn around the square (Fig. 3-16B), all pieces

can be the same size (Fig. 3-18D). Check the sizes against the divisions. If you are uncertain of the accuracy of your work, a little extra can be left at the overlapping end to be planed off after assembly.

4. Mark on the divisions the positions of the outside strips. The lower one is 1/2 inch up, to allow space for cleaning. The upper one is level with the top edge of the short division.

5. Glue the divisions together. Make sure they finish squarely and with their bottoms level.

6. Mark the eight outside strips with their positions on the divisions and with the overlaps.

7. Glue and nail the strips to the divisions, then nail the overlapping corners. Strength will be increased if the nails are driven in an alternate diagonal manner to produce dovetail nailing (Fig. 3-16C).

8. Sink the nail heads below the surface and cover them with stopping.

9. The bottom (Fig. 3-17D) is a simple square attached to the divisions. Because the division end grain does not provide a very good grip for nails, it would be better to attach the bottom with screws. For cutlery the bottom could be lined with cloth stuck on. That would be easier to do if one piece of cloth is stuck all over before screwing on, than if four pieces are added later. However, it would then be advisable to finish all the wood before gluing on the cloth and attaching the bottom.

Materials List for French Cutlery Carrier

1 division	1/2 × 6 × 12
1 division	1/2 × 6 × 6
1 bottom	1/2 × 6 × 6
8 sides	1/2 × 2 × 7

CHILD'S STEPS

A young child wants to see what mother is doing or try to help, but is not tall enough. This twin step (Fig. 3-19A) allows a child to step up 5 inches or 10 inches safely to reach a table or work surface.

Fig. 3-15. This French carrier will take knives, forks, and spoons vertically.

54

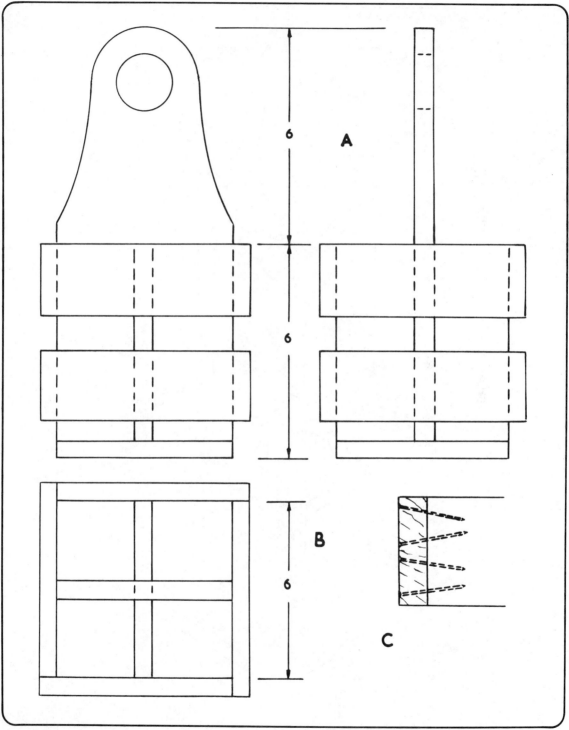

Fig. 3-16. Sizes of a French cutlery carrier.

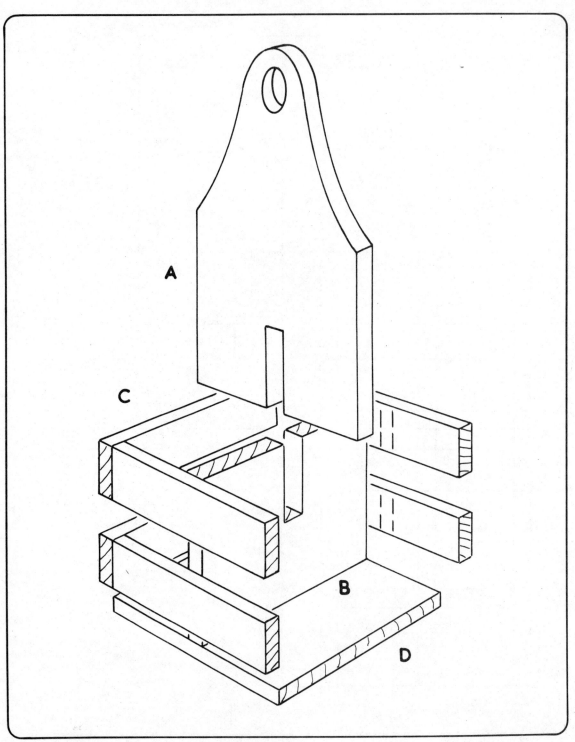

Fig. 3-17. How the parts of the French cutlery carrier fit together.

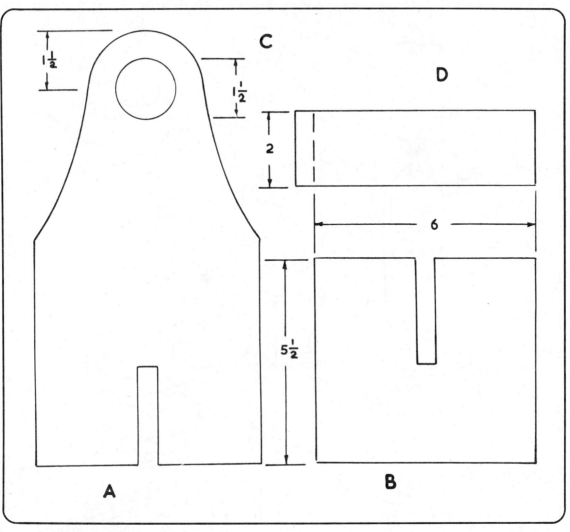

Fig. 3-18. Sizes of parts of a French cutlery carrier.

Any but the smallest child could move the steps themselves. Construction is strong enough to stand up to rough use, either by the child or by an adult using the steps to get at an otherwise inaccessible shelf or other high storage place. If the steps are intended for adult use, the treads should be made wider—6 inches would give a better bearing surface for larger feet.

The parts are made from solid wood. They could all be cut from 1-by-12-inch softwood, but 3/4-inch would be adequate and lighter. Hardwood might look better, but it would add to the weight. The sides and back have their grain vertical.

Construction is shown with the treads set into dadoes in the sides. There is then no risk of them slipping down in use. Merely screwing or nailing through the sides would not be safe. The back is shown let into a rabbet (Fig. 3-19B). This is not so important—you could just screw the overlapping edges—but using rabbets makes better joints and covers the top dadoes. Shaping the edges softens appearance, but straight lines could be used (Fig. 3-20A). Hand holes in the sides make lifting easy.

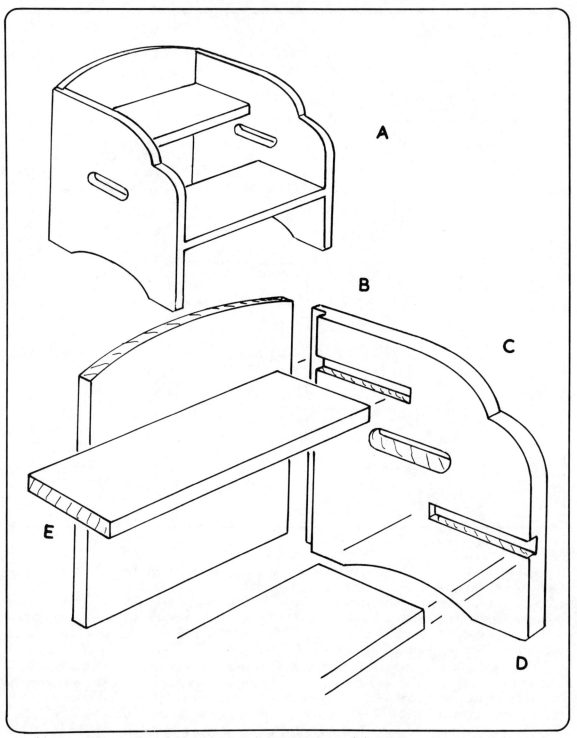

Fig. 3-19. These steps (A) allow a child to reach a worktop. Treads fit into dadoes (B-D).

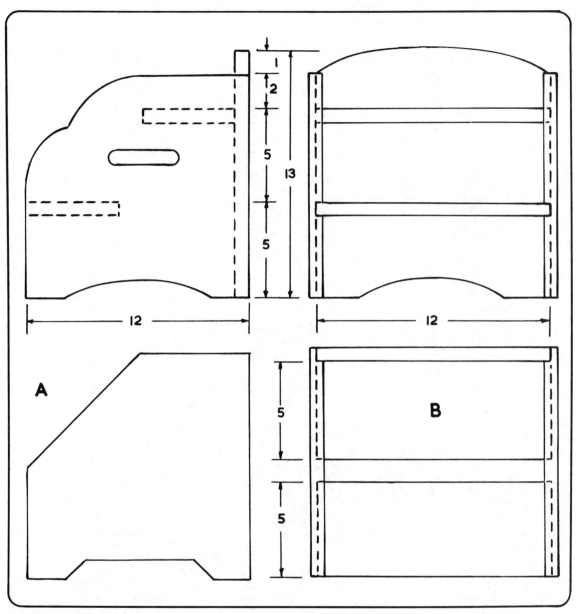

Fig. 3-20. Suggested sizes for child's steps.

If sizes are altered, make the rise the same from the floor to the top of the first tread, and from that tread to the top of the second tread. This is important in any series of steps, so the feet raise the same amount at each step.

1. Start with the two sides (Fig. 3-19C), mark-ing out from the squared drawing (Fig. 3-21).

2. Mark the sizes of the dadoes and rabbets the same as the actual wood you are using, allow-ing for the thickness it will be after final planing.

3. Cut the rabbets and dadoes to about half thickness. The dado for the bottom step could be stopped so the joint does not show on the front

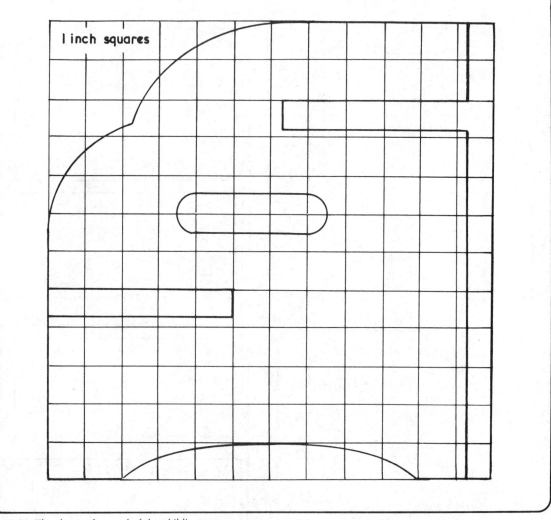

I inch squares

Fig. 3-21. The shape of an end of the child's steps.

edge, but for this piece of furniture is should look satisfactory exposed (Fig. 3-19D).

4. Make the hand holes by drilling the ends and cutting away between them. Round the edges to make comfortable grips. Round the top and front outside edges.

5. If the wood for the back is not exactly 12 inches wide, it does not matter. It fits into the rabbets and will determine the overall width of the steps.

6. The curve at the bottom of the back is the same as in the ends and can be marked from them. The ends of the top curve can also be marked from them and joined. Round the thickness of the top.

Materials List for Child's Steps	
2 sides	3/4 × 12 × 13
1 back	3/4 × 12 × 14
2 treads	3/4 × 5 × 13

7. Make the two treads (Fig. 3-19E) the same as the width of the back. See that they have square ends so the assembly can be made without twist (Fig. 3-20B).

8. Glue the parts, but screws should be driven through the sides into the back and treads. Round-head screws could be regarded as decoration under a clear finish, or flat heads could be painted over. Round all exposed edges after assembly.

Chapter 4

Stools and Seats

It is natural to sit when it is not necessary to stand, so it is fairly safe to say that we cannot have too many seats. In a weekend you cannot hope to make a large and elaborate chair, but there are plenty of simpler seats that can supplement your stock or serve in special circumstances, such as outdoors or at a bar or work surface.

The simplest seats are stools, which can be anything from foot height to tall alternatives to standing. If you put a back or arms on a stool it might not be as form-fitting as a chair with more time spent on its shaping, but it could make good exterior furniture or be comfortable in a play room if fitted with cushions.

DRESSER STOOL

A seat in front of a dressing table is appreciated. It has many uses in a bedroom and if it is a suitable height it can be pressed into use when every seat in the home has to be used for a houseful of guests.

Particleboard already veneered on the sides

and ends allows simple construction of a stool. In this stool (Fig. 4-1A) sizes are mainly controlled by an available cushion. Although one could be made, it might be simpler to find a cushion and make the stool to fit it. In the example the cushion is assumed to be 12 inches by 15 inches and about 3 inches thick when not compressed (Fig. 4-2A). The seat top is then 19 inches above the floor, but the cushion will probably compress to about 17 inches.

The particleboard could have wood veneer or be a white or other shade of plastic, depending on anything else you want to match in the room. Careful squaring of the parts you cut is important because the modern angular outline does nothing to hide any errors.

1. From the cushion obtain the size of the top panel (Fig. 4-1B). It should be about the same length as the cushion so the projections of the stool ends will grip well enough to prevent the cushion from moving too freely.

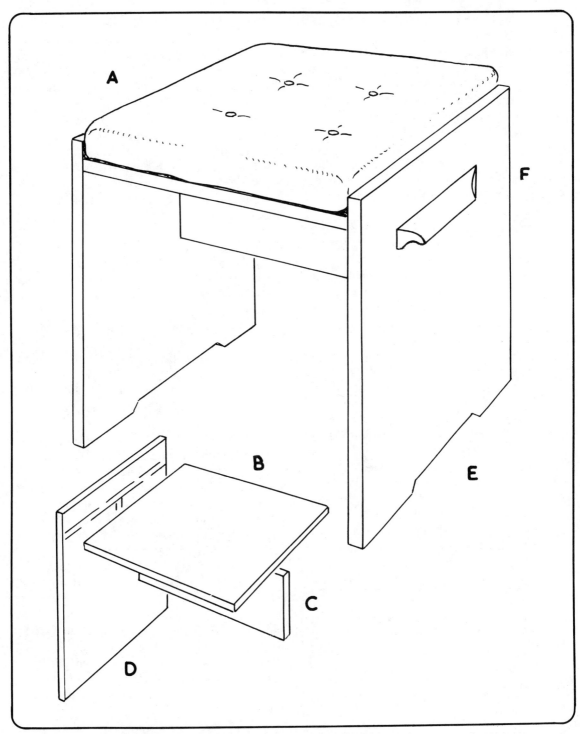

Fig. 4-1. This dresser stool is made of veneered particleboard and has a loose cushion top.

2. Make the brace (Fig. 4-1C) the same length as the top.

3. Make the two ends (Fig. 4-1D). Veneer the top edges. There is no need to veneer the bottoms. The bottoms could be left cut straight across, but the stool will stand better on slight unevenness if you cut away to form feet (Fig. 4-1E).

4. Rigidity of the stool depends on the strength of the joints. Dowels or screws could be used. Whichever are used, they should be in sufficient number—probably five across the seat end, three down the stay end, and four between seat and brace.

5. Dowels should go as deeply as possible into the thickness (Fig. 4-2B) and the parts held with clamps while the glue sets.

6. If screws are used, they can be wood screws, self-tapping screws, or special screws intended for particleboard. Counterbore and drill undersize holes in the inner part as far as the screw is intended to go. It is unwise to try to make a screw cut its own way, so drill full depth for the threaded part (Fig. 4-2C). Counterbore deep enough to allow a matching plastic plug to be glued in (Fig. 4-2D). The seat and brace could be joined with dowels, even if screws are used at the ends. Use glue with screws, but they pull the joints together and clamps will not be needed.

7. Lifting handles could be added (Fig. 4-1F). Besides their practical value, they break up the plain appearance of the ends. They could be plastic or metal, or you could shape and varnish wooden ones. Wood veneer on the particleboard can be finished like wood, but plastic veneer does not need any special finishing.

Materials List for Dresser Stool

1 top	5/8 × 12 × 16
1 brace	5/8 × 6 × 16
2 ends	5/8 × 12 × 18
2 handles	1 1/8 × 1 1/8 × 6

BATHROOM STOOL

It is convenient to be able to sit rather higher than chair level when drying yourself in a bathroom. It is also better to have a soft seat against bare skin. If the stool can also provide somewhere to put odds and ends, its value is further increased. This stool (Fig. 4-3) satisfies all these requirements. It is 19 inches high, and has an upholstered seat and a tray/shelf underneath.

The stool could be made of softwood, but would be stronger if made of a close-grained hardwood that would be better able to stand up to rocking onto two legs and taking the rough treatment unintentionally meted out by a bather with soap-filled eyes.

Joints are shown doweled, using 1/4-inch or 5/16-inch dowels. They could be tenoned for added strength, but close-fitting joints and well-glued dowels should be adequate. The stool is square, so sizes are the same both ways (Fig. 4-4A).

1. Mark out the four legs together with the positions of the rails (Fig. 4-4B).

2. Mark out the eight rails together. Make sure they match and the ends are square.

3. Groove the four lower rails for the tray bottom (Fig. 4-4C). This could be oil-tempered hardboard or thin exterior-grade plywood.

4. Mark out the dowel positions on the rails and legs (Fig. 4-4D). They can be evenly spaced for the top rails, but for the lower rails the hole positions must miss the grooves. The dowels will meet in the legs and their ends should be mitered to allow maximum penetration.

5. Hollow the top edges of the lower rails (Fig. 4-4E) and round all edges that hands might touch.

6. The tray bottom fits into the grooves in the rails, but at the corners it could be notched around the legs, although it will be better to notch the legs in line with the grooves, so the bottom can be cut across (Fig. 4-4F). Do not cut the notches any deeper than necessary, to avoid weakening the legs.

7. Remove all sharpness from the legs and

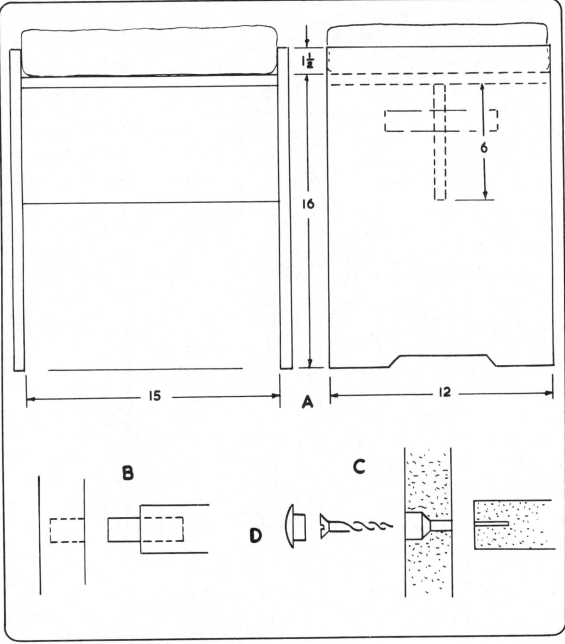

Fig. 4-2. Sizes and construction of the dresser stool.

rails. Sand everything, then first assemble two opposite sides. See that they are square and match each other as a pair. Use them as a guide to the size of the tray bottom, which need not reach to the bottoms of the rail grooves, or it might prevent rail joints closing tightly. Fit in the tray bottom and

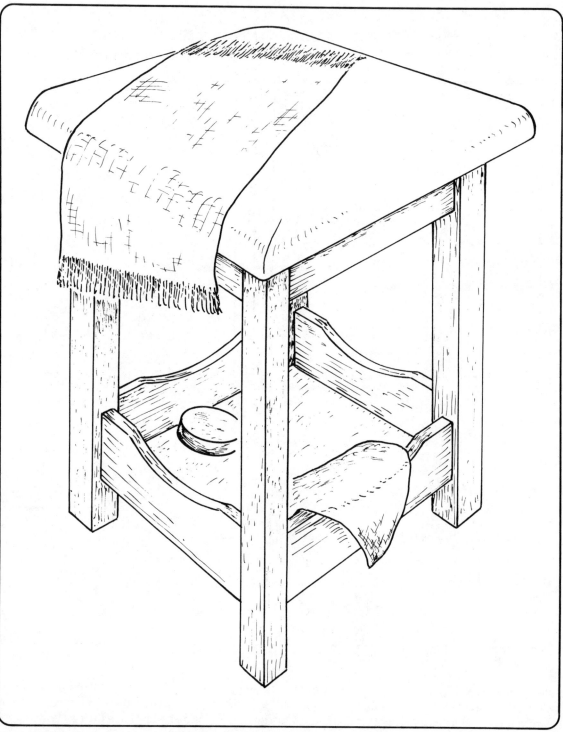

Fig. 4-3. This bathroom stool has a padded top and a deep shelf.

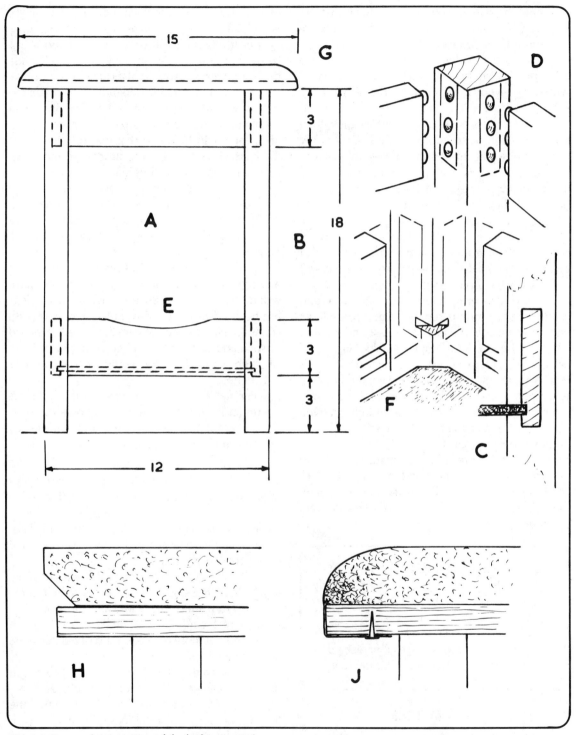

Fig. 4-4. Sizes and construction of the bathroom stool.

assemble the rails the other way. Check that the assembly is square in all directions and stands upright on a level surface.

8. When the glue has set, check that the top rails and legs will present a flat surface to the top, which is plywood and should overlap about 1 1/2 inches all around (Fig. 4-4G).

9. Round its edges and corners slightly, then screw down through it into the rails. Drill a few holes to allow air in and out of the upholstery.

10. Padding is a piece of rubber or plastic foam. For this purpose a thickness of 1 inch should be enough, but you can make it thicker if you wish.

11. Cut the foam slightly larger than the top. How much depends on the softness of the foam, but 1/2 inch all around should be satisfactory. Cut away the underside (Fig. 4-4H), so the edge will compress to a curved shape.

12. The covering should be waterproof and plastic-coated fabric is suitable. Cut a piece large enough to go over the foam and tuck underneath.

13. Use 3/8-inch copper tacks. First pull across the center one way and tack underneath (Fig. 4-4J). Do the same across the center the other way, then work towards the corners at a suitable interval to pull the covering to a smoothly curved edge. With many materials, a spacing of 1 1/2 inches should be satisfactory.

14. At the corners fold the material under so as to show a smooth curve on top. Trim the edges of the fabric inside the line of tacks underneath.

15. Give the woodwork a water-resistant paint or varnish finish.

Materials List for Bathroom Stool	
4 legs	1 1/4 × 1 1/4 × 19
8 rails	5/8 × 3 × 12
1 bottom	11 × 11 × 1/8
	oil- tempered hardboard
1 top	15 × 15 × 1/2 plywood

TWO STOOLS

Any stool is attractive if you want to sit with your feet up, but a substantial stool of one step height is useful for reaching shelves in the kitchen or elsewhere. It might have uses in the yard and it can be used as a seat by a young child. If it is well made of strong wood it should stand up to rough use.

How a stool is made depends on the intended uses. If you are only concerned with utility, it can be plain. If you want it to have a better appearance there can be some shaping. In this project there are two stools, but construction is the same. Only the profiles are different.

The plain stool (Figs. 4-5 and 4-6A) provides a steady platform or low seat. The other stool (Fig. 4-6B) is generally similar, but the outlines have been softened with curves, which results in a folk appearance.

In both cases the wood may be hard or soft and 5/8 inch thick, although with a strong hardwood this could be reduced to 1/2 inch. The legs are notched into the sides, but assembly is with screws, which can be left with their heads exposed or sunk and covered with plugs or stopping. With 5/8-inch wood all screws could be 8 gauge by 1 1/4 inches.

For stability the legs extend so their corners are under the corners of the top. If you alter sizes, do not let the top overhang the area covered by the feet more than a very small amount.

1. The slope of the legs governs the layout of other parts. Make a full-size drawing (Fig. 4-6C) on the edge of a scrap of plywood and use this as a guide to angles of cuts and the lengths of the legs. An adjustable bevel set to the angle can be used on all related parts.

2. For the plain stool make the two sides (Fig. 4-6D). Mark the slopes of the legs and their thicknesses. From these mark and cut the slots (Fig. 4-7A), which could be 3/16 inch deep in 5/8-inch wood and not more than one-third of the thickness of other wood.

3. Make the two legs (Fig. 4-7B). The length (Fig. 4-7C) can be obtained from the full-size drawing (Fig. 4-6C). Cut away the sides to match the tops so the outsides of the legs will be level with the outsides of the sides when fitted into the slots.

Fig. 4-5. The simpler of the two stools.

Bevel the ends, but final planing of the top can be done after joining to the sides.

4. Cut Vs to about half the length of the legs, to provide feet.

5. The top (Fig. 4-6E) is a plain rectangle. It could be left a little oversize for planing level after assembly.

6. Glue and screw the legs into their slots. Two screws in each place should be sufficient. Check squareness of the assembly. It should stand level, but if not, the feet can be planed later. Plane top surfaces level.

7. Fit the top with glue and screws—3 inches apart along the sides and 1 at the centers of the legs will be adequate.

8. Plane edges level, take sharpness off all around, and sand all surfaces. Finish with paint or varnish.

9. The second stool has the same slope to the legs (Fig. 4-6C). The top overlaps the sides by 1/2 inch and the feet are carried out to the same width, so they provide a stable base.

10. Make the two sides (Fig. 4-6F). Mark out first in the same way as for the plain stool and cut the slots.

11. Draw the shaped edges (Fig. 4-7D) and cut the two sides symmetrical and to match each other. Leave cutting the curves at the ends until after making the top, as they have to match its shaped ends.

12. Make the two legs (Fig. 4-7E), getting the length and angle in the same way as for the first

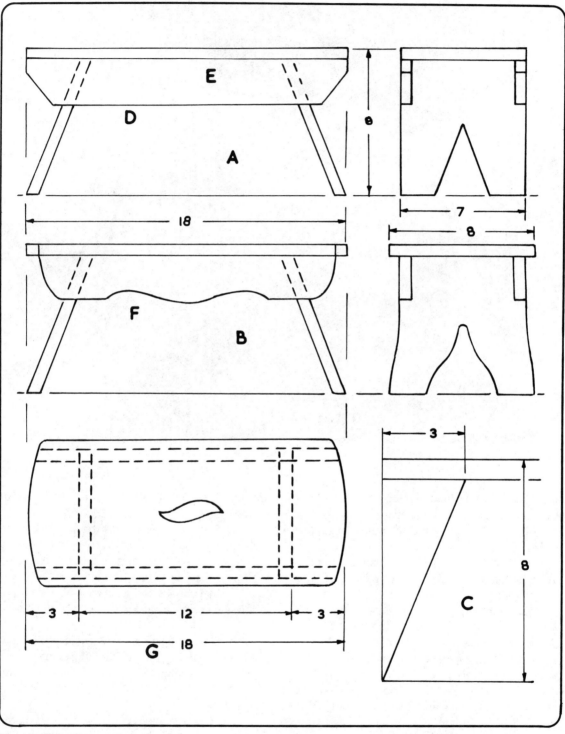

Fig. 4-6. Sizes of two versions of a stool.

70

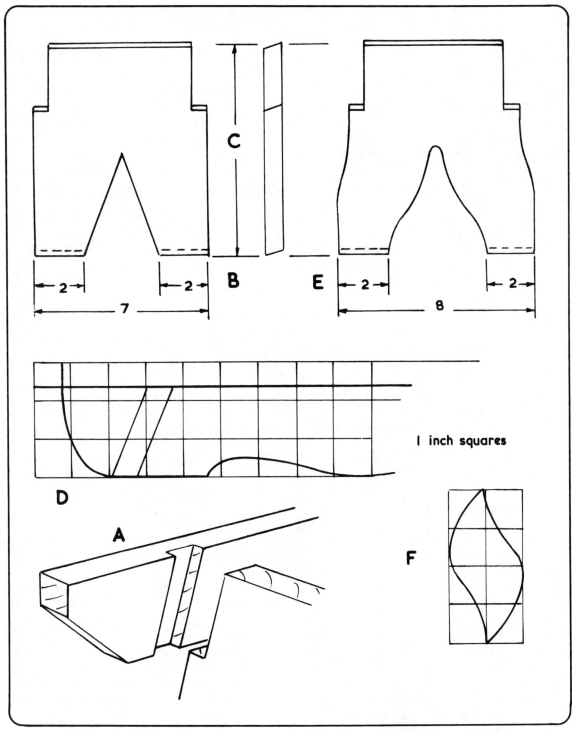

Fig. 4-7. Parts of the two stools.

stool. The sides will be 7 inches apart, but the feet extend to 8 inches. Draw the curves to give a symmetrical shape. A hole can be drilled at the top of the cut-out.

13. Mark out the top (Fig. 4-6G). The end curves are 12-inch radius. From this shape get the length of the stool sides and complete shaping their ends.

14. There could be a hand hole at the center of the top. Simplest would be a slot with rounded ends, made by drilling two 1-inch holes 4 inches apart and cutting away the waste wood between them. A leaf shape, in keeping with the traditional appearance, is suggested (Fig. 4-7F). It can be cut with a fretsaw or coping saw.

15. Assemble the stool in the same way as the first one. Finish it with paint or varnish. A traditional finish to a painted stool would be to add floral or other designs to the sides and top, either painted on by hand or applied with decals, which can be protected with varnish.

Materials List for Two Stools	
First Stool	
2 sides	5/8 × 2 3/8 × 19
2 legs	5/8 × 7 × 19
1 top	5/8 × 7 × 19
Second Stool	
2 sides	5/8 × 2 3/8 × 19
2 legs	5/8 × 8 × 9
1 top	5/8 × 8 × 19

CAMP STOOL

A folding stool with a cloth or canvas top is one of the most compact seats. Although it is usually described as a camp stool, it has many open-air uses, such as sitting on the waterside fishing or relaxing between bouts of gardening. Indoors it can be used by children or pressed into use when ex-tra seating is required. You could make six and put them in the car trunk and still leave plenty of room for other things.

This stool (Fig. 4-8) is of a reasonable size and height for normal use (Fig. 4-9A). If you alter the sizes, make sure the feet spread at least to the same width as the top. The design suits cloth 12 inches wide. This should be fairly stout and a type with little stretch. If you can buy it 12 inches wide it will have manufactured selvedges that can be used as they are. If you have to cut from wider cloth or canvas, the edges will have to be turned under and sewn.

It would be unwise to use softwood because it would not be strong enough in the joints. A close-grained hardwood would be better. The strongest joints between tops and legs would be mortise and tenon, but dowels could also be used. If the stool will be kept under cover when out of use there is no need for special precautions. If it will spend much time outside in wet conditions, the cloth should be waterproofed, the wood treated with preservative, and the tacks and bolts made of corrosive-resistant metal.

1. Mark out and make the four legs (Fig. 4-10A). Allow extra for a tenon, if that is to be used. Round the bottom ends in the direction of opening (Fig. 4-9B). This is better than cutting the ends to go flat on the ground, because the ground is rarely level and that would make weak points. Drill for 1/4-inch bolts.

2. The two tops are the same length, but the inner edges of the legs on one (Fig. 4-10B) come level with the outer edges of the legs on the other (Fig. 4-10C).

3. Mark out the joints and cut them before doing any rounding. Mortises are blind, so the tenons go about three-fourths of the way through (Fig. 4-10D). If you choose dowels, they should be 1/2 inch diameter and go about 5/8 inch into each part (Fig. 4-10E).

4. Round the outer edges of the tops (Fig. 4-9C). Round the ends, which will extend about 1/2 inch outside the cloth top.

5. Join the legs to the tops. Check square-

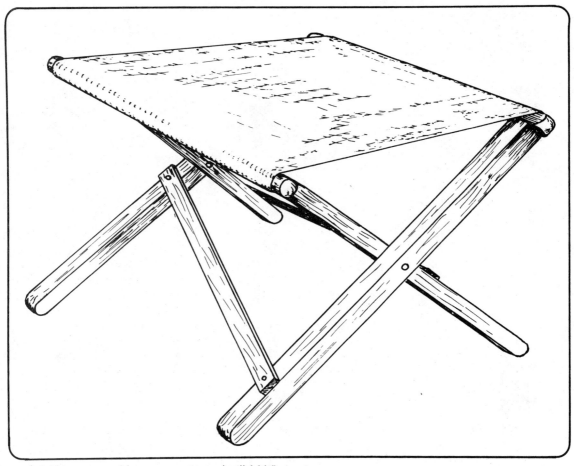

Fig. 4-8. This camp stool has a canvas top and will fold flat.

ness. Also try one assembly over the other to see that they are parallel and match each other.

6. Any 1/4-inch bolts can be used, but a round head outside is neater. Inside there could be some form of locknut or you could hammer over the end of the bolt to prevent the nut from loosening in use and coming off. In any case, put washers between the legs and under the nuts. Assemble temporarily, while you make and fit other parts, then the wood can be separated for varnishing.

7. The diagonal braces are important to stiffen the stool and prevent strain if the user rocks it. They go on what will be the outsides when the stool is folded (Fig. 4-9D) and are arranged between the marks on the legs in opposite directions

(Fig. 4-9E). Glue them in place, with a central screw at each crossing (Fig. 4-9F).

8. Within an inch or so either way you can adjust the width and height of the stool according to the length of cloth you allow. The stool is drawn with the tops at about the same distance apart as the feet, giving a width of 15 inches and a height of 13 inches. Altering one size affects the other. For instance, increasing the height reduces the width of the top.

9. Have the cloth longer than it will finally be. Turn it under and tack below a top rail (Fig. 4-9G). Notch around the legs. Tacks at 1 1/2-inch intervals, with extra at the ends, should be strong enough.

10. Open the stool to the correct width and

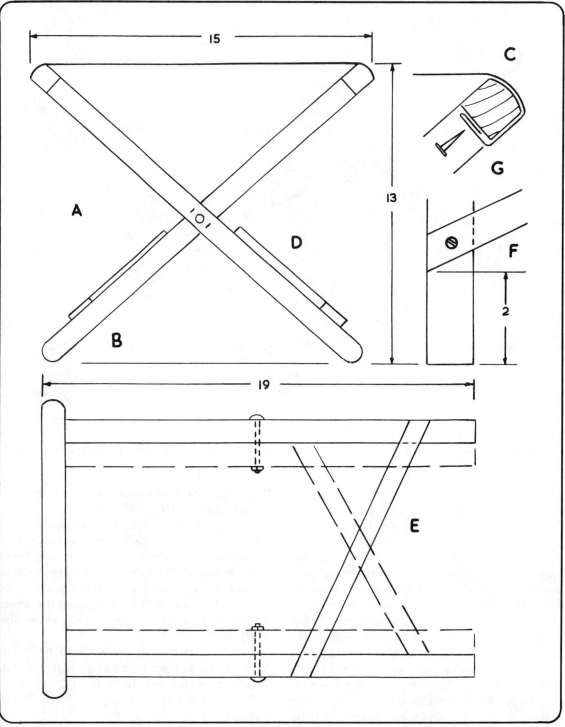

Fig. 4-9. Sizes and construction of the camp stool.

tack under the other top rail in the same way.

11. Test the action of the stool, then remove the bolts and varnish the wood, using boat or external varnish. Varnishing under the cloth does not matter, but the wood can be varnished before tacking if you wish.

12. Bolt the legs finally and lock the nuts.

Materials List for Camp Stool

4 legs	1 × 1 × 19
2 tops	1 × 1 × 14
2 braces	3/8 × 3/4 × 14
1 piece cloth	12 × 22
2 bolts	1/4 × 2 1/2 with nuts and washers

BAR STOOL

If you have a breakfast bar or a drinks bar at a height to suit standing, any seating has to be higher than a normal chair. You have similar needs when you are working in the shop or at a hobby where you want to rest from standing, yet need to be able to use your hands with the same reach and height.

A tall stool tends to be rocked by the user and the strain on leg joints is greater than in a lower chair, so the construction must be stiff and strong. This stool (Fig. 4-11) has double lower rails, as well as a rigidly-connected seat. The low back will also contribute to stiffness.

A furniture-quality hardwood is advised, although softwood might stand up to careful use. Joints can be mortise and tenon or dowels. Well-fitted tenons should be stronger.

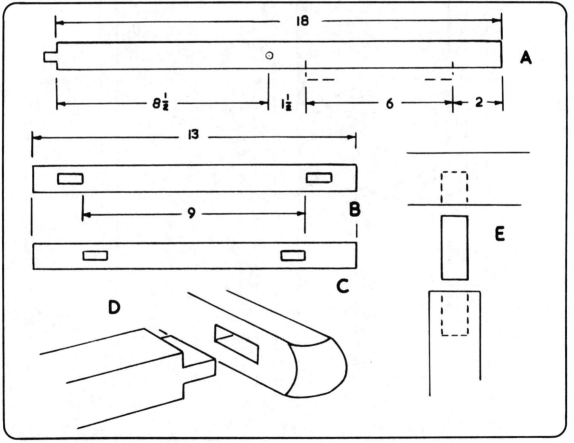

Fig. 4-10. Leg details of the camp stool.

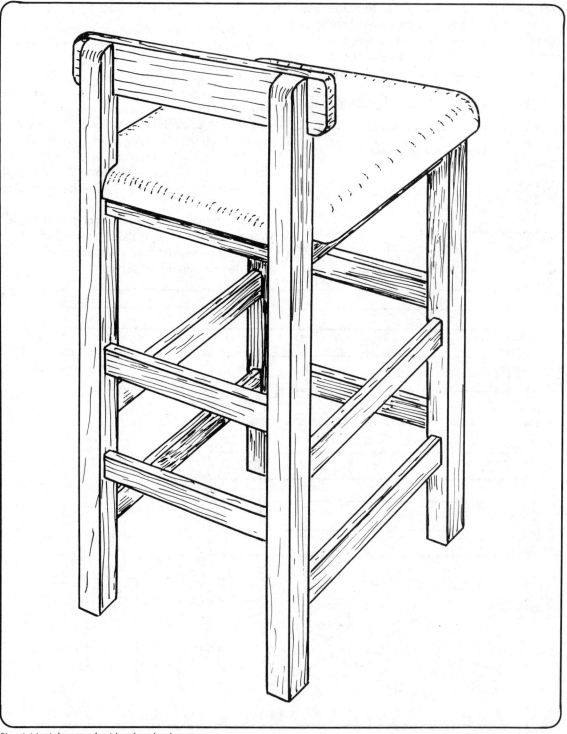

Fig. 4-11. A bar stool with a low back.

The seat height should suit your bar, but those shown (Fig. 4-12) should be satisfactory at a bar or work place. Wood sections shown should make a stool that is light and strong. All sizes could be altered to suit your needs or available wood.

1. Mark the legs together so joint positions match. The rear legs extend upwards (Fig. 4-12A). The rail levels are staggered so the joints do not interfere with each other (Fig. 4-12B). All rails are the same. Mark their positions on the legs.

2. Mark and cut the rails. For tenons allow 3/4 inch at each end (Fig. 4-13A). For dowels, cut to the length between legs (Fig. 4-13B).

3. Mark out and cut the joints in legs and rails.

4. The back (Fig. 4-12C) is a flat piece with rounded corners and front edges. Let it into the rear legs by half its thickness (Fig. 4-13C).

5. To ensure accuracy it is wiser to assemble in two stages. Make up two sides, checking squareness and lack of twist, then join the rails the other way. The back could have dowels to the legs or be glued and screwed. See that the assembly is square when viewed from above.

6. The seat is a piece of 1/2-inch plywood, which extends about 1 inch outside the legs at sides and front, but it need not extend at the back. Notch it around the rear legs (Fig. 4-13D), then nail or screw and glue to the top rails.

7. The seat could be left as bare wood, but it is better to lightly upholster it after the wood has been finished with varnish. Use a piece of 1-inch rubber or plastic foam. A piece of plastic-coated cloth will make a good covering. Pull it underneath the plywood and tack it there. A tack spacing about 1 1/2 inches should give an even finish on top. Fold under at the front corners. Notch around the rear legs. Appearance will be improved if you put a piece of gimp all around the edge of the seat.

STRIP CHAIR

A simple robust chair is useful on the patio or in the yard. A similar chair might have uses in a den or hobby room. For exterior use it should be made of a durable wood and treated with preservative. If it is kept indoors it could be made of softwood then stained and varnished, or you could make it of hardwood and give it a clear finish.

Most of the construction in this chair (Fig. 4-14) is screwed or nailed. Much depends on the quality of finish you want. Screws or nails should be galvanized steel or corrosion-resistant metal. Joints should also be glued. The only joint where glued dowels would be better than screws is between each arm and front leg.

All of the parts are made from 1-by-3-inch sections of wood. Other closely-sized sections could be used, with some modification of detail sizes. Have sufficient wood ready so allowances can be made for variations. The sizes shown (Fig. 4-15) give a seat height of 16 inches, which might be increased a little with a cushion. There is plenty of size front to back to allow for a cushion behind you. The overall width is about 27 inches and the total height is 33 inches.

The best way to tackle the work is to make the pair of sides, then add the pieces that fit between them, and finally make the arms.

1. Mark out and cut the two rear legs (Figs. 4-15A and 4-16A). With them as guides to rail and seat height make the front legs (Figs. 4-15B and 4-16B).

2. The two bottom rails (Fig. 4-15C) are 21 inches long. The seat rails (Fig. 4-15D) are similar, but extend forward 1 1/2 inches to beveled extensions (Fig. 4-17A).

3. Join these rails to the legs squarely, so the opposite assemblies make a pair. Waterproof glue and three or four nails or screws at each crossing should make strong joints. Choose screws that go

Materials List for Bar Stool	
2 legs	1 1/2 × 1 1/2 × 25
2 legs	1 1/2 × 1 1/2 × 33
8 rails	3/4 × 1 1/2 × 12
1 back	1/2 × 3 × 15
1 seat	13 × 14 × 1/2 plywood

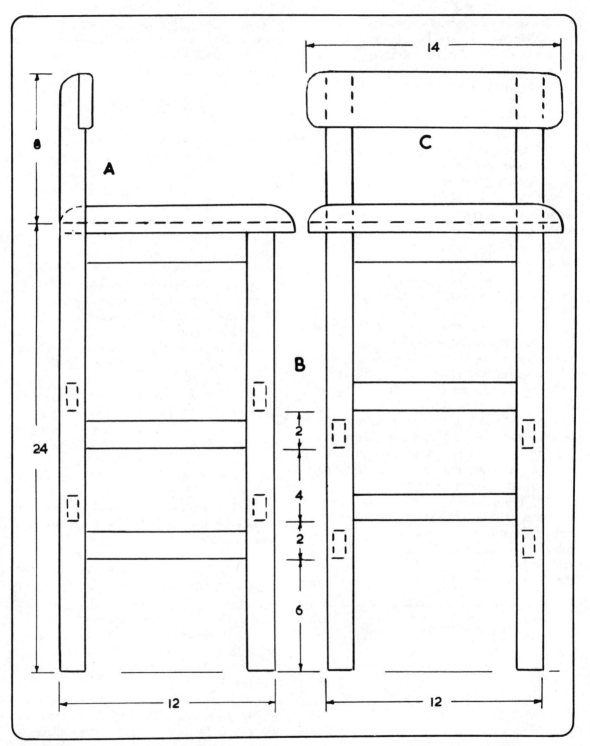

Fig. 4-12. Sizes of the bar stool.

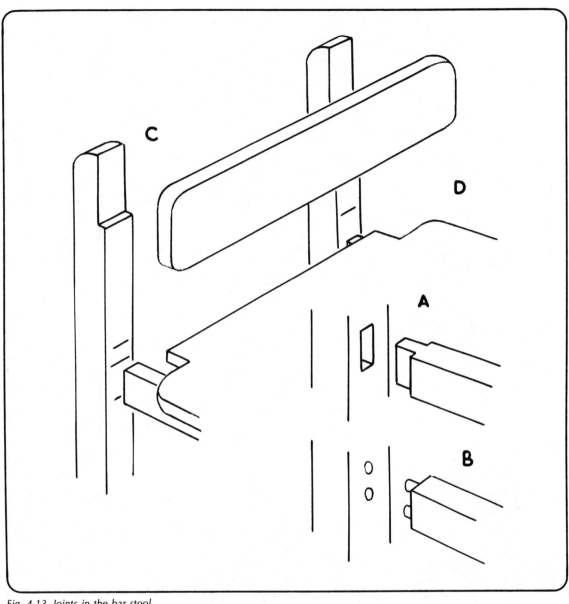

Fig. 4-13. Joints in the bar stool.

almost through. Nails could be the same or they could go right through so their points can be clenched.

4. The two crosswise rails (Figs. 4-15E and 4-16C), the seat slats (Fig. 4-15F) and the back slats (Figs. 4-15G and 4-16D) are all 24 inches long. Round the top edges of the seat slats and the front edges and ends of the back slats. Drill for screws

or nails, but do not assemble yet.

5. The slope of the back is provided with wedge-shaped pieces (Fig. 4-17B), which are made by cutting a 13-inch length of 3-inch width diagonally. Glue and nail these pieces to the tops of the rear legs. Round the back corners of the legs.

6. Join the end assemblies first with the lower rails, then add one seat slat and one back

79

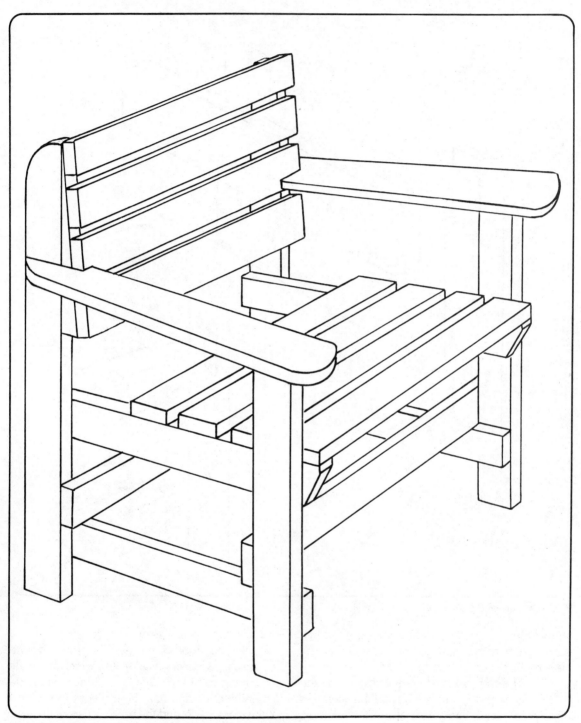

Fig. 4-14. A chair for indoor or outdoor use, made from strips.

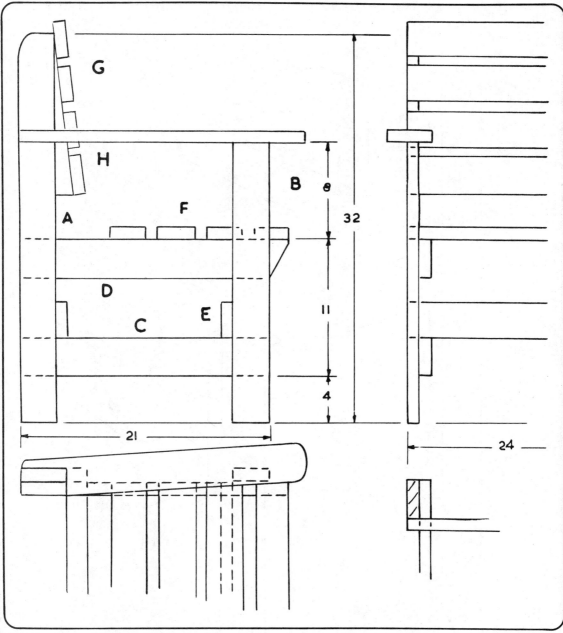

Fig. 4-15. Suggested sizes for the strip chair.

slat. Check squareness before adding the other slats. The top back slat extends about 1 inch above the leg. Leave the chair on a level surface for the glue to set.

7. The arms could be made square to the chair frame, but they look better and are more comfortable if they are spread outwards at the front. An arm comes central at a rear leg, but its inner

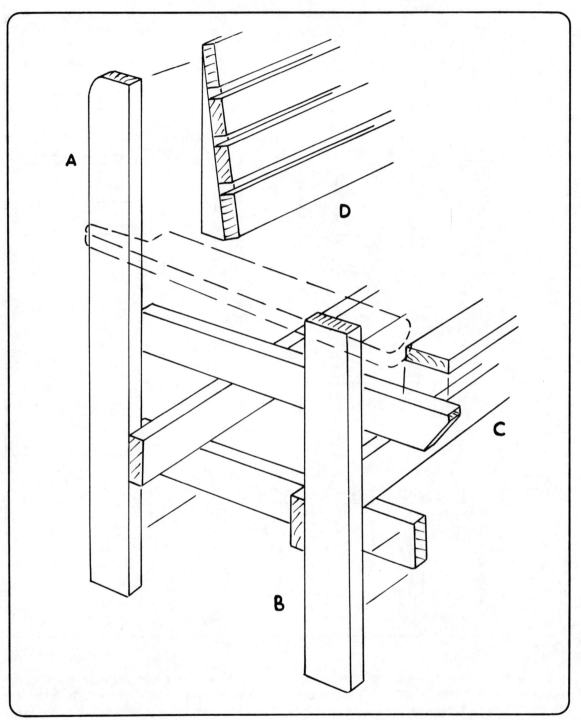

Fig. 4-16. The parts of the strip chair.

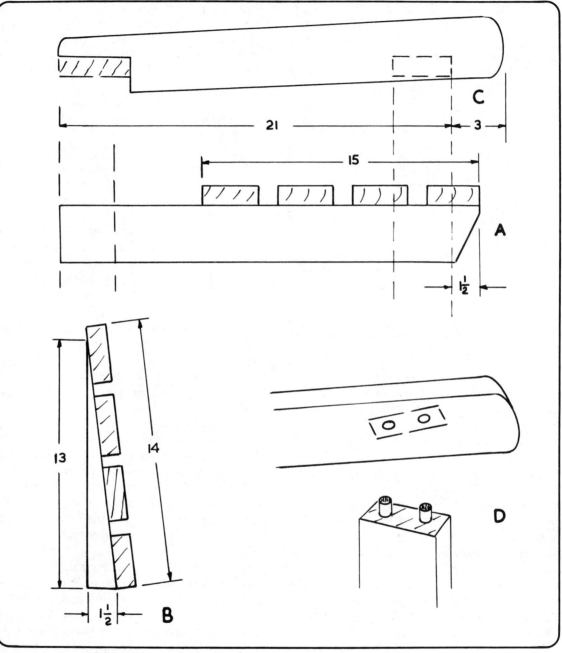

Fig. 4-17. Arm and back arrangements for the strip chair.

edge is level with the front leg (Fig. 4-17C). At the back the arm has to be cut around a back slat (Fig. 4-15H). Allow for about 1 inch to come outside

the leg. At the front leg mark where it comes under the arm and drill the arm and the leg for 1/2-inch dowels (Fig. 4-17D). Round the extending end of the arm and take sharpness off all edges. At the back screw through the narrow part of the arm into the leg. Make sure the two arms form a pair and are level.

8. Remove surplus glue and any sharp edges. Apply a finish to suit intended use.

Materials List for Strip Chair

2 rear legs	1 × 3 × 33
2 front legs	1 × 3 × 24
2 end rails	1 × 3 × 22
2 seat rails	1 × 3 × 23
2 lower rails	1 × 3 × 25
4 seat slats	1 × 3 × 25
4 back slats	1 × 3 × 25
2 back wedges from	1 × 3 × 14
2 arms	1 × 3 × 25

MILKING STOOL

Maybe it is very unlikely that you will ever want to milk a cow by hand, but a traditional milking stool still has attractions. Besides its obvious use as a seat, it could also serve as a stand for a plant. In the garden it allows you to sit instead of crouch as you plant seeds or attend to sprouting crops.

Three legs are a characteristic of a milking stool. A tripod arrangement will stand without rocking on any surface, however uneven it may be, so there was little risk of a milkmaid tipping her seat. This is still an advantage on an uneven garden or elsewhere. The basic stool was made as simply as possible. You could make one with elaborate turning, but it will be more authentic if kept simple. Not all milking stools had handles, but one is suggested as a help in moving the stool about.

A turned stool (Fig. 4-18) is more like a traditional stool, although many old stools were whittled round and were not produced on a lathe. An alternative hexagonal stool is shown (Fig. 4-19A), if you wish to make your stool without a lathe. The sizes shown (Fig. 4-19B) are reasonable

for garden use, a plant stand, or a seat for a child, but they can be altered to suit your needs or available wood. Use hardwood of fairly large sections—a top at least 1 1/4 inch thick and legs 1 1/2 inch diameter would be appropriate.

1. For the turned stool, make the top as a disc 11 inches diameter. Soften the edge with slight rounding.

2. Mark the positions of the three leg holes on the top surface. They are on a circle about 2 inches in from the outside edge and come on alternate points as you step off the radius around this circumference.

3. The legs must slope outwards and this is controlled by the angle at which you drill the holes. The bottom of a leg should be 1 1/2 inches to 2 inches outside the circumference of the top. Draw the side view of one leg (Fig. 4-19C). That will give you the angle to drill each hole.

4. If you drill by hand, cut a piece of scrap wood to indicate the angle of the drill (Fig. 4-20A). If you use a drill press, tilt the wood so the angle the drill makes with it is correct (Fig. 4-20B). For 1 1/2-inch legs the holes could be 1 inch in diameter.

5. The legs are turned parallel with rounded feet, but at the top they reduce to a parallel part that will fit the holes (Fig. 4-19D). Make the reduced part too long, so it goes through and can be planed level. Be careful to make all three legs the same and check the reduced size with a hole made by the same drill bit in a piece of scrap wood.

6. So the leg tops can be tightened with wedges, saw across the ends (Fig. 4-20C).

7. Assemble with glue. Put each leg in so its saw cut is across the lines of grain in the top, then the wedge will not have a splitting action on the surrounding wood. Put in all three legs and check that the top is parallel with the surface the feet are standing on. Adjust as necessary before tightening the wedges. When the glue has set, plane the tops of the legs level.

8. The handle (Fig. 4-19E) comes directly opposite one leg and midway between the others. Make it not more than 1 1/4 inch maximum di-

Fig. 4-18. This stool with a handle is based on the traditional milking stool pattern.

ameter and taper it to a parallel part to fit in a 3/4-inch hole (Fig. 4-20D). It is shown fitted level, but it could be given a slight upward tilt.

9. If you choose the other stool, use wood of similar thickness. Mark out the hexagonal top by joining the points obtained by stepping off the radius around the circumference of a circle (Fig. 4-19F).

10. Mark the hole positions 2 inches in from alternate points. Drill in the same way as described for the round stool.

11. The legs could be given hexagonal sections, but that would mean complicated prepara-

tion of the wood. It is easier to start with square wood and plane the corners off to make an octagonal section (Fig. 4-20E). The top round parallel parts will have to be carefully pared by hand. Make these ends and the whole legs too long at this stage.

12. Assemble the legs to the top with glued joints and wedges, in the same way as the round stool. Plane the tops of the legs level.

13. Invert the stool and mark the ends of the legs the same height all around, then cut the feet so they will be flat on the floor.

14. The handle (Fig. 4-19G) goes into a hole

in a flat surface made across one corner. Make it like the round handle, but taper it square, then take the corners off to make it octagonal before rounding the end to glue into the hole.

15. Traditional milking stools were left untreated, but you might wish to treat it with preservative or varnish.

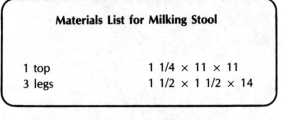

Materials List for Milking Stool	
1 top	1 1/4 × 11 × 11
3 legs	1 1/2 × 1 1/2 × 14

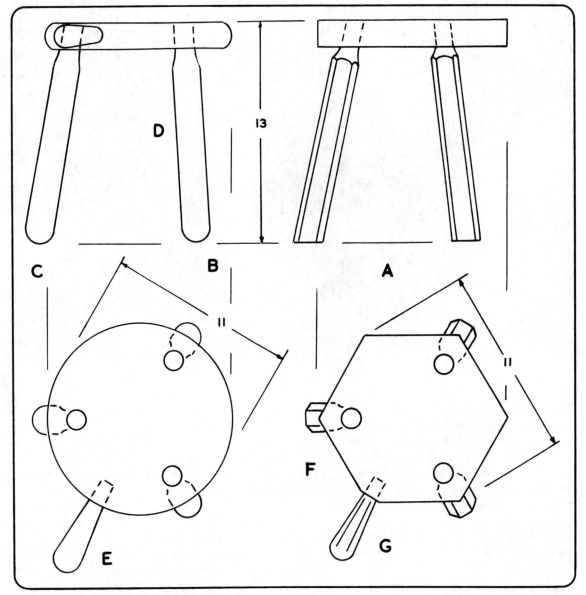

Fig. 4-19. Sizes of milking stool turned or planed.

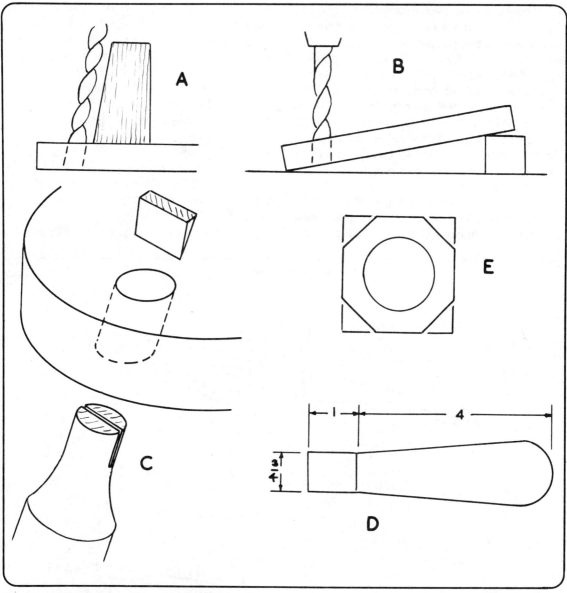

Fig. 4-20. Drilling for the milking stool legs and handle.

FOLDING STEPS

For use indoors, folding steps three treads high should be sufficient for you to reach as high as you will need in a normal room. Such steps would then be at a tall stool height for sitting on, so they serve a dual purpose.

A reasonable amount to step up is 9 inches,

so the steps can be 27 inches high. If you alter sizes, keep the distances between the surfaces of treads the same amount all the way. A change in distance could be disconcerting and might lead to an accident.

These folding steps (Fig. 4-21) include some simple joints, while other parts are screwed. Any wood could be used. Even if hardwood is chosen, the weight should not be too much for comfortably moving about. For use, the steps cover a floor area about 14 inches by 27 inches, but when folded the 27-inch way reduces to about 7 inches. Choose wood with reasonably straight grain in the sizes you cut, so the assembly has maximum strength. When set for use the steps slope at 60 degrees to the floor, which simplifies marking out. The slight taper in width is not enough to require special angular cuts the other way.

1. The key parts are the pair of sides (Fig. 4-22A). Draw a line across at 60 degrees, then draw other lines measured square to it (Fig. 4-22B)

to get the spacing even. Mark the widths of the dado grooves to take the treads.

2. Set the taper out full-size the other way (Fig. 4-23A). either half or full width. This will give you the length of the treads. Allow for them to go into the legs a little less than halfway.

3. Both treads could have screws driven into them from outside the legs, but it would be better to include a tenon at each end of the bottom tread (Fig. 4-22C). This goes through the leg and can have a wedge into a saw cut as well as glue. The other tread could also be tenoned, but with the bottom one tenoned and the top secured, simple dado joints should be sufficient.

4. Make the back (Fig. 4-22D) with its lower

Fig. 4-21. These low steps fold flat.

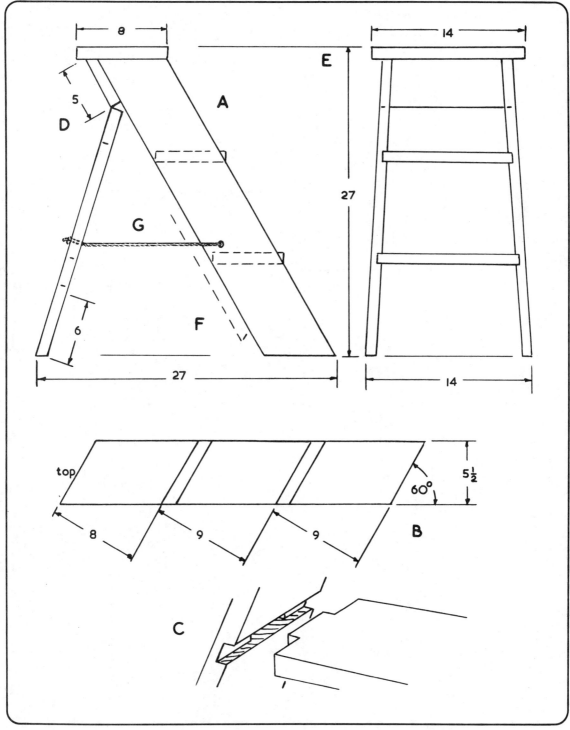

Fig. 4-22. Sizes and leg details of the folding steps.

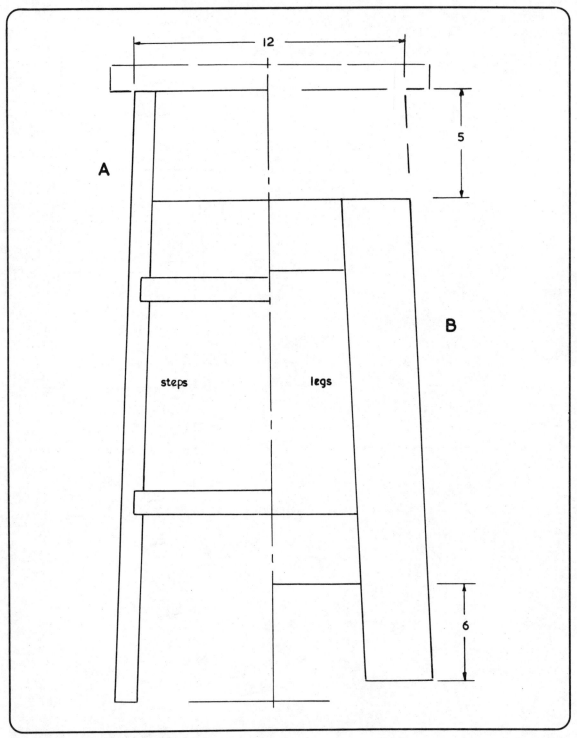

A

B

12

5

6

steps

legs

Fig. 4-23. Layout for the steps and legs.

90

edge square and the top matching the angle of the sides.

5. Assemble the treads, sides, and back. Glue and screw the back into place. Check that the assembly is symmetrical by comparing diagonals.

6. Make the top (Fig. 4-22E). Screw it downwards into the back and sides. Round its edges and corners. Round the edges of the treads slightly. The screws could be counterbored and covered with plugs.

7. The legs are intended to extend so the treads come level. It will be advisable to hold your assembly in this position and measure from the underside of the back to a suitable position on the floor for the leg length. This will allow for any differences in size in your steps. When folded, the bottoms of the legs should be a short distance above the bottoms of the sides (Fig. 4-22F).

8. The assembly of legs and their rails must match the parts you have already assembled (Fig. 4-23B). Cut the legs to length with the end angles matching the step assembly, and the bottoms to fit flat on the floor.

9. The rails should be securely joined to the legs. You could use mortise and tenon joints or they could be doweled. Three 1/2-inch dowels in each joint should be satisfactory. Cut the rails to length and join them to the legs, so they match the other part.

10. Two 3-inch hinges may be put on the surface of the back and the tops of the legs.

11. To control the spread of the folding steps, put ropes through holes in the legs and sides (Fig. 4-22G).

Materials List for Folding Steps	
2 sides	1 × 5 1/2 × 36
2 treads	1 × 6 × 14
1 top	1 × 8 × 15
1 back	1 × 5 × 14
2 legs	1 × 3 × 24
2 rails	1 × 3 × 13

Chapter 5

Tables

Like chairs, it is almost impossible to have too many tables. They are useful in every room, as well as in garden sheds, on patios and decks, or anywhere that people want to work, eat, or read. Large well-finished tables, possibly with drawers or extensions, are more than you can expect to make in a weekend. There are small pieces of furniture, such as coffee tables and other occasional types, as well as larger less-elaborate tables for outdoor or shop use, that need not take more than a weekend to construct.

Any table, even the smallest, must stand firmly on all its legs. It must also be square and upright. More than most other pieces of furniture, a table that is out of shape is very obvious to an observer. To ensure accuracy, it is usually best to assemble in two stages: opposite assemblies, then join parts the other way after the glue has set in the first direction. Always assemble on a flat surface.

SIMPLE COFFEE TABLE

A small table may be made fairly plain to let the

emphasis be on the interesting grain markings. Alternatively, with plainer wood turning or carving could be employed, so the interest is then in the form of the table and away from the wood. The table in the photograph has a plain form to display the markings of the oak used. The basic design could be adapted to suit plainer wood, with turned legs and the lower edges of the top rails shaped (Fig. 5-1).

The sizes suggested (Fig. 5-2A) will make a chairside table of useful size, but the same method of construction can be used to build to a different size.

1. Prepare all the wood to width and thickness, so the actual pieces can be used when marking the sizes of joints.

2. Mark out the four legs, with the rail positions on two faces (Fig. 5-2B) of each leg. Leave a little extra length at the top. The bottom ends can be beveled all around.

3. Mark and cut the four top rails to the lengths between the legs. Plow grooves in the short

Fig. 5-1. A small table can be fairly plain to emphasize details of the grain.

rails (Fig. 5-3A) to take the buttons that will hold the top (Fig. 5-3B). Grooves 3/16 inch wide and deep, 1/4 inch down from the top edge will do.

4. Mark the lower rails with tenons (Fig. 5-3C), the same lengths between shoulders as the top rails.

5. Mark and cut mortises in the legs for the lower rails. The tenon ends might have to be mitered in the legs.

6. Mark for 3/8-inch dowel holes in the legs and top rails (Fig. 5-3D). Allow the leg holes to meet. When you assemble the table, miter the meeting ends of the dowels.

7. First assemble the two long sides (Fig. 5-4). Check that they are flat, square, and a match for each other.

8. Add the rails the other way. Besides

checking squareness in end view, check from above by comparing diagonals. See that there is no twist. Leave on a level surface for the glue to set.

9. Cut the tops of the legs level with the rails and see that all top surfaces are level.

10. The top will probably have to be made by gluing several boards. Match the grain as far as possible.

11. Cut the top to size to overlap the framing by the same amount all around.

12. The top edges could be left square, but they will be better molded; a suitable section is shown here (Fig. 5-3E).

13. As a top of this size may expand and contract by as much as 1/4 inch in the width, it should not be fastened down rigidly. Instead, there are buttons screwed under the top and engaging with

93

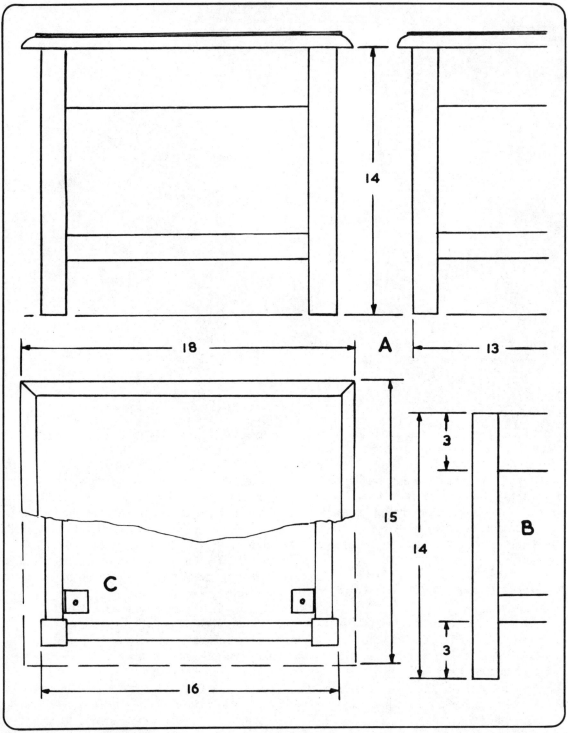

Fig. 5-2. Sizes of the simple coffee table.

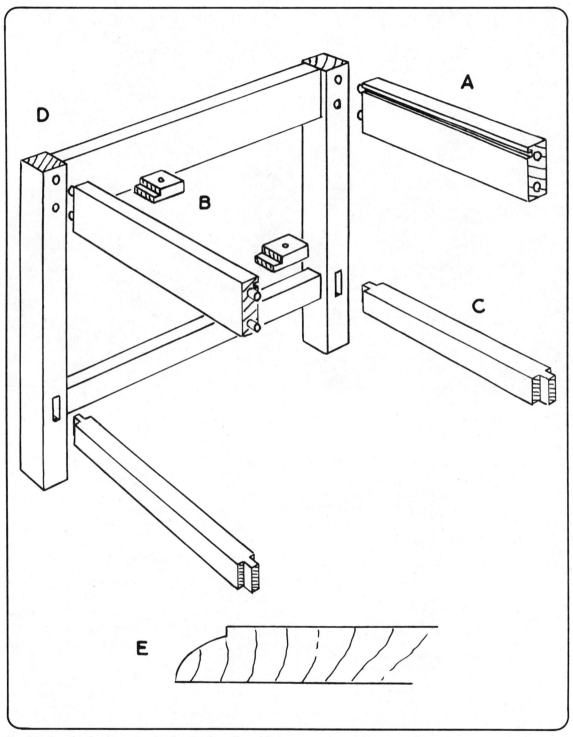

Fig. 5-3. Details of construction for the simple coffee table.

Fig. 5-4. Opposite sides of the table are assembled before adding the rails the other way.

grooves in the short top rails (Fig. 5-3B), so they can slide if there is movement in the wood. Their exact size does not matter, but when screwed to the top they should pull it tight onto the rails.

14. Invert the framework on the underside of the top and screw on the buttons about 1/4 inch

from each leg (Fig. 5-2C). After a trial assembly you might wish to remove the top for convenience in final sanding and applying a finish to all parts. If it is an attractive wood the finish should be clear varnish, lacquer, or polish.

DRINKS TABLE

A chairside table that will hold bottles in its base is obviously convenient, but it also has the advantage of stability. Some small, light tables are easily knocked over, but up to four bottles low down will make the table very steady, even when the bottles are only partly full.

Size has to suit the bottles. Fortunately, many soft drink and wine bottles are all similar sizes, but if you want to use unusual sizes of bottles, the table sizes will have to be adjusted to suit. This table (Fig. 5-5) is designed to hold four bottles about

Materials List for Simple Coffee Table	
4 legs	1 3/8 × 1 3/8 × 15
2 rails	3/4 × 3 × 14
2 rails	3/4 × 1 3/8 × 16
2 rails	3/4 × 3 × 11
2 rails	3/4 × 3 × 13
4 buttons	1/2 × 1 3/8 × 2
1 top	3/4 × 15 × 19

Fig. 5-5. This drinks table has storage below for four bottles.

4 inches diameter and 15 inches high, and to give clearance for their removal. Smaller bottles and slightly larger ones would fit also (Fig. 5-6A).

The suggested materials are 1-by-2-inch softwood with 1/2-inch plywood. There could be Formica or other material on the top. With these materials a painted finish is advised. If you want a better-quality furniture finish, use hardwood and veneered plywood.

1. The key parts that control other sizes are the long legs and the shelf with holes. Make them first.

2. Choose straight-grained strips for the long legs (Fig. 5-7A). All of the notches are 3/8 inch deep (Fig. 5-6B). At the top allow for the depths of the rails and check the lower dadoes with the thickness of the plywood.

3. Make the shelf square (Fig. 5-7B) with curved corners. Mark out the positions of the bottle holes. You might be able to drill these with an expansive bit, but otherwise you will have to drill many small holes and saw and shape the large hole outlines. Round the edges of the bottle holes and the exposed outer edges of the shelf.

4. Make the bottom (Fig. 5-6C) the same size as the shelf, but without the holes.

5. Make the two short legs (Fig. 5-6D), getting the notch spacing from the long legs. Round the extending tops of these legs.

6. Make the two top rails (Fig. 5-6E) to fit into the leg notches, but there is no need to notch the rails. Let them extend 15 inches (Fig. 5-7C) with tapered ends.

7. Make the crosswise rail (Figs. 5-6E and 5-7D), checking the length so the legs will stand upright when the shelf and bottom are tightly in their notches.

8. Drill for two 1/2-inch dowels in each end of the crosswise rail, through the top rails, and as deep as possible in the legs without going through.

9. Assemble the parts, taking care to get the plywood pieces central. At each leg drive a screw diagonally up through the bottom to strengthen each leg joint (Fig. 5-6G). See that parts are square to each other and the table stands upright.

10. Cut the top to size 1 1/2 inch outside the legs and rail ends, which should be about 18 inches square (Fig. 5-7E). Round the corners. If it is to have Formica or other covering, add that now and true the edges. The edge could be left square or given a slight rounding. Most plywood is unsuitable for a molded edge.

11. The top can be glued to the rails, but this may be reinforced with screws driven diagonally upwards near the tapered ends of the rails (Fig. 5-8).

12. Remove surplus glue and sand the wood, if necessary. Finish with paint.

Materials List for Drinks Table

2 legs	1 × 2 × 23
2 legs	1 × 2 × 10
2 rails	1 × 2 × 16
1 rail	1 × 2 × 14
1 shelf	14 × 14 × 1/2 plywood
1 bottom	14 × 14 × 1/2 plywood
1 top	18 × 18 × 1/2 plywood

TRAY TABLE

At one time the butler brought in food or drink on a tray that fitted onto its own stand and became a serving table. In these days when we do our own waiting something similar can be very useful, particularly if the whole thing can fold away to take up little space when out of use. You can have the stand ready and bring in the tray of food to fit on it, then if you want to pick up the tray to take to guests, or to remove used things, it can be lifted off again.

This tray table (Fig. 5-9) has a tray 15 inches wide and 21 inches long. It stands about 23 inches from the floor and there is a removable shelf underneath that provides extra space and keeps the legs in place when the tray is removed. When the tray and shelf are removed the stand folds flat.

1. The sizes shown (Fig. 5-10A) depend on the crossing arrangement of the legs. The width

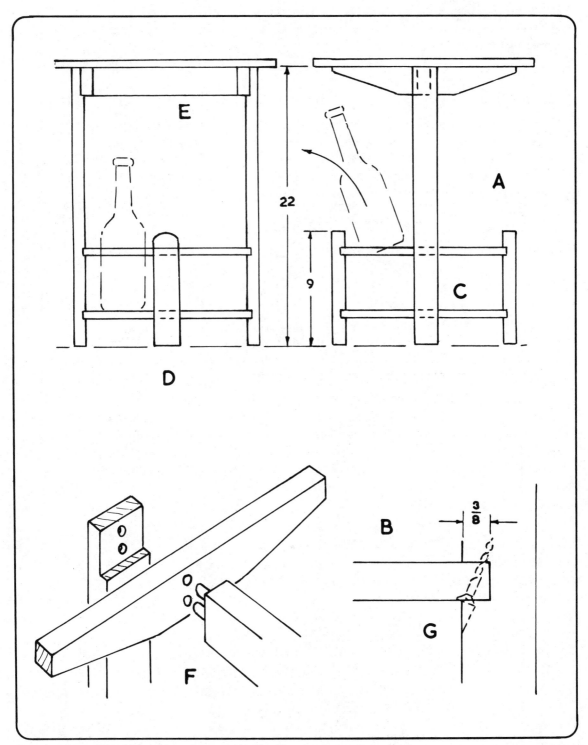

Fig. 5-6. Layout of the drinks table and construction details.

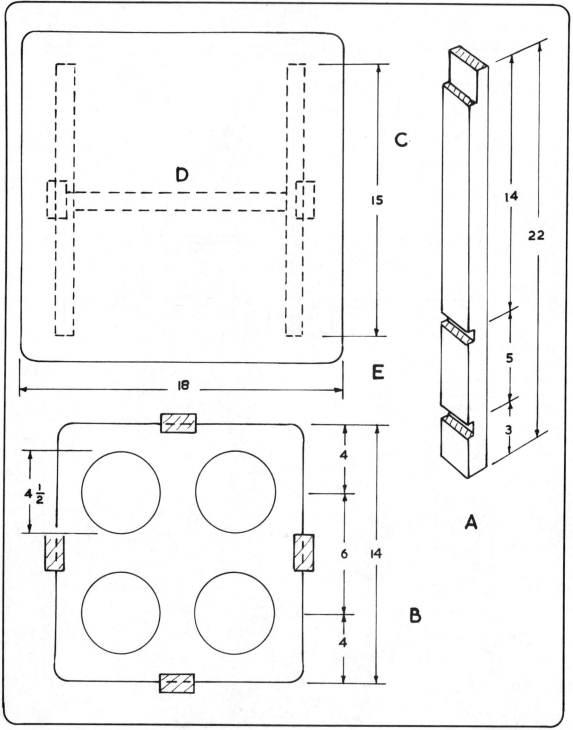

Fig. 5-7. Sizes of top, shelf, and legs of the drinks table.

Fig. 5-8. The top rests on the framing and is held with glue and screws.

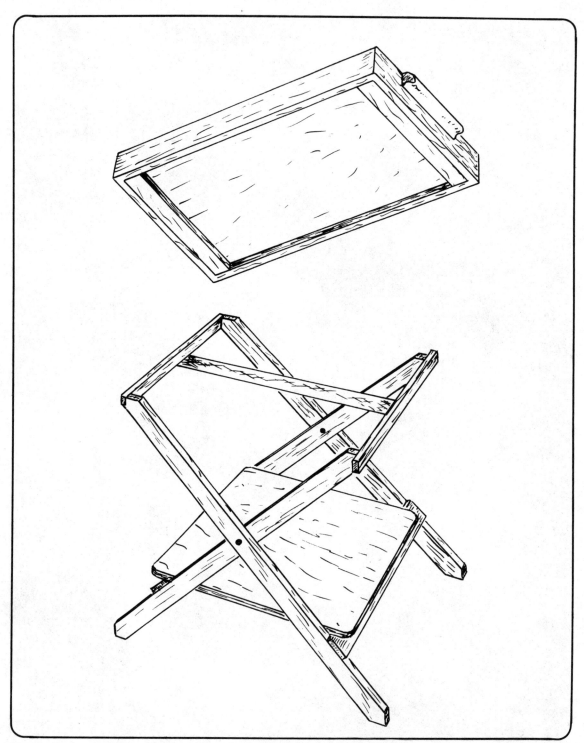

Fig. 5-9. The tray table has a lift-off top. When the shelf is removed, the legs will fold.

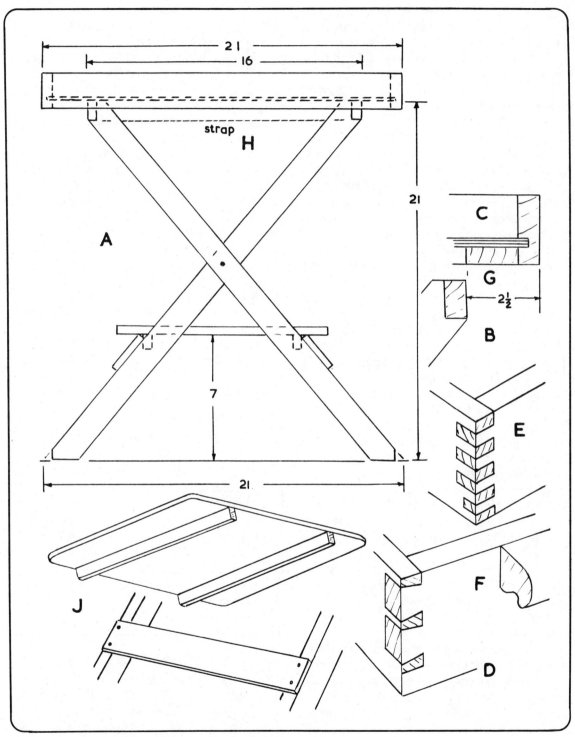

Fig. 5-10. Sizes and alternative construction for the tray table.

(Fig. 5-11A) could be altered without affecting the action of the table. To set out the leg sizes, draw a square with 21-inch sides (Fig. 5-11B), mark in 3 1/4 inches from the top corners, and join these points to the bottom corners. These lines are the upper edges of the legs (Fig. 5-11C). The drawing also gives you the angles to cut on the legs.

2. Make the four legs (Fig. 5-11D). Cut the tops to the angles and notch them to take the crossbars (Fig. 5-10B). At the bottom the extreme points might be fragile, so cut them back about 3/4 inch. On your drawing, mark the widths of the legs so you can get the locations of bolt holes (Fig. 5-11E). A line 7 inches up will show you the position of the top edges of the leg braces (Fig. 5-11F).

3. Make the crossbars and the leg braces. One pair of legs crosses inside the other pair, but the crossbars at the top should be the same length (Fig. 5-11G). Have these pieces prepared, but slightly too long, so they can be adjusted to suit the tray after that has been made.

4. The tray is made as a box with the base let into grooves (Fig. 5-10C). Cut the grooves 3/8 inch from the bottom edges.

5. Corners could be dovetailed (Fig. 5-10D), with the part from the groove down mitered to hide the groove. You could use a comb joint (Fig. 5-10E), with the groove enclosed in the next comb to the bottom.

6. It would be possible to put hand holes in the ends of the tray, but lifting handles are shown (Fig. 5-10F). They could be glued and doweled if you want to avoid screw heads showing inside the tray. Alternatively, you could use metal or plastic handles.

7. Assemble the tray. Put two stops under the ends (Fig. 5-10G). If all other parts are to size these will be 1 7/8 inch wide, but you might wish to wait until after a trial assembly before settling on their widths and fitting them.

8. Check the lengths of the crossbars, which should be an easy fit between the tray sides (Fig. 5-11H). Drill the legs for 1/4-inch bolts. Glue and screw the crossbars to the legs and screw on the braces so the assemblies are square and parallel, and the inner pair of legs fit between the outer pair.

9. Make a trial assembly. The crossbars should come upright against the tray stops and the feet should be flat on the floor.

10. You will probably delay pivoting the legs permanently until the wood has been stained and polished. When you fit bolts, choose 1/4-inch coach bolts with their shallow heads outside. Put washers between the legs and under the nuts. If possible, use lock nuts.

11. Although the leg assembly will remain in shape while the tray is in place, it could spread—if nothing is done to hold it—when the tray is removed. Make a strap across the crossbars. (Fig. 5-10H). This could be webbing, stout tape, or a leather strap. Attach it with screws through washers. Arrange its length so it holds the crossbars at the right distance to fit into the tray.

12. For the lower shelf (Fig. 5-10J) cut a piece of plywood to fit easily between the inner pair of legs. Round its edges and corners. On its underside fit guides to go between the leg braces when the tray table is in use. The strap will prevent the legs spreading, while the shelf will prevent them closing and hold the assembly square when the tray is lifted off.

Materials List for Tray Table	
2 tray sides	5/8 × 2 × 22
2 tray ends	5/8 × 2 × 16
2 tray handles	1 × 1 × 8
1 tray base	15 × 21 × 1/4 plywood
2 tray stops	3/8 × 1 7/8 × 15
4 legs	3/4 × 1 1/2 × 30
2 crossbars	5/8 × 1 × 15
2 leg braces	3/8 × 2 × 15
1 lower shelf	12 × 12 × 1/2 plywood
2 shelf guides	5/8 × 1 × 12

TILED TABLE

Ceramic tiles of the type used for bathroom walls have other uses. One is to make a table top. Glazed tiles, either plain or patterned, fitted into a wooden frame, will make an attractive top that will keep

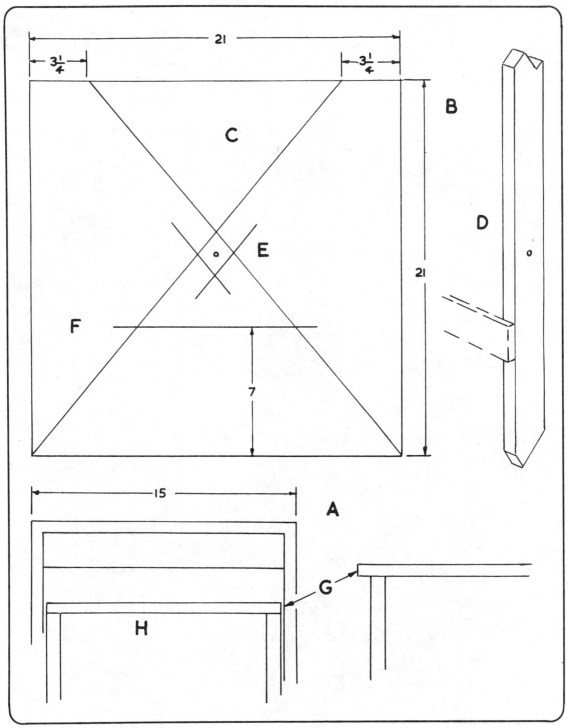

Fig. 5-11. Laying out and fitting the tray table parts.

its appearance, be hygienic and easy to clean, and stand up to moderate heat and most liquids. Table size is governed by the size of tile used. The example (Fig. 5-12) uses six 6-inch-square light-colored tiles in a dark hardwood coffee table (Fig. 5-13A), but the number of tiles could be increased.

In this larger table there could be three rows of four tiles instead of two rows of three tiles, with the wood parts increased by 6 inches each way, but other details unaltered.

The tiles can be mounted on plywood. How they are fixed depends on their type. With those

Fig. 5-12. This table has a tiled top framed in wood.

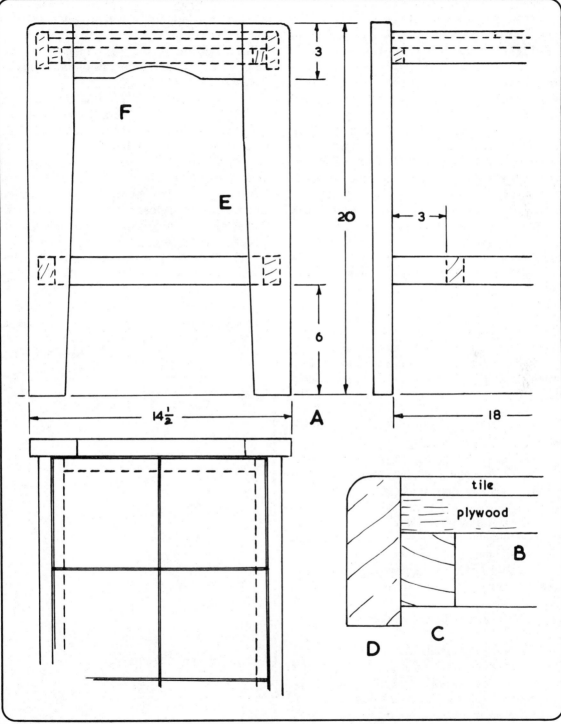

Fig. 5-13. Sizes and sections of the tiled table.

intended primarily for walls, they can be set in the same plaster compound, but care is needed to prevent this from soaking into surrounding wood and spoiling its appearance. That can be avoided if the borders and ends are polished or varnished to seal their surfaces before the plaster is used. It will then be possible to wipe off plaster and leave the wood unmarked.

Although it would be possible to use softwood, if you want a natural pine or painted finish, a better table is made of hardwood that is finished dark around light-colored tiles, or light if they are dark.

The table is best constructed as four units, with each made up before they are assembled together: the top, underframing, and two ends. Parts are shown joined with dowels, but you could use mortise and tenon joints, if you wish. Because many sizes are controlled by the tiles, have them ready before cutting any wood.

1. Put the tiles together and measure their overall size. Some tiles are made to have a narrow line of plaster between them. Allow for this at the edges as well when you cut the plywood base (Figs. 5-13B and 5-14A).

2. Make a frame under the plywood (Figs. 5-13C and 5-14B), across the ends as well as along the sides. Use glue and nails because the nail heads will be hidden.

3. Make the two side rails (Figs. 5-13D and 5-14C). Round the outer top edges. Drill the ends for 1/2-inch dowels into the legs.

4. Stain and polish or varnish these rails, avoiding the end grain, which is better left bare to take glue later.

5. Drill the side framing strips under the plywood for screws that will be driven outwards into the side rails.

6. Set the tiles in plaster or other compound on the plywood.

7. Add the side rails while the plaster is still soft, pulling them in with screws. Make sure their tops are level with the tops of the tiles and any gaps are filled with plaster. Wipe off any surplus plaster so there are no holes or gaps between or around the tiles.

8. Make the four legs (Fig. 5-13E). Keep them 2 1/2 inches wide for a length of 6 inches at the top, then taper to 2 inches. Mark where the side rails and underframing come, 1/2 inch in from the outer edges. Allow for the tops of the legs being 1/2 inch above the tiles.

9. Make the rails between the legs (Fig. 5-13F) to hold the legs the correct distance apart. The lower edges can be hollowed to provide hand holds when the table is lifted.

10. Assemble the legs and their rails, with three dowels in each joint. Check that the width is correct and the legs are parallel. If necessary, put temporary struts across the bottoms of the legs. Round the top corners of the legs and take off sharpness on all edges.

11. Make the two sides of the underframing (Fig. 5-14E) the same length as the side rails at the top. Cut the two crossbars (Fig. 5-14F) to hold the side rails at the correct spacing to match their markings on the legs. Drill the ends of the rails for dowels and assemble the crossbars to the underframing sides, and check squareness with the top.

Materials List for Tiled Table

Top	
1 piece	12 × 18 × 1/2 plywood
2 frames	3/4 × 1 × 19
2 frames	3/4 × 1 × 12
2 sides	3/4 × 2 × 19

Ends	
4 legs	1 × 2 1/2 × 21
2 rails	1 × 3 × 11

Underframing	
2 sides	1 × 1 1/2 × 19
2 crossbars	1 × 1 1/2 × 13

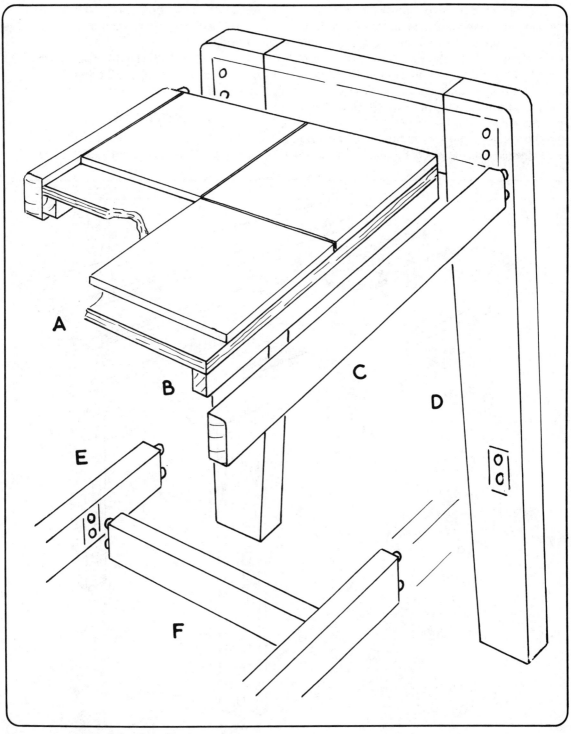

Fig. 5-14. Main parts of the tiled table.

12. Stain and polish or varnish the end assemblies and the underframing to match the finish applied to the top side rails. Avoid getting finishing materials into dowel holes. To keep the holes clean, drilling the dowel holes in the legs could be left until after applying the finish.

13. Join the units with dowels and glue. If necessary, add a little plaster between the end tiles and the leg assemblies so that no gaps show between the tiles and the wood. Pad any clamp heads to reduce the risk of damage to the finish.

14. Check squareness and see that the legs stand upright.

15. It will probably be necessary to touch up the finish and give a final coat all over, but be careful not to discolor the plaster.

STRIP TABLE

This table (Fig. 5-15) can have several uses, but it is intended as a companion to the Strip Chair (Fig.

Fig. 5-15. A strip table for outdoors or den use.

4-14). It is made entirely of strips 1 by 3 inch, the same as the chair. If both are given the same finish, they will match.

The table is particularly suitable for exterior use, on a patio, lawn, or deck. If made of durable wood or if treated with preservative, it could be left outside for long periods. If made of furniture hardwood and given a better-quality finish, the table could find a place in a den or game room.

Sizes are suggested (Fig. 5-16), but they can be altered to suit your needs without affecting the sections of wood needed or the method of construction. Parts should be glued and either screwed or nailed. For greatest strength use screws that will go almost through. Nails should be the same length, although where flat parts overlap they could go through so the points can be clenched. Screws and nails should be galvanized steel or a corrosion-resistant metal.

Get sufficient wood of the correct section before starting construction, to allow for any differences of size.

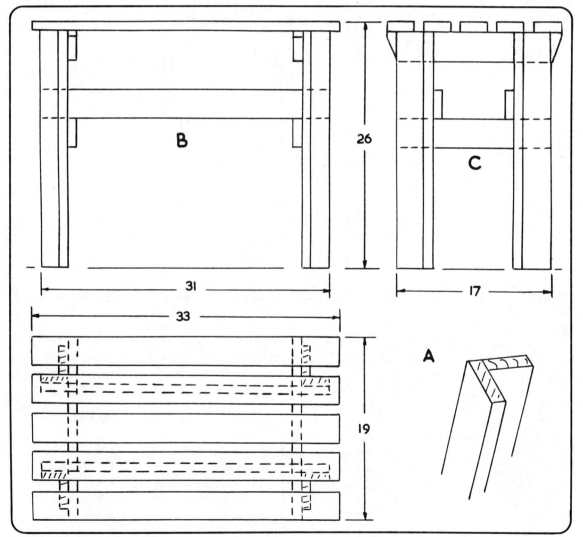

Fig. 5-16. Sizes of the strip table.

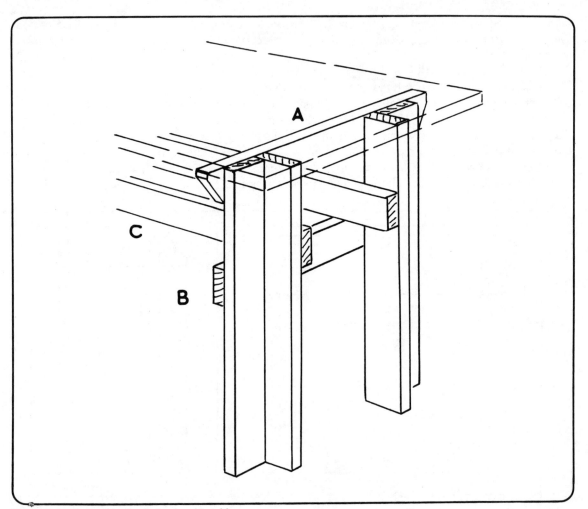

Fig. 5-17. End assembly details for the strip table.

1. Make the four legs first. They have one strip overlapping the other (Fig. 5-16A) and are arranged with the 4-inch side across the table, so they must be marked out in pairs. Table rails cross them at the top, then there are lengthwise rails (Fig. 5-16B) 3 inches below them and crosswise rails (Fig. 5-16C) immediately below them.

2. Make the table rails (Fig. 5-17A) to extend 1 inch on each side of the legs, with beveled ends. The crosswise rails (Fig. 5-17B) are 2 inches shorter.

3. Make up the two ends, with the rails squarely across the legs.

4. Join the ends with the lengthwise rails (Fig. 5-17C). At this stage, check squareness in all directions and see that the assembly stands level.

5. The five pieces that make the top should

Materials List for Strip Table	
8 legs	1 × 3 × 26
2 table rails	1 × 3 × 22
2 crosswise rails	1 × 3 × 18
2 lengthwise rails	1 × 3 × 32
5 tops	1 × 3 × 34

be checked for straightness. Take off sharp edges all around before fitting. Screw downwards into the table rails. They should extend 1 inch past the legs at the ends, and the outer pieces should come level with the ends of the table rails. Space the intermediate rails evenly, which will give gaps of 1 inch. For an indoor furniture finish the screw heads should be counterbored and covered with plugs.

6. Treat the wood with preservative or stain and finish it to suit the intended situation.

Chapter 6

Racks and Shelves

There is considerable scope for a weekend wood-worker in making small pieces of furniture that provide storage, particularly for books, magazines, ornaments and similar things—resulting in neat displays where there was previously an untidy jumble. It is usually possible to find hanging space on a wall, or it might be convenient to put a rack beside a chair. None of these racks or shelves has to be very elaborate and the work involved need take no more than a day, even if you try your skills at making more advanced joints.

Before starting such a project, establish a need and make sure your solution is the right one. Check sizes, both the available space and the contents. It should be possible to remove books easily, there should be clearance above ornaments. It is no use making a magazine or other rack into which the contents have to be forced. Remember, final sizes are the result of your forethought.

SMALL DISPLAY RACK

Souvenirs of trips, figurines, and other small decorative items will look their best if displayed in a special rack or compartmented shelf. Although the rack itself should be attractive, its main purpose is to form a background to the items it contains, so it should be well-made, but comparatively plain. It will make a good background to many things if it is painted one or more pastel colors. The inside could be one color and the outside another. This rack (Fig. 6-1) is intended to show individual items in their own compartments, so they will not be spoiled by forming part of a confusion of other items. The top can take smaller things or those the wrong shape for a compartment.

The wood should be thin to avoid a clumsy appearance; 1/4 inch is suggested. There could be dovetails at the corners and dadoes for the divisions, but because construction details will not show under a painted finish and loads on the joints should be light, it should be sufficient to glue and pin the parts. Any softwood without pronounced grain markings can be used. A coarse wood might split when pins are driven.

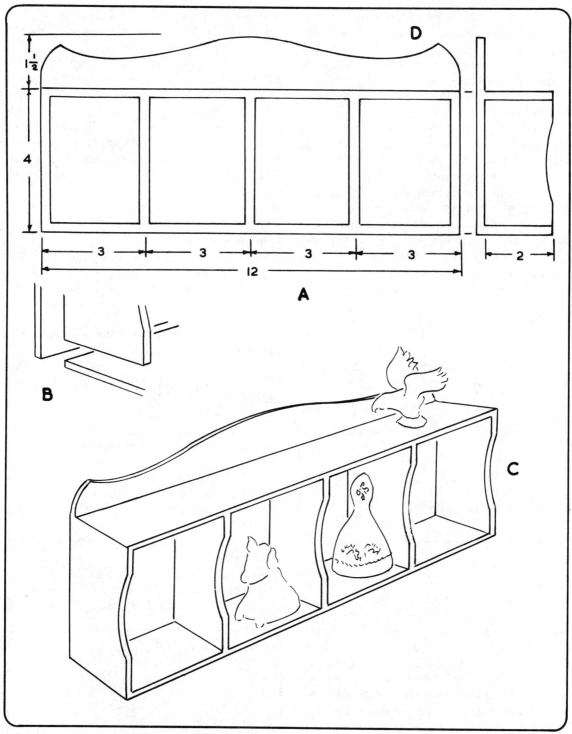

Fig. 6-1. This small display rack is intended to feature individual items.

1. Prepare all the wood. Make sure the strips to cut the main parts are all the same width and thickness.

2. Mark out the top and bottom with the positions of the other parts (Fig. 6-1A).

3. The five upright pieces are all the same and fit between top and bottom (Fig. 6-1B). The hollows at the front are not essential, but they draw attention to the displayed items (Fig. 6-1C). Arrange them with a little more straight edge below than above, for the best effect.

4. Fit the pieces between the top and bottom with glue and pins, keeping the fronts level and the assembly square and free from twist. After the glue has set, level the rear edge, if necessary.

5. Make the back (Fig. 6-1D) to fit over the other parts and extend far enough above to provide a background to things displayed there. Shape the top edge. Glue and pin on.

6. Paint all over, using sufficient undercoats to hide the grain and joint details before giving the final coats.

7. Mounting can be with screws high inside the end compartments, where they will not show.

Materials List for Small Display Rack

2 pieces	1/4 × 2 × 13
5 pieces	1/4 × 2 × 4
1 piece	1/4 × 5 1/2 × 13

ARROW BOOKENDS

There is an endless variety of bookends. The basic types are either heavy enough to prevent books from tilting, or they may be lighter with thin metal plates extending under the end books to provide stability. Any bookends can be decorated.

These bookends (Fig. 6-2) are made with plates to go under books and with an arrow motif, as if passing through the books. The sizes (Fig. 6-3) suit books of average size, but the design could be modified to make bookends of any size.

Any wood can be used. The effect is increased if the arrow parts are lighter or darker than the main parts. This can be achieved by using woods of contrasting colors or by staining.

In each bookend the two main parts could be joined with any of the usual corner joints. The best would be dovetails, but there should be little strain on the joints and construction is shown with notches and screws (Fig. 6-3A). The same screws hold the metal plate, which could be aluminum or brass. If the wood is glued, three 8-gauge by 1-inch screws should be adequate in each joint.

1. Prepare the wood for all main parts together. One piece about 21 inches long can be planed to width and thickness.

2. Mark out the parts, including mortises for the arrow ends, 2 inches down from the top edges.

3. Separate the parts and chamfer the ends, then chamfer the sides of each piece from about 1 inch from the joint (Fig. 6-3B).

4. Cut the rabbets in the bases (Fig. 6-3C) to match the uprights.

5. Mark out and drill the metal plates (Fig. 6-3D). Countersink so the screw heads will not project. Smooth all edges.

6. Cut shallow rabbets for the metal plates in the bases. Drill the wood for the screws, using undersize holes where the threads have to pull into end grain.

7. Mark and cut the arrow parts (Fig. 6-4). The tenons are shown 1/2 inch long, but the mortises should be cut about three-fourths through the uprights and the tenons trimmed to fit. Remove any roughness and round the edges of the projecting arrow parts.

8. Sand all parts and check that they will match each other (Fig. 6-5).

9. Assemble the main parts with the metal

Materials List for Arrow Bookends

Main parts from	1 piece 5/8 × 4 × 21
Arrow from	1 piece 1/4 × 2 × 8
2 metal plates	3 × 4 × 18 gauge

Fig. 6-2. These bookends have plates under the end books and the arrow appears to go through them.

plates. If these or the arrow parts are to be stained, do that now.

10. Glue in the arrow parts. Check that they are straight and in line with each other.

11. Finish the wood with polish or varnish.

12. Although the bookends could be used as they are, any tendency to slip can be reduced and the risk of scratching a table top removed if the undersides of the wood and metal have cloth glued on.

TAKE-DOWN BOOK RACK

A rack to hold 10 or 12 books is useful on a desk or table top. It can contain the books you are currently reading or they may be reference books. For a student the rack could hold test books conveniently within reach. For anyone travelling, or for a student who might change his place of work, a rack or trough that can be reduced to four flat boards for easy transport can be very useful.

This rack (Fig. 6-6) is intended to be primarily useful, although that is no reason why it should not also look attractive. It could be made of solid wood and finished with stain and polish, or made of plywood.

The shelves fit into the ends with tusk tenons, projecting through their mortises and tightened with wedges. If the wedges are knocked out, everything can be packed flat (Fig. 6-7).

The sizes suggested will take books of average size and hold them with their bottom edges at 30 degrees to the desk top. The angle could be modified if you wish, and the shelves made wider

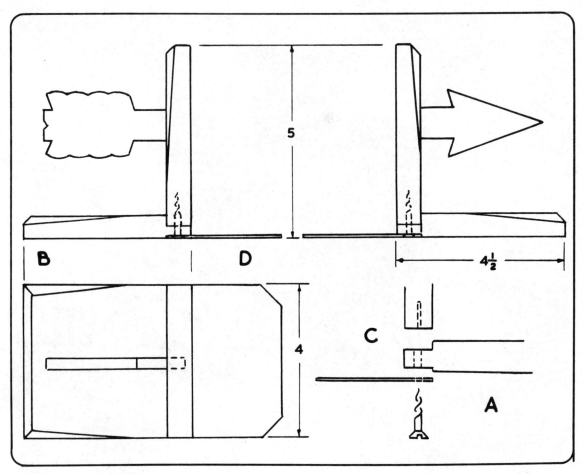

Fig. 6-3. Sizes and construction of the arrow bookends.

if you want to fit large volumes. With the shelf arrangement drawn, both shelves are 4 inches wide and positioned so the bottom one would be at the center of a book 6 inches wide, and the rear one would be central on the back of a book 8 inches high. They would be just as suitable for books several inches bigger or smaller.

1. The key parts—those that control sizes, are the ends (Fig. 6-8A). Mark them out from the pattern of squares (Fig. 6-9A). Mark on the actual thicknesses of the wood to be used for the shelves. The shelf angles are 30 degrees and square to each other. The mortises are 2 inches wide. An angular outline is shown, but that could be softened with curves if you wish. Cut the outlines, but leave cut-ting the mortises until the tenons are marked and cut.

2. Mark and cut the two shelves (Fig. 6-8B), which are identical. Squareness of the bearing surfaces at the ends is very important if the rack is to assemble properly and stand level. Cut the tenons (Fig. 6-9B) and make the mortises in the ends so the parts go together as an easy push fit.

3. The slots in the mortises have to match the wedges which are cut from 3/4-inch-square wood. The exact taper is unimportant, but the wedges should be the same so they are interchangeable. From 3/4 inch to 9/16 inch in the 1 1/2-inch length should be satisfactory (Fig. 6-9C).

4. The back of each slot must come within the thickness of its end (Fig. 6-9D) when the wedge

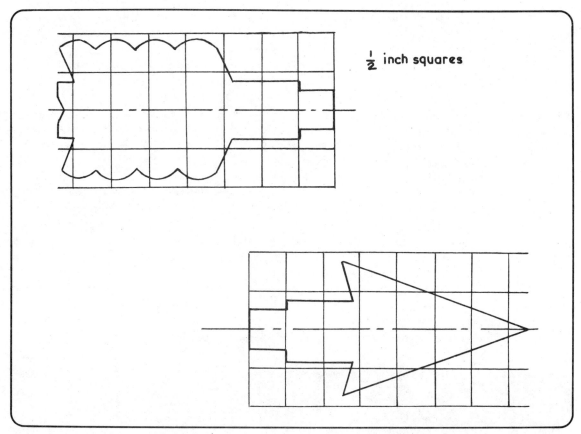

½ inch squares

Fig. 6-4. Shapes of the arrow parts for the bookends.

is tight, so the wedge bears on the surface of the end to force the joint tight. The outer part of the slot should match the slope of the wedge and be cut so the wedge extends about the same amount each side when tight.

5. Make a trial assembly. If the shelves fit better in one position than another, mark the joints. Bevel the ends of the tenons and wedges, then take sharpness off edges all around and finish the wood with stain and varnish or polish.

Materials List for Take-Down Book Rack	
2 ends	1/2 × 8 × 11
2 shelves	1/2 × 4 × 19
4 wedges	3/4 × 3/4 × 2

LOW BOOKCASE

A low block of shelves can have many uses. Although usually to hold books, the shelves can be used to store and display other items. If the bookcase is located under a window, it makes use of space that might not be usefully occupied. Plants or flowers can be stood on top so they benefit from the daylight through the window.

This bookcase (Fig. 6-10) is a size that will hold many books of popular sizes and its height should fit below many windows. However, before starting work, check on the sizes of what you want to fit in the shelves and the total height and width that will suit the intended location. Variations in size will not affect construction unless the difference is considerable.

The parts can be solid wood; it is also possible to use veneered particleboard. A long shelf

119

filled with books has considerable weight, which could cause sagging. All the parts could be 3/4 inch thick, but if you decide to use thinner wood for most parts, do not reduce the middle shelf if it is to take the weight of books.

As shown (Fig. 6-11A), the top shelf overhangs and the others are between the sides. The bottom is stiffened with a plinth and there is a rail around the top. The back is open. There could be a hardboard or thin plywood back, and you could leave off the top rail if you wish.

1. Decide on the method of construction. There could be stopped dadoes (Fig. 6-12A) for the shelves and top. Top corners could be dovetailed (Fig. 6-12B). Certain parts will have to be dowelled in any case, and you might decide to dowel everything (Fig. 6-12C). This would have to be the method with particleboard, but it is optional for solid wood. Shelves can have three or four 1/4-inch or 5/16-inch dowels. The top rails and plinth can have them widely spaced. When you know which joints you will use, allow for them when you cut the wood.

2. Make the shelves and ends the same width (Fig. 6-11B). Leave some excess length on the top until after the dadoes have been cut. Make the other two shelves the same length as the distance between the dadoes. Mark out in a similar way if dowels are to be used (Fig. 6-12C). For through dovetails, the top does not overhang (Fig. 6-12B).

3. Mark the positions of the rails (Fig. 6-11C and 6-11D) on the top. Allow for dowels, but because there is very little load, they can be short. If the end rails come over the bookcase ends, stagger the dowel positions so the holes above are not in line with those below.

4. Cut the end rails to shape (Fig. 6-12D) and hollow the center of the back rail (Fig. 6-12E). Round all the upper edges. Drill for dowels. The back rail fits between the end rails.

Fig. 6-5. Parts of the arrow bookends before assembly.

Fig. 6-6. This book rack stands on a table and holds books at a convenient angle.

5. The plinth (Fig. 6-11E) is a strip set back a little below the bottom shelf. Drill it for dowels into the ends and the shelf. Cut back its underside, so only its ends bear on the floor.

6. Mark where the plinth comes on the ends. Cut back in a similar way to the plinth (Fig. 6-11F). The bookcase will then stand on its corners only and is more likely to remain steady if the floor is slightly uneven.

7. If dadoes are used the joints can be strengthened by screws—two in each top and bottom joint (Fig. 6-12F). They can be driven from inside at the top and from under the bottom shelf.

8. Join the top rails to the bookcase top. Have the other parts and their dowels ready, then join all parts at one session. Check squareness and see that the assembly stands upright on a flat surface.

Materials List for Low Bookcase

1 top shelf	3/4 × 8 × 38
2 shelves	3/4 × 8 × 36
2 ends	3/4 × 8 × 25
1 plinth	3/4 × 3 × 36
1 top rail	3/4 × 2 × 36
2 top rails	3/4 × 2 × 8

CORNER SHELVES

The corner of a room is often wasted space. If any

Fig. 6-7. By removing wedges the book rack can be taken down and packed flat.

ordinary furniture is put across the corner, it has to be at an angle and there is an unused triangle behind it. Corner furniture can be basically triangular so it fits in with its front diagonal to the walls.

This corner shelf unit is intended to hang (Fig. 6-13) with three shelves on which you can store or display a variety of things. The unit can be given a good-quality furniture finish and used in the living room to display some of your treasures. It could be used for pot plants or flowers in vases. A similar block of shelves made of less-expensive wood and given a painted finish could be used in a kitchen or laundryroom for storage. A simpler version might find a use in your shop, so a corner could store some of the many cans of paint, boxes

of nails, and other similar things you accumulate.

The block of shelves is shown with a wider space below a narrower one (Fig. 6-14A). Apart from practical considerations, any design looks better that way than with equal spaces. The shelves are not simple triangles, but are squared from the walls (Fig. 6-14B), which gives a useful increase in storage area.

For a good-quality finish, the unit should be made of an attractive solid wood and finished with stain and polish or varnish. Plywood could be used throughout, but that would be better painted to disguise the otherwise unattractive edges.

1. Check the angle of the corner of the room.

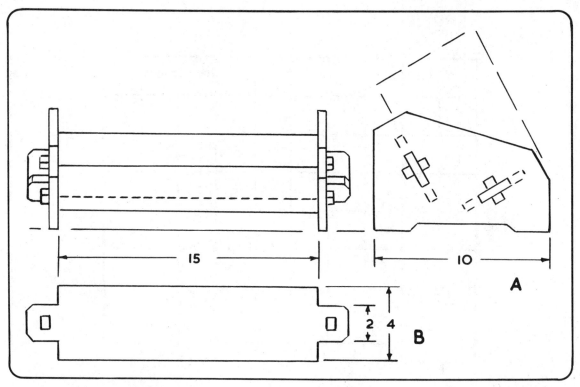

Fig. 6-8. Main sizes for the take-down book rack.

It might not be square. That would not matter or even be noticed in ordinary circumstances, but if you made the unit square and put it in an inaccurate corner, it would not fit and gaps at the edges could be noticeable. Set an adjustable bevel to the angle of the corner of the room and test this with a square. If there is an error, use the bevel instead of a square for marking out the shelf angles.

2. Mark out the two backs, with the positions of the grooves. As the parts overlap in the corner, one piece will be 1/2 inch wider than the other (Fig. 6-14C).

3. Cut the dado grooves for the shelves (Fig. 6-14D) the full width of both backs. It does not matter about the grooves of the overlapping piece extending over the other; it will not show in the corner.

4. Make the three shelves all the same. Cut them to fit in the dadoes and overhang to the wall (Fig. 6-14E), so the ends of the grooves will be hidden. For maximum strength have the grain lines diagonal across each shelf. Round the outer corners.

5. For simple corner shelves the back edges can be left straight and the tops and bottoms bevelled (Fig. 6-14F).

6. The backs are shown with their edges shaped, which would be preferable for display shelves in most rooms. Do all the joint cutting and main cutting to size before marking out and cutting the curves.

7. Mark and cut the tops and bottoms of the backs the same (Fig. 6-15A).

8. The front edges could be marked with a compass, but a curve that is deeper below its center is more attractive (Fig. 6-15B). The curves on the ends and fronts are shown broken with steps. This little extra work gives a more classical effect to the shaping.

9. The overlapping backs could be screwed together, or a few dowels might be used (Fig. 6-14G).

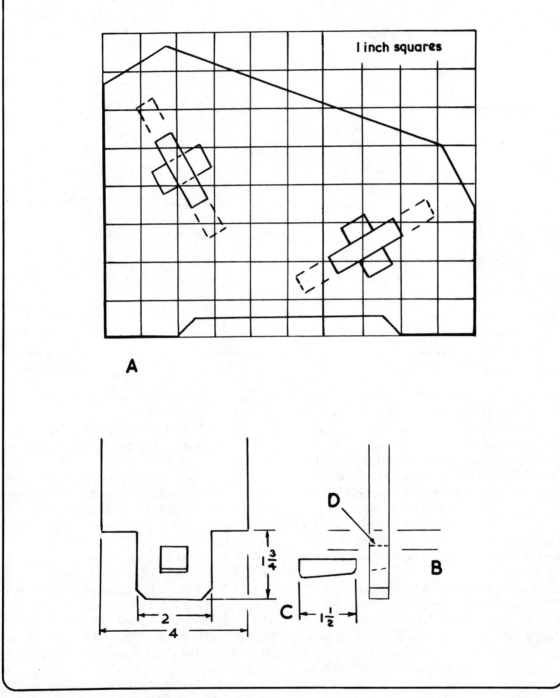

Fig. 6-9. End and tenon details for the take-down book rack.

Fig. 6-10. A low block of shelves can have many uses besides holding books.

10. Glue in the shelves. There can also be one or two screws driven into them because the screw heads will not show when the unit is attached to the wall.

11. It will probably be sufficient to drill for a screw into each wall below the top shelf, but others could also be used, particularly if you expect to

Materials List for Corner Shelves

1 back	1/2 × 7 1/2 × 25
1 back	1/2 × 8 × 25
3 shelves	1/2 × 8 × 14

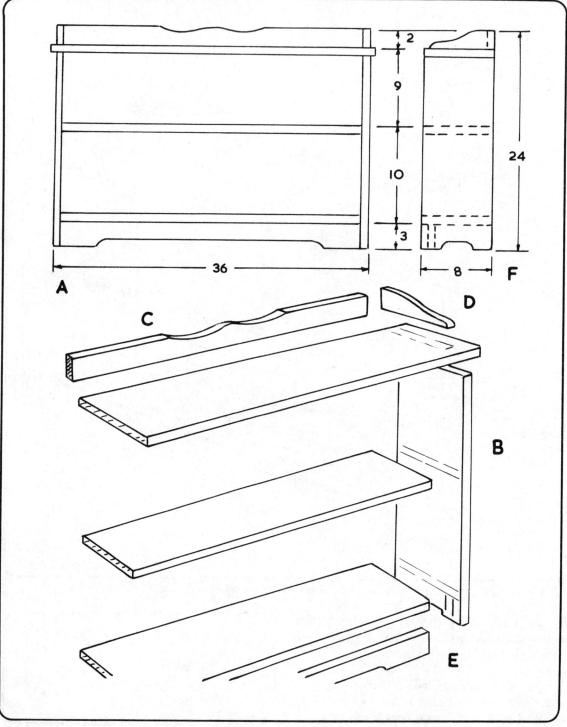

Fig. 6-11. Sizes and parts of the low bookcase.

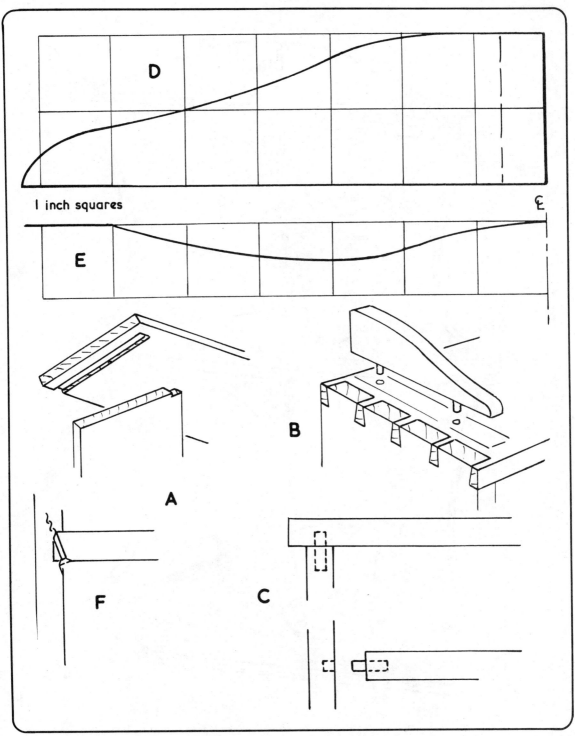

I inch squares

Fig. 6-12. Shapes and joints of the low bookcase.

Fig. 6-13. Corner shelves use space that might otherwise be vacant.

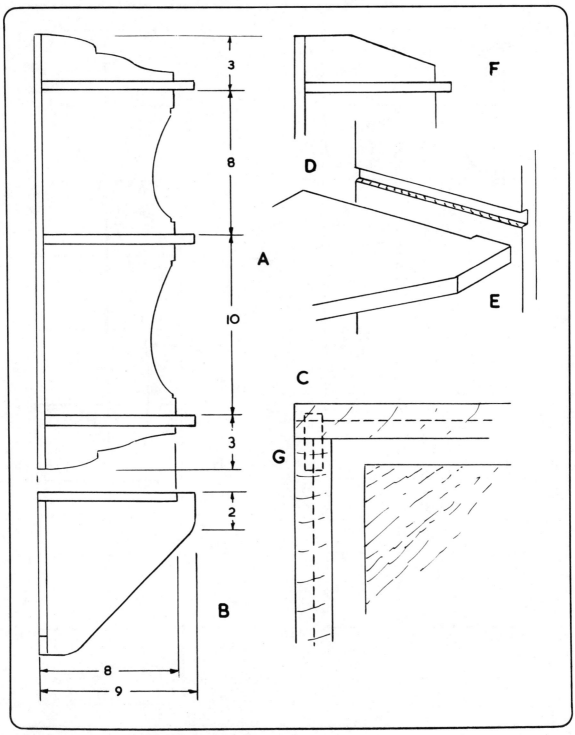

Fig. 6-14. Sizes and construction of the corner shelves.

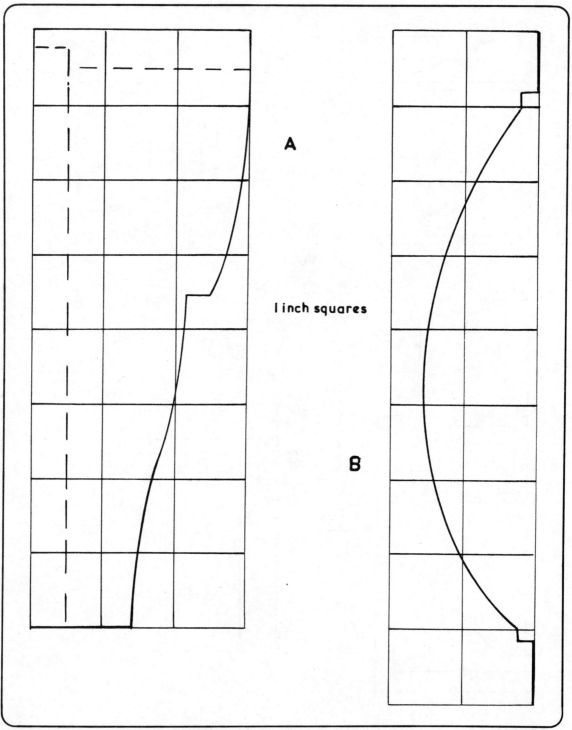

A

1 inch squares

B

Fig. 6-15. Shaped parts of the corner shelves.

add heavy items. Make a trial positioning, then apply finish before finally screwing to the wall.

MAGAZINE RACK

If you have a large number of magazines they can become untidy, and you might have difficulty in locating the one you want if they are scattered around the room. A shelf under a table will take care of many of them, but then you have the problem of pulling out a pile to find the one you want. A bin is almost as bad and there is the additional problem of pages folding and creasing, particularly the thinner ones printed on limp paper. All of these difficulties can be overcome if the magazines are arranged to hang independently of each other. They will be kept in a way that reduces the risk of damaging them and you can see where each one is and pull it out without moving the others.

This rack (Fig. 6-16) holds 10 or 11 magazines hung over rails. It can stand out of the way and be lifted beside your chair or anywhere else you need it. When out of use it folds almost flat. It is adjustable to three positions. In a restricted place it can be at the narrowest setting, but if space is available or the magazines are very thick, you might prefer one of the wider settings.

The suggested sizes (Fig. 6-17A) should suit most magazines, but it is advisable to measure those you subscribe to in case some are unusual. The important measurements are between the end supports for clearance of the length of the magazines and the height of the lower rails from the floor for the width of a hanging magazine.

The rails are hardwood dowel rods. The end supports could be any wood, possibly chosen to match existing furniture.

1. The rails may go right through the legs, but if you prefer them not to show on the outside they could go into blind holes (Fig. 6-17B). Rigidity of the assembly depends on the rail joints, so go at least three-fourths of the way through and choose a drill that will give a tight fit on the rods.

2. The top rail is thicker and will go right through the inner legs, but may be stopped in the

outer ones or taken through them (Fig. 6-18A). As one frame swings inside the other, the rail lengths have to be adjusted to suit (Fig. 6-17C). Allow an easy clearance between the legs.

3. Make the four legs (Fig. 6-18B). Both ends are semi-circular and the rail holes are 2 1/2 inches apart, so the lowest one is 12 1/2 inches from the top one, which serves as a carrying handle. Drill all holes. Take the sharpness off all edges.

4. The stay pivots on the middle thin rail on the inner frame. It is shown hooked on the next lower rail at the other side (Fig. 6-17D). This gives the intermediate setting. If it is hooked on the rail straight across the legs are opened to about 50 degrees and the bottoms are about 21 inches apart. When it is hooked on the lowest rail the angle is about half that and the legs are about 11 inches apart (Fig. 6-17E).

5. Make the stay (Fig. 6-18C) with a hole to fit on its rail and a notch that will easily hook over the other rails. Round the ends and edges. One stay should be enough, but you can fit another at the other end if you think it necessary.

6. Assemble the inner frame first. Remember to include the stay on its rail. Check squareness by measuring diagonals. Use this frame as a guide when assembling the other frame to it.

7. Finish with stain and varnish or polish, as required.

Materials List for Magazine Rack	
4 legs	3/4 × 1 1/2 × 24
1 stay	1/2 × 7/8 × 10
1 rail	19 × 1/2 dowel rod
10 rails	19 × 1/4 dowel rods

PORTABLE MAGAZINE BIN

A rack or bin that can be carried about allows you to put magazines and books alongside a chair or take them into other rooms. The same bin could

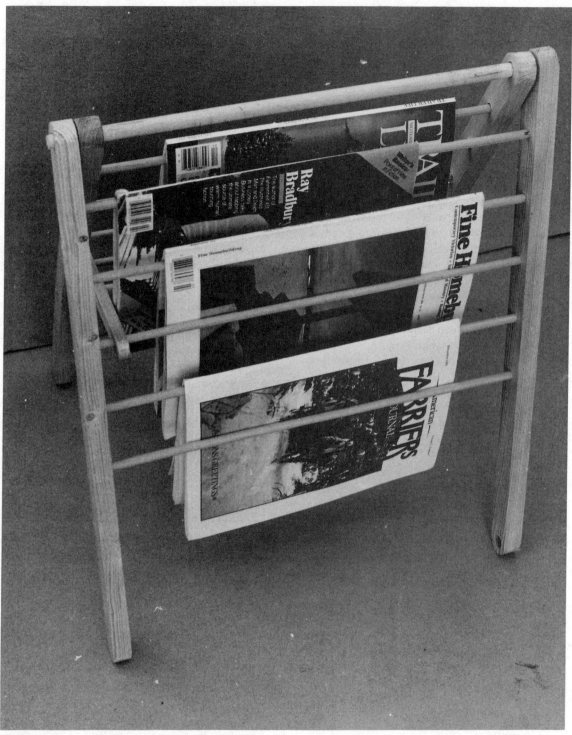

Fig. 6-16. This rack allows magazines to hang from rails.

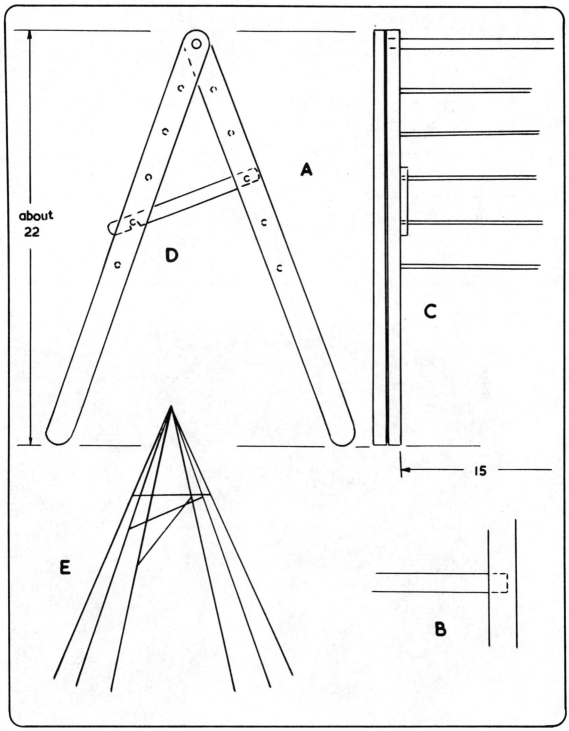

Fig. 6-17. Size and layout of the magazine rack.

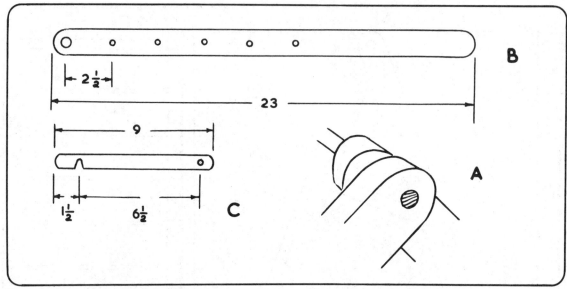

Fig. 6-18. Sizes of magazine rack parts.

Fig. 6-19. The portable magazine bin has space for a large number of magazines, which can be carried about with the central handle.

be used for knitting or sewing materials. It might even be taken into the yard when gathering flowers.

This bin (Fig. 6-19) is intended to have its flat parts made of plywood, with solid wood strips and dowels rods at the sides. Solid wood could be used throughout if you have wide enough pieces. The complete bin could be stained to even the colors of different woods, or it could be painted. A bright color would make an attractive contrast with the whites and pale shades of newspapers and magazines.

The sizes shown (Fig. 6-20) should suit most purposes and will certainly hold plenty of magazines, but this project can be made other sizes without affecting the methods of construction.

1. Start with the two ends (Fig. 6-21A). The top edges are shaped (Fig. 6-22A) and at the sides allow for the ends being notched into all four bars (Fig. 6-22B), but the outside edges should come level. Mark for the position of the central division and the bottom, which comes inside the ends.

2. Make the central division (Fig. 6-21B), which fits between the ends and on top of the bottom. Shape the top and make the hand hole (Fig. 6-22C). Well round the shaped edge and the edges of the hand hole.

3. The four bars are the same (Fig. 6-21C). At their ends cut notches to fit the bin ends (Fig. 6-20A). Make sure the distance between the inner edges of the notches is the same as the length of the central division. After cutting the notches, round the extending ends.

4. The rods are 1/4-inch dowels. Seven each side are shown (Fig. 6-20B), but you could use a

Materials List for Portable Magazine Bin

2 ends	10 × 11 × 1/2 plywood
1 central division	13 × 17 × 1/2 plywood
1 bottom	9 × 17 × 1/2 plywood
4 bars	3/4 × 1 1/2 × 19
14 rods	9 × 1/4 diameter

different number or different sizes. Space them evenly, which will result in 2-inch centers (Fig. 6-20C) if you make the bin to the sizes on the drawings.

5. Allow for the dowel rods entering their holes in the bars about 1/2 inch. When you assemble the bin, however, the bar spacing will have to be adjusted to match the ends and you will avoid movement being restricted if you make all holes slightly too deep (Fig. 6-22D).

6. Although the simplest bottom would be a piece of plywood nailed or screwed upwards into the other parts, its edges would show and the bin will look better with the bottom inside the ends and lower bars (Fig. 6-21D).

7. Use glue and thin screws into the plywood edges. Join the ends to the central division. Glue the dowel rods into the bars. Before the glue has started to set, join the notches in the bars to the ends, so the dowel ends will automatically adjust correctly in their holes.

8. It helps to start with the bottom slightly oversize and plane its edges to a close fit after the other parts are assembled.

9. You could fit feet if you wish. Squares under each corner would be satisfactory (Fig. 6-22E).

10. Remove any excess glue and finish the bin with stain and varnish, polish, or paint.

VASE STAND

If you have a large vase of flowers or a pot containing a plant, or an ornamental jar you wish to display, it will probably be better on a stand, rather than directly on a table or shelf. The stand will protect the surface, particularly if there may be water dripping, and a nicely-finished wood stand will complement the ornament and enhance the display. The stand does not have to be elaborate. In a greenhouse or on a deck it could be severely plain, but for use indoors some shaping will soften appearance and emphasize any grain markings showing through the finish.

This stand (Fig. 6-23A) is designed to form a base to a fairly large ornament, giving a good spread of the feet for steadiness. It could go under

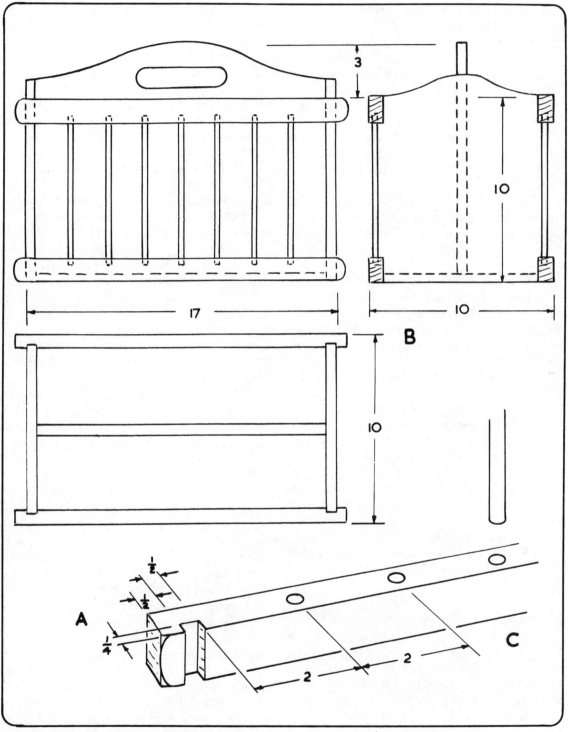

Fig. 6-20. Sizes of the portable magazine bin.

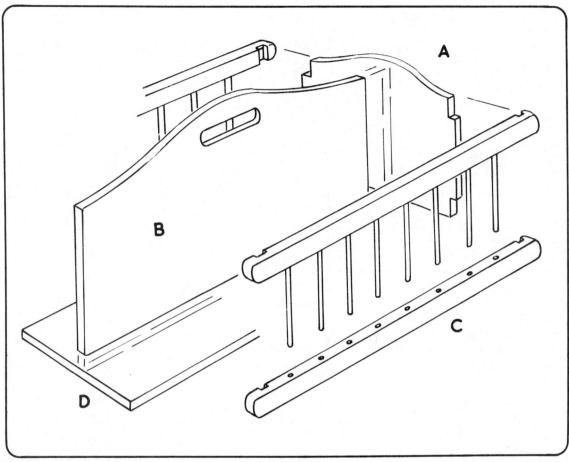

Fig. 6-21. How the parts of the portable magazine bin are assembled.

a tall jar or vase, with its contents of flowers, or under a broad and heavy pot containing a plant. Several stands of different sizes, but all the same wood and pattern could make a set that would give uniformity to a display and be attractive in themselves. The sizes given (Fig. 6-23B) can be regarded as standard, to be altered to suit your needs.

1. The top (Fig. 6-23C) is 7 inches square with its corners cut back (Fig. 6-24A). Mark carefully to get the four corners the same and make cuts vertically. If the straight cuts are marked down the edges they can be cut squarely and slight errors in the curves will not be so apparent. Remove saw marks and take the sharpness off all edges.

2. The feet (Fig. 6-23D) should be marked

out completely on a 1-by-2-inch strip (Fig. 6-24B) before cutting any part of them, including the halving joint notches (Fig. 6-24C).

3. Cut the outlines, being careful to keep the cuts square to the surface. Remove saw cuts and sand the projecting ends, which will be the most obvious parts in the finished stand.

4. Cut the halving joints to make a push fit. Be careful of breaking at this stage. The joint will

Materials List for Vase Stand		
1 top	5/8 × 7 × 7	
2 feet	1 × 2 × 13	

137

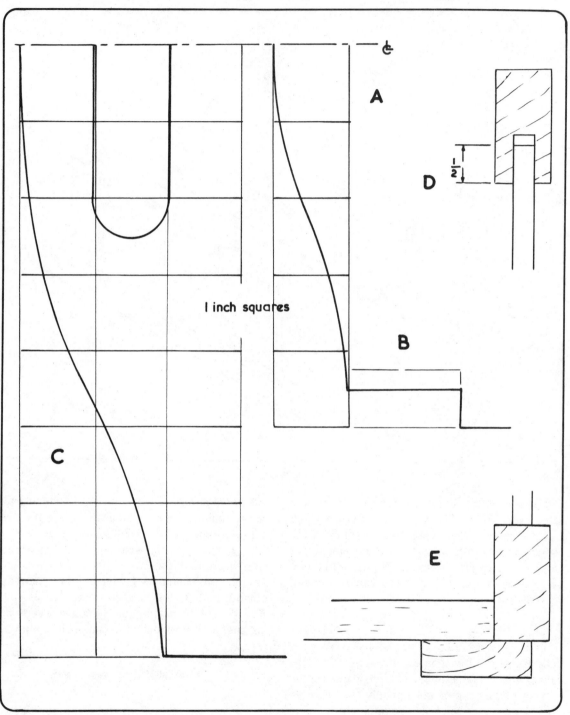

1 inch squares

Fig. 6-22. Shapes and sections of parts of the portable magazine bin.

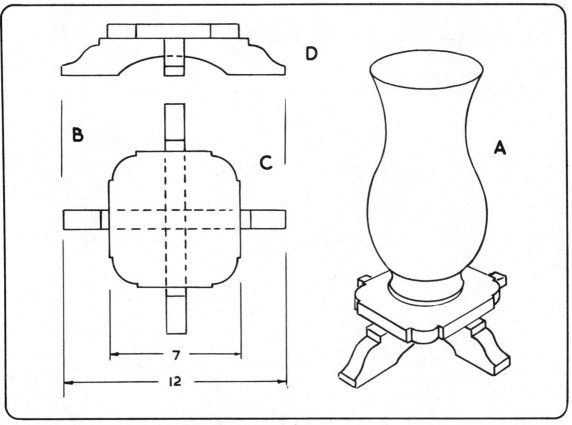

Fig. 6-23. A vase stand supports and adds to the appearance of a vase or pot.

have ample strength when the feet are attached to the top.

5. Mark the positions of the feet on the underside of the top. Drill for two screws upwards through each foot. Put the feet together and check squareness and fit against the top. Join all parts with glue and screws.

6. Finish with stain and polish. Cloth glued under the ends of the feet will protect a polished table top and prevent slipping.

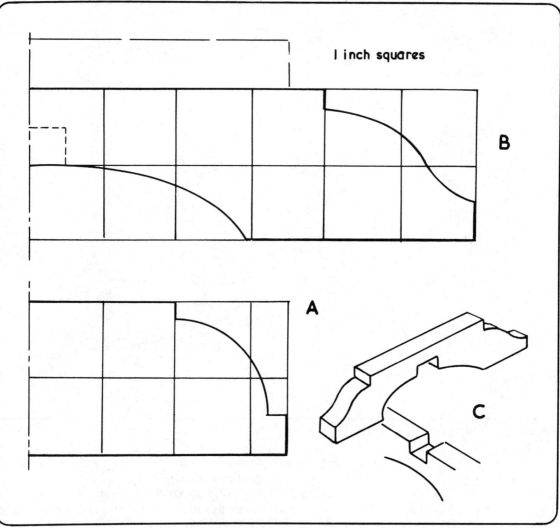

1 inch squares

B

A

C

Fig. 6-24. Shapes and assembly of parts of the vase stand.

Chapter 7

Bedroom

We spend about one-third of our lives asleep in the bedroom, but before and after sleep we can make use of many items of furniture to help us prepare for night or day. Many of these things are small enough and simple enough to be made in a weekend.

Some beds are too large an undertaking to be made in the time, but there are simple ones and you may be able to improve the one you have. Space is often limited in a bedroom. Some things you construct will help to conserve space by accommodating things that would otherwise be scattered around. Make sure there is space for what you intend to make. An inch or so more or less can make considerable difference. It is in this control of size that you have advantage over the person who has to buy a stock item. You might also be making a unique item; something that could not be bought.

BEDSIDE CABINET

Veneered particleboard makes possible the con-

struction of furniture that would certainly take longer than a weekend to make if the parts had to be prepared from solid wood. This item uses particleboard already veneered on both sides and both edges. The cabinet in the photograph (Fig. 7-1) has wood-grain plastic veneer for most parts, but the door is a contrasting white. The whole cabinet could be made with the same wood or plastic veneer throughout. The back is hardboard.

The sizes shown (Fig. 7-2) allow for most parts being cut from panels 12 inches wide, then only a few exposed edges will have to be covered with iron-on strip veneer. Sizes can be altered with minimum effort if other stock width panels are to be used. Accurate squaring of the panels is important for a good fit and for appearance. Joints with 1/4-inch dowels are suggested, but they could be made with the screw-on plastic fittings used with some knock-down furniture. Dowels are better for a permanent assembly.

1. Make the two sides (Fig. 7-3A) with the positions of other parts marked on them.

141

Fig. 7-1. This bedside cabinet is made of particle-board veneered with wood-grain plastic, but the door is white.

2. Make the two shelves to match each other (Fig. 7-3B).

3. Make the plinth (Fig. 7-3C) and the top rail (Fig. 7-3D) to the same lengths as the shelves. Dowel the plinth 3/4 inch in from the front of the bottom shelf.

4. Mark the dowel positions on the sides and on all other parts. Drill as deeply as possible in the sides and at least as deep in the other parts.

5. Cut sufficient dowels and glue all these parts in one operation. Check squareness and leave the assembly standing level for the glue to set.

6. Make the top (Fig. 7-3E) level at the back and front, but overhanging 1/4 inch at each side. Veneer its cut ends. Dowel it to the sides and rail.

7. Make the hardboard back (Fig. 7-3F). Cut its edges to half the thickness of the top and sides, so it does not show. Glue and nail it on.

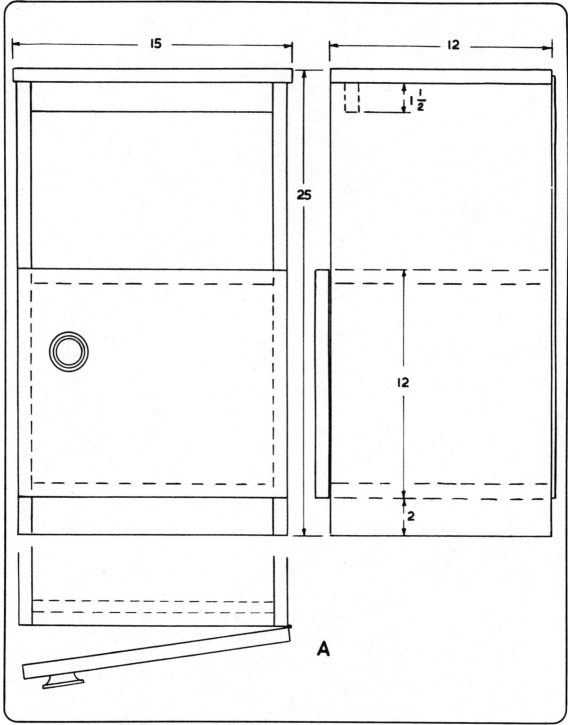

Fig. 7-2. Main sizes of the bedside cabinet.

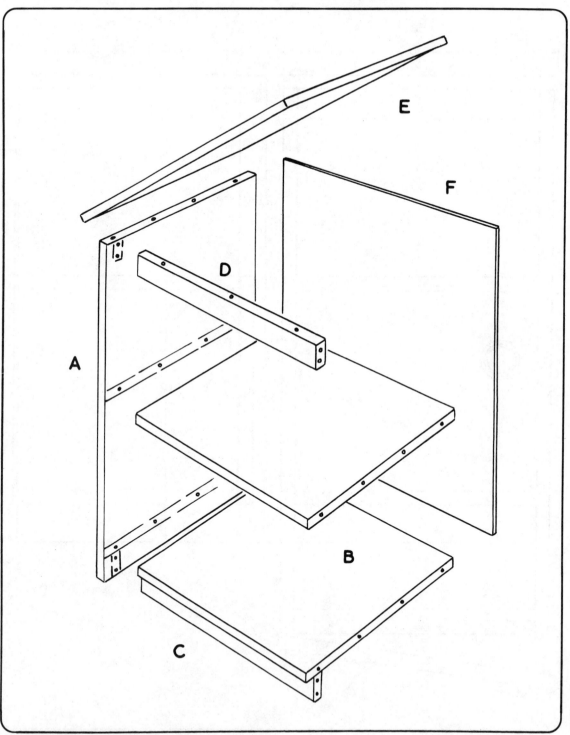

Fig. 7-3. How the parts of the bedside cabinet are assembled.

8. Make the door to overlap the sides and shelves (Fig. 7-2A). Veneer its cut edges. Fit a handle fairly high on the side towards the bed and hinges at the other side. Add a magnetic or spring catch.

Materials List for Bedside Cabinet

Veneered particleboard 5/8 inch or 3/4 inch thick

2 sides	12	× 25
2 shelves	12	× 14
1 plinth	2	× 14
1 rail	1 1/2	× 14
1 top	12	× 16

Hardboard 1/8 inch thick

1 back	14	× 23

BED TABLE

A meal or refreshments in bed may be appealing, whether you are ill or just lazy, but balancing a tray or separate plates, cups, and cutlery could be disastrous. The answer is a bed table, which has legs to stand on each side of you. This bed table (Fig. 7-4) has legs that fold and extend with a spring action, so the table can be carried as a tray or stored flat, then opened with a simple action to give rigid support when needed on a bed.

The top of the tray has raised ends with hand holes (Fig. 7-5A). There is a back, but the side towards you is open. Underneath there are two pairs of legs hinged at the ends of the table. Along the center of the table is a springy piece of wood that presses against the crossbars of the legs to keep them folded against the underside of the tray (Fig. 7-5B). When the legs are to be extended they are pulled down and the spring will press into notches in the crossbars to hold the opened legs against the box ends under the table.

The main parts of the table could be made from 1/2-inch plywood. The legs could be any wood. The springy bar could be ash or hickory, but whatever is chosen must have some spring in it.

The sizes suggested (Fig. 7-5C) will probably suit your needs, but they can be altered—although because the legs must fold within the table, a large increase in height would necessitate making the table longer.

1. Cut the wood for the table top (Fig. 7-5D). The top parts will be at the edges (Fig. 7-6A) with screws upwards. The parts underneath are set in 1/2 inch with screws downwards (Fig. 7-6B).

2. Make the pieces underneath in the form of a box. At the corners the wood could be overlapped and screwed, but a better joint for plywood is a variation of the finger joint (Fig. 7-6C). This allows you to glue the parts and drive pins both ways.

3. Cut the pieces for the ends (Fig. 7-6D). Make the hand holes by drilling and sawing out the waste.

4. Make the back (Fig. 7-5E) to fit between the ends. It could be left parallel, but it is shown cut down. Round all the upper edges of the top parts. Make the corner joints in the same way as those underneath.

5. Make the two leg assemblies (Fig. 7-6E) to fit easily between the sides under the table. The joints could be mortise and tenon or dowelled, but they should be strong because sometimes there might be considerable leverage on them. Round the bottoms of the legs, which will rest on the bed.

6. At the center of the underside of the table glue and screw a 2-inch-square block the same thickness as the legs (Fig. 7-5F). Over this will go the springy strip.

7. There might have to be some experimenting with the spring (Fig. 7-5G). Start by making it a 1/4-by-2 inch section. If this proves too stiff it might have to be planed thinner throughout or towards the ends. Much depends on the choice of wood. Make it too long at first.

8. Cut shallow notches across the leg rails (Fig. 7-6F). At first make them 1/8 inch deep and wide enough to let the spring fit in easily.

9. Make deeper similar notches in the box ends. They should be deep enough to let the spring drop in without touching, when it is holding the

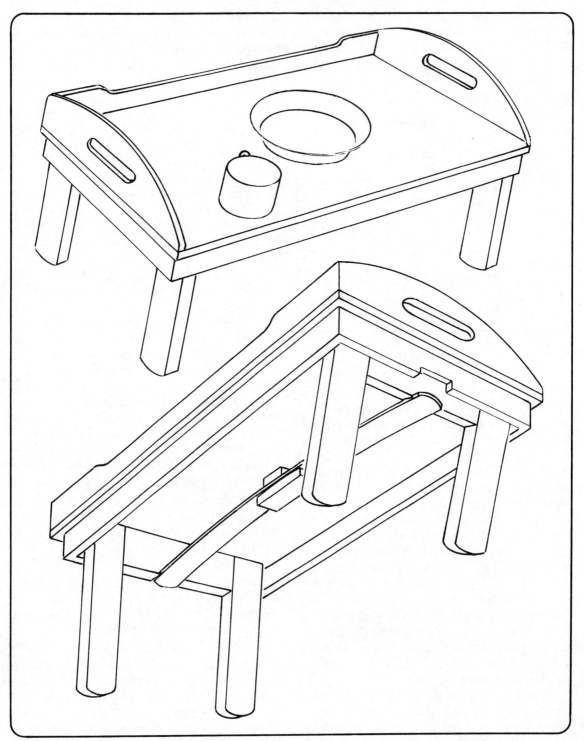

Fig. 7-4. This bed table has legs to stand on the bed, but they will fold flat with a spring action when the table is carried.

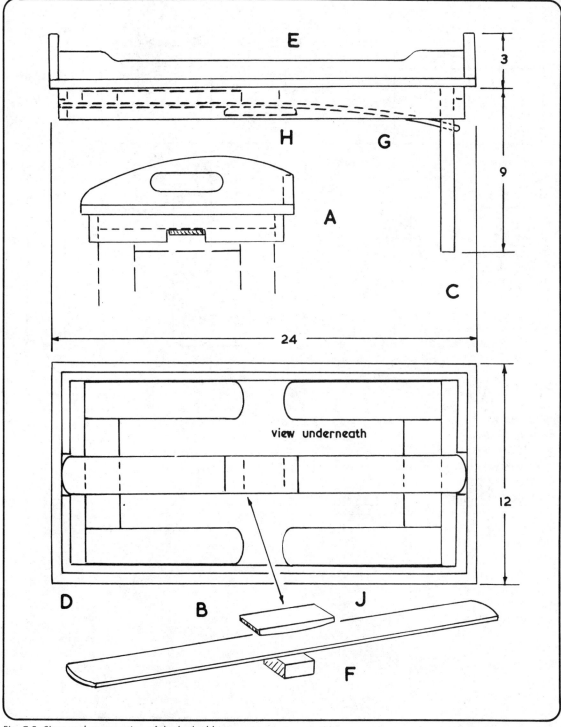

Fig. 7-5. Sizes and construction of the bed table.

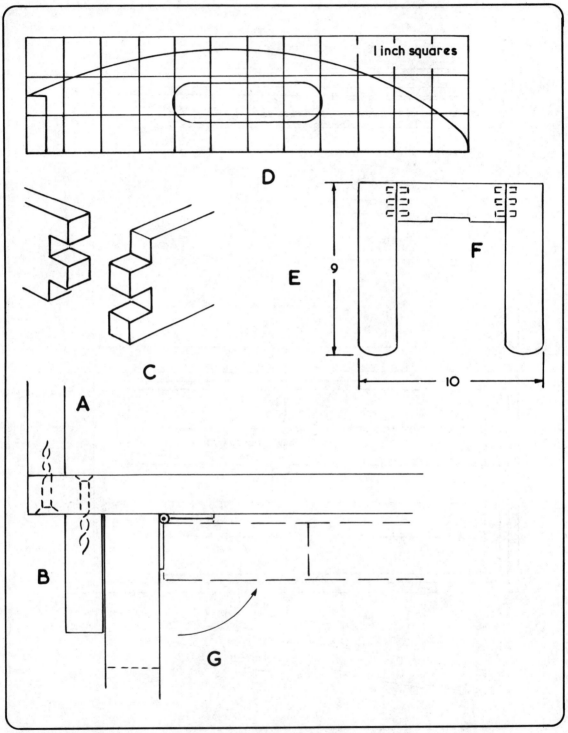

1 inch squares

A
B
C
D
E
F
G

9

10

Fig. 7-6. Assembly and action of the bed table legs and the end shape.

legs in the folded position. Leave finally trimming its depth until a trial assembly.

10. Fit 2-inch hinges to the tops of the four legs. They need not be let in, but position them so when the legs are down their tops press against the table and their outer surfaces are against the box ends (Fig. 7-6G). That will allow them to fold inwards between the box sides. Screw the legs to the table and test their action.

11. Make a block to fit over the center of the spring (Fig. 7-5H and 7-5J). Curve the side that will come against the spring slightly—just enough to approximate to the curve the spring will take when the legs are extended. Drill for two thin screws at its center (6-gauge will do).

12. Screw the spring in place with its block. Try the action of the legs. The spring should hold them flat against the table when folded. You might have to deepen the notches in the box ends to allow this. When the legs are opened the spring should press in the notch in their crossbar and hold them tight against the box ends. Examine the notches and note how much you might have to alter them so the spring beds flat against their bottoms. Note where the ends of the spring have to be cut, so they extend through the leg notches only a short way.

13. Take the spring assembly apart so its ends can be cut and notches adjusted.

14. You might wish to also remove the legs so all parts can be stained and polished. Reassemble and test the action of the legs. The top of the table could have non-slip plastic glued on, or you might depend on a separate cloth.

TIE RACK

This rack is intended to be attached to a wall or inside a clothes closet door and will hold up to eight ties, belts, ribbons or other long, narrow items. It can be made from oddments and sizes adjusted to suit available materials. Light-colored dowel rods look good against dark wood or the whole rack can be the same color. It would be possible to use plywood, but solid wood looks better (Fig. 7-7).

1. Both parts are 4 inches wide, so a piece long enough for both may be prepared.

2. Mark the back piece with a centerline and the position of the other part (Fig. 7-8A). Shape the corners with 5/8-inch radius and drill for screws to the wall at these centers. Drill for two screws to hold the front—8 gauge by 1 inch are suitable for 1/2-inch wood.

3. On the front (Fig. 7-8B) mark the centers of the top and bottom holes in the positions shown. Join these points and space the other hole positions equally.

4. Drill squarely for the dowel rods. Round the exposed edges of both parts.

5. Cut the dowel rods to the same length (Fig. 7-8C), although the lengths could be graduated, if you wish, particularly if you plan to hang wider belts. Round the ends.

6. Glue the dowel rods in place, then glue

Materials List for Bed Table				
Plywood				
1 table	12	× 24	× 1/2
2 ends	3	× 13	× 1/2
1 back	1 1/2	× 24	× 1/2
2 box sides	1 1/2	× 24	× 1/2
2 box ends	1 1/2	× 12	× 1/2
Solid wood				
4 legs	3/4	× 2	× 10
2 crossbars	3/4	× 2	× 11
1 spring	1/4	× 2	× 25
1 spring block	3/4	× 2	× 2
1 spring block	3/4	× 2	× 5

Materials List for Tie Rack
Back and front from 1 piece   1/2 × 4 × 16
Rods from one piece   18 × 1/2 diameter

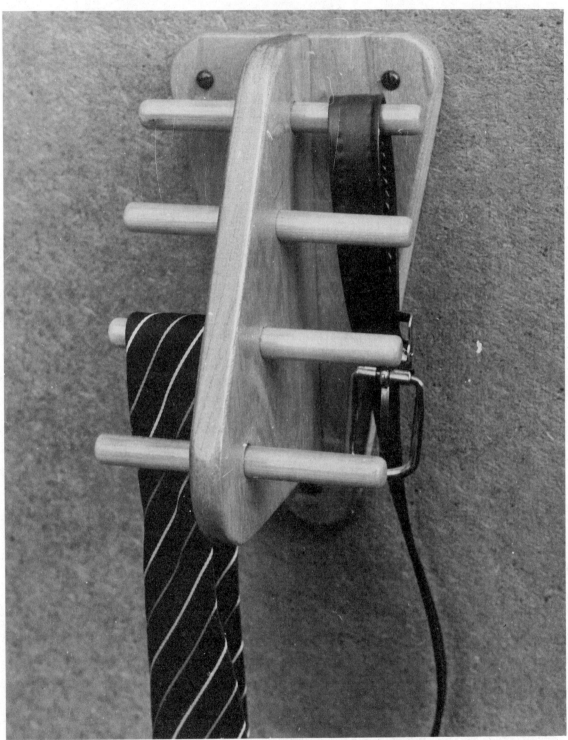

Fig. 7-7. This rack will hold ties or belts and can be mounted on a wall or inside a clothes closet.

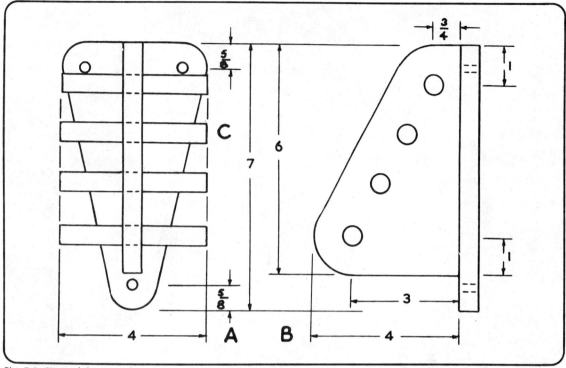

Fig. 7-8. Sizes of the tie rack.

and screw the back to the front. Finish with stain and polish.

VICTORIAN MIRROR

During the last century the only mirror in a bedroom was often a small one, arranged to tilt, and standing on a table or chest of drawers. Only plate glass would give an undistorted reflection. Such glass was heavy and expensive and silvering it was more costly than modern treatments, so the ordinary household could not afford the lavish spread of mirrors that we now regard as normal.

A tilting mirror modeled on the Victorian style forms a useful extra mirror and its design makes a pleasant change from the more stark outlines of much modern furniture. Construction makes an interesting project for a woodworker with a modestly equipped shop.

In Victorian days the most popular furniture wood was mahogany, but this project could be made of any wood. If you want to match natural pine furniture it could be softwood, but otherwise it is better made of one of the more common furniture woods. Most parts are 1 inch thick and it is not advisable to use wood that finishes much less, for the sake of stability.

You could make a frame and get a mirror cut to fit, or you might prefer to look for a stock mirror and make the frame to suit it. The Victorian mirror shown (Fig. 7-9) is made of oak and the frame is 10 inches wide and 14 inches high, with the glass about 8 1/2 by 12 1/2 inches (Fig. 7-10A), but it would not matter if you used a mirror an inch or so bigger or smaller and adjusted wood sizes to suit. In any case it is advisable to make the frame first and use it as a guide to the sizes of the stand.

If you alter sizes, the proportions look best if the base is about as long as the overall height and its width about half that.

The pivots on the mirror frame come a short distance above the halfway point—7 1/2 inches up on a 14-inch side. Although friction helps hold the mirror at the set angle, gravity helps prevent

Fig. 7-9. This tilting mirror is given a Victorian appearance.

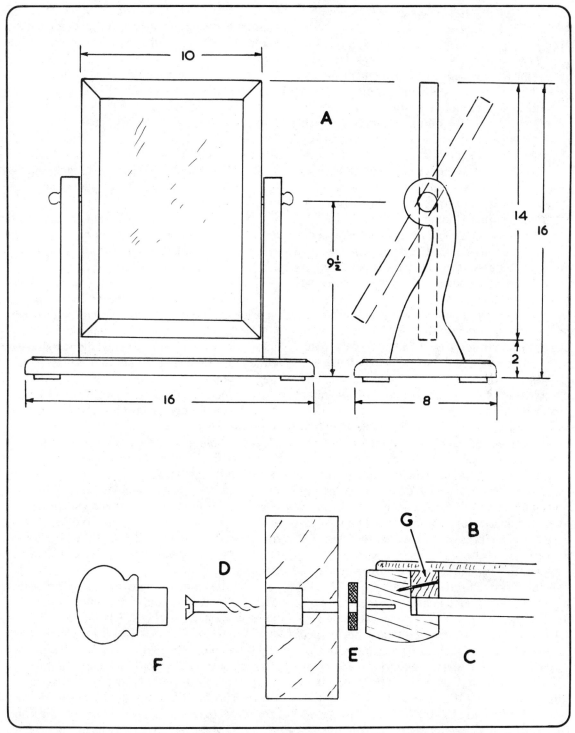

Fig. 7-10. Sizes of the Victorian mirror (A) and section showing the frame assembly and tilting arrangements (B-G).

the mirror turning over because it pivots above the center.

1. Prepare the wood for the mirror frame by cutting the rabbets (Fig. 7-10B). It might be easiest to do this on a wider board and cut off to size after rabbeting. The amount of rabbet might have to be adjusted to suit the mirror. A recess 3/8 inch wide can be as deep as the mirror thickness plus about 3/8 inch for the fillets.

2. The front of the frame could be left flat, molded in any way you wish, or curved (Fig. 7-10C)—which was a common treatment on original Victorian mirror frames.

3. The frame should be made to allow a little clearance around the edge of the mirror. A tight fit might cause the glass to crack eventually.

4. Miter the corners of the frame. They could be strengthened with pieces of veneer glued into saw cuts across the corners, but it will probably be better to drill diagonally for 1/4-inch dowels, planed level outside (Fig. 7-11A). Check squareness and be sure that the frame is held flat as the glue sets. A temporary piece of plywood the same size as the mirror could be used to keep the frame in shape under a weight.

5. Make the two supports suitable heights to bring the pivot points about 1/2 inch above the center of a frame side. Square the ends of 1-by-4-inch strips before marking out the shapes. Accurate square ends are needed to make the supports stand upright with close joints at their bases. Mark the pivot centers the same height above the base on both pieces, then draw the outlines (Fig. 7-11B).

6. Clean up the edges to remove saw marks. They might be left square, but the top part could have its edges rounded to match the curves on the front of the frame, with the curve blending into square edges a short distance below the shaped top. The Victorian look can be emphasized by carving or filing a tapered V to follow the circle of the top, either outside each support or on both sides of it (Fig. 7-11C).

7. The mirror frame pivots on two screws (Fig. 7-10D), with fiber washers between the sur-

faces to provide friction (Fig. 7-10E). Obtain the washers and measure the width over them and the frame. That will be the distance apart for the supports.

8. Cut the wood for the bottom. It is a plain rectangle extending about 2 inches outside the supports all around. Mark on it the positions of the supports at the correct distances apart (Fig. 7-11D). Although tenons could be used, three 1/2-inch dowels at each place will make a strong joint (Fig. 7-11E). Do not join these parts until the pivot details have been prepared and the edges of the bottom finished.

9. Although the edges of the bottom could be left square and its corners rounded, it would look better if molded. A simple form is suggested (Fig. 7-11F).

10. Counterbore for the pivot screws (8 gauge by 1 inch or 1 1/4 inch). Victorian mirrors of this type have the screws covered with knobs (Fig. 7-10F), which are a push fit in the counterbored holes, so they can be pulled out if the screws need tightening. Suitable knobs are sold as drawer handles, or you can turn your own.

11. Join the supports to the bottom. Check that they are upright and that the mirror frame will fit between them.

12. There could be turned feet under the corners of the bottoms, but small squares are just as suitable (Fig. 7-11G).

13. Make a trial assembly, then remove the frame for fitting the mirror. It will usually be advisable to prepare everything for holding the mirror, then stain and polish all the wood before finally fitting the mirror and mounting it in the stand.

14. The mirror should drop into the recess (Fig. 7-11H) easily. Hold it with fillets held to the frame with a few pins (Figs. 7-10G and 7-11J). Arrange the size of fillets to come level with the back of the frame or just below its surface. To protect the back of the mirror pin on a piece of thin plywood or hardboard (Fig. 7-11K), but let it be about 1/8 inch in from the outsides of the frame and around its edges so it is not obvious from the front.

15. Tighten the pivot screws sufficiently, then

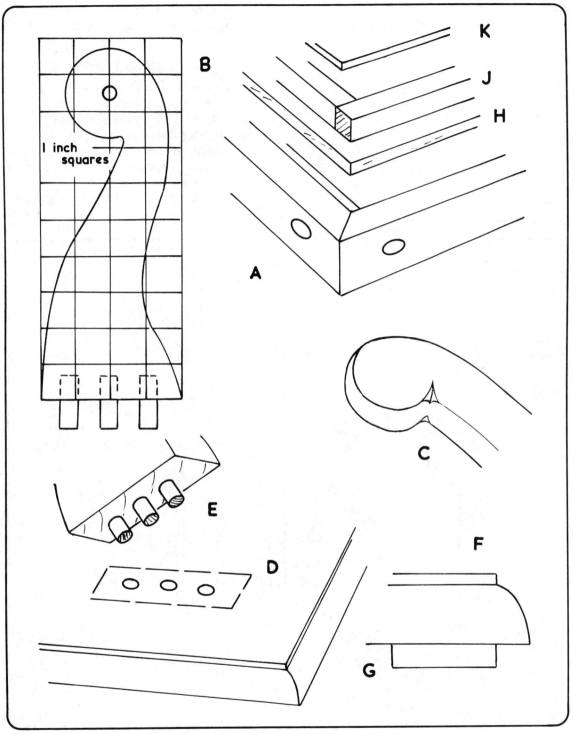

Fig. 7-11. Mirror frame assembly and shape and assembly of the supports.

push in the knobs. As the screws bed down they will probably have to be tightened further after a little use.

PANELED BED ENDS

Some beds would take more than a week to construct, but a pair of bed ends for an iron-framed or other mattress can be made quite simply. These bed ends are traditional in appearance, with a head high enough for pillows to be stacked against for sitting in bed and a foot that could have clothing or blankets hung over it. There are two identical panel assemblies on legs of different heights (Fig. 7-12).

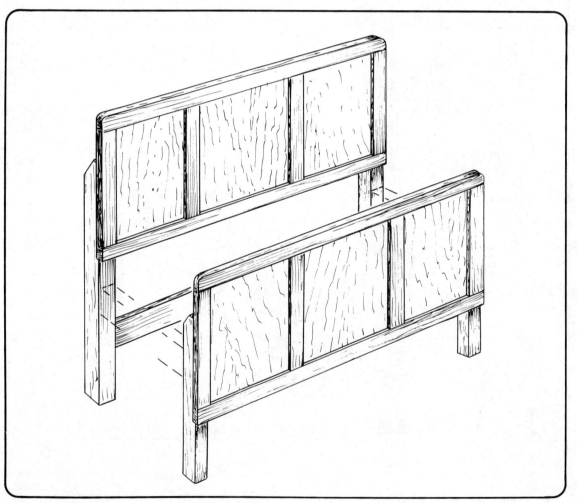

Fig. 7-12. Paneled head and foot ends for a bed.

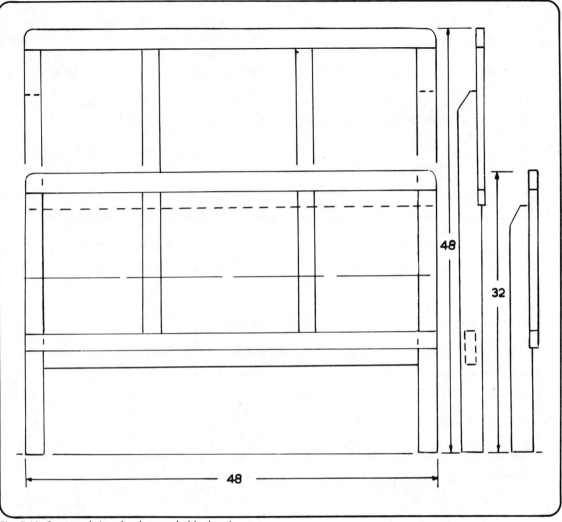

Fig. 7-13. Suggested sizes for the paneled bed ends.

Sizes will depend on the mattress to be used, but in the drawing a width of 48 inches is assumed (Fig. 7-13). Other measurements could be kept the same unless your bed is to be a very different size. The number of panels may be varied and either made all the same or with a wider one at the center, as shown. Bed assemblies vary, but it is assumed that the mattress level is about 20 inches above the floor (Fig. 7-14A). If you want to make it a very different level, some other heights might have to be altered. The lower edge of the head panel should not be so high that pillows can be pushed under it. Measurements of legs are from floor level. If your bed is to stand directly on the floor, that is the length of the wood, but if there will be casters, allow for their depth. If you will be using glides, the depth of most of them can be ignored.

This is a project that should be made of a good hardwood for strength and appearance. When a bed is moved there is often considerable strain on the legs and other parts; softwood might not stand up to the loads. It will be best if the plywood panels are veneered to match the solid wood, but an attractive appearance can be obtained with a different veneer. Available plywood, already veneered, might govern the choice of solid wood.

1. Mark and cut the bed foot legs (Fig. 7-14B). The recess for the panel is 1/2 inch deep in each leg, so it takes half the thickness of the panel frame. Reduce the length to allow for casters, if they are to be fitted. Bevel the tops at about 30 degrees.

2. Make the bed head legs in the same way

(Fig. 7-14C). Mark on the position of the rail.

3. Check the width of the mattress frame and allow for the ends being a little wider—1 inch extra would be acceptable, but much depends on the spacing of the frame fittings that have to be attached to the legs.

4. Mark and cut the pieces for the tops and bottoms of the panels, leaving them overlong at this stage (Fig. 7-14D).

5. Cut the pieces for the eight uprights, with enough extra at the ends for making the joints.

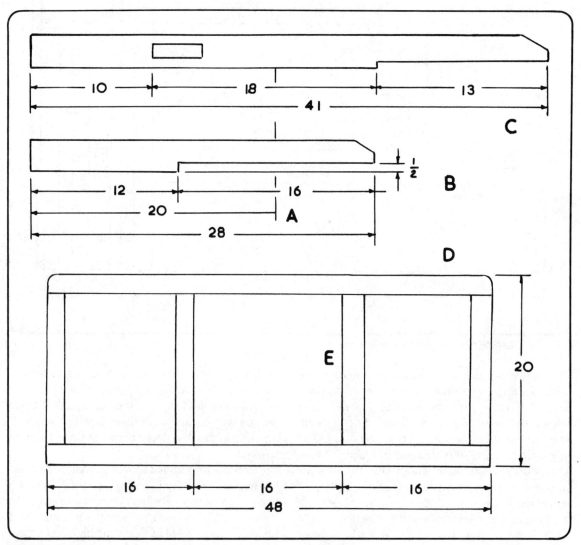

Fig. 7-14. Sizes of parts of the paneled bed ends.

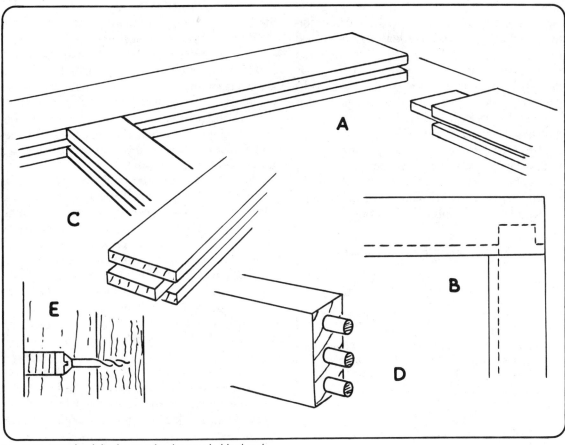

Fig. 7-15. Details of the framing for the paneled bed ends.

6. Plow grooves in one edge of the four long pieces and the four short ones that will be outside.

7. The intermediate uprights (Fig. 7-14E) need grooves in both edges. It should be sufficient to make all grooves 3/8 inch deep and wide enough for the plywood to slip in without undue force.

8. Mark the positions of the uprights on the long pieces.

9. Although it would be possible to use dowelled joints, it is better to cut mortise and tenon joints, which can be adapted to suit the grooves. The tenons can be the same thickness as the grooves (Fig. 7-15A).

10. For the corner joints, mark the shoulders of the uprights and allow for the tenons going about 1 inch into the long pieces. Cut the tenon back to the groove depth and allow for a haunch outside (Fig. 7-15B).

11. Mark the mortises to match the tenons. Cut them a little too deep so the shoulders will pull tight instead of the tenons hitting the bottoms of the mortises.

12. There should be little strain on the intermediate joints after assembly, so stub tenons need only go as deep as the grooves (Fig.7-15C).

13. Cut the plywood pieces so they will not quite reach the bottoms of the grooves.

14. Assemble both end panels. Glue the joints, but there is no need to put glue all around each piece of plywood. A little glue at occasional spots in the grooves should be sufficient.

15. Trim any excess wood, round the top corners, and take off sharp edge all around.

16. Make the rail. It can be tenoned into the legs, or dowelled (Fig. 7-15D). So that the front surfaces are without marks, the legs may be joined to the panel ends with screws in counterbored holes, which are then stopped with plugs (Fig.7-15E). Alternatively, there could be dowels. In either case four screws or dowels will be needed at each leg. Check squareness and see that the two ends match during assembly.

17. If casters are used, the type that fit into holes in the leg ends are convenient, but there is sufficient area for those that screw through a plate.

18. A trial assembly with the mattress frame is advisable before finishing the wood.

Materials List for Paneled Bed Ends	
2 legs	2 × 2 1/2 × 42
2 legs	2 × 2 1/2 × 29
4 panel parts	1 × 2 × 49
8 panel parts	1 × 2 × 20
4 panels	15 × 19 × 1/4 plywood
2 panels	17 × 19 × 1/4 plywood
1 rail	1 × 4 × 47

SOFTWOOD BED

Some beds are elaborate and would take more than a weekend to make, but one of quite attractive basic design can be made in a limited time. Although there is more wood than in many other projects, not much has to be done to it and the joints are simple. If the wood is obtained already planed to the finished sections, or you only have a small amount of work preparing stock, the construction should not take long.

Modern mattresses, whether internally-sprung or made of rubber or plastic foam, have ample cushioning without needing springs in the support beneath. Therefore the bed can be made with solid supports, which simplifies construction.

This bed (Fig. 7-16) is shown without a raised foot, so the bedding can drape over the end as well as the sides. At the head there are two pieces to form the headboard. The sizes are shown to suit a 36-inch mattress (Fig. 7-17), possibly for a child's bed, but the bed could be made to suit other mat-

tresses without altering the way it is made. Unless the bed is to be considerably bigger there is no need to increase wood sections.

Softwood makes a lighter bed than hardwood and for this bed it has ample strength. It could be given a clear finish for the popular natural pine appearance, or stained first to match other furniture. If hardwood is used, the wood sections could be reduced slightly. Hardwood is unnecessary for the under-mattress slats in any case, where cheaper softwood can still be used.

Even this narrow bed might be too large to move completely through doors and up stairs, so it is arranged to take down and assemble in position. The sides are held to the ends with shelf brackets, which can be unscrewed, then the slats are lifted out and you have the parts flat: two ends, two sides, and the slats. It is unlikely that you will want to disassemble the bed very often and wood screws in the brackets will be adequate. If you expect to take the bed apart frequently, however, there could be bolts through in place of the wood screws.

The bed has to be made to fit its mattress, so obtain that first. The sizes given in these instructions are for a mattress 36 inches wide and 78 inches long. Thickness is not so important, but it is assumed to be 5 inches or 6 inches.

The leg lengths are from the floor. If you intend to fit casters, reduce the wood lengths to suit. The leg section is large enough to take the type of caster with a stem to fit in a hole or the sort with a baseplate to screw on.

1. Mark out the pair of rear legs (Fig. 7-17A), with the positions of the headboards and bed framing (Fig. 7-18A).

2. Mark out the front legs (Fig.7-17B) from them so as to get the side heights the same (Fig. 7-18B). Round the tops of all legs.

3. The parts that provide rigidity in the width of the bed are the head and foot rails (Fig.7-17C), so their joints to the legs should be strong. You could use mortise and tenons, but four 3/4-inch or 7/8-inch dowels taken at least 1 inch into legs and rails should be satisfactory (Fig.7-17D) and simpler to make.

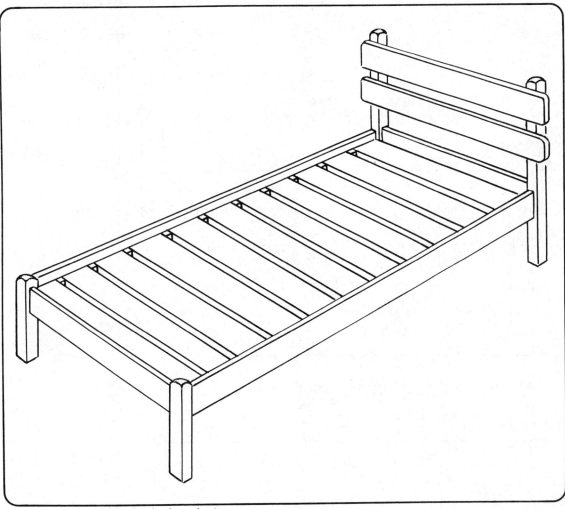

Fig. 7-16. A bed made mostly of softwood strips.

4. Before assembling the rails to the legs prepare the two headboards (Fig. 7-17E). Round their corners (Fig. 7-18C) and round all edges. They will probably be left plain, but if there is to be any decoration on the bed, this is where you put it. The top board could be pierced, either with a formal or floral design, or you could cut out initials. Softwood is not strong enough to take fine detail, so the pattern should be bold. Carving cannot be done unless you settle for a design that only involves a few bold strokes, such as large flourishes or very bold lettering.

5. The headboards might be screwed from the front, if you do not mind the appearance of screw heads in the finished bed. You could use dowels (Fig. 7-18D), or it may be stronger to use counterbored screws driven from the back (Fig. 7-18E). You could plug over the screws for a neat finish, but because beds are nearly always pushed against a wall, this might not be necessary.

6. Assemble both ends. Get the head end assembled square with its rail and headboards. Use it as a guide to squareness when assembling the foot end.

7. Make the two sides (Fig. 7-18F) to fit between the end legs and of a length to take the mat-

161

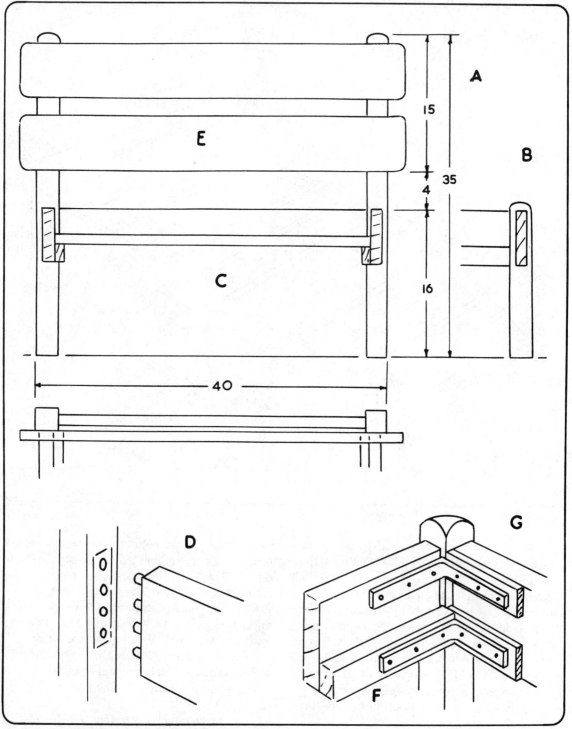

Fig. 7-17. Sizes and construction details of the softwood bed.

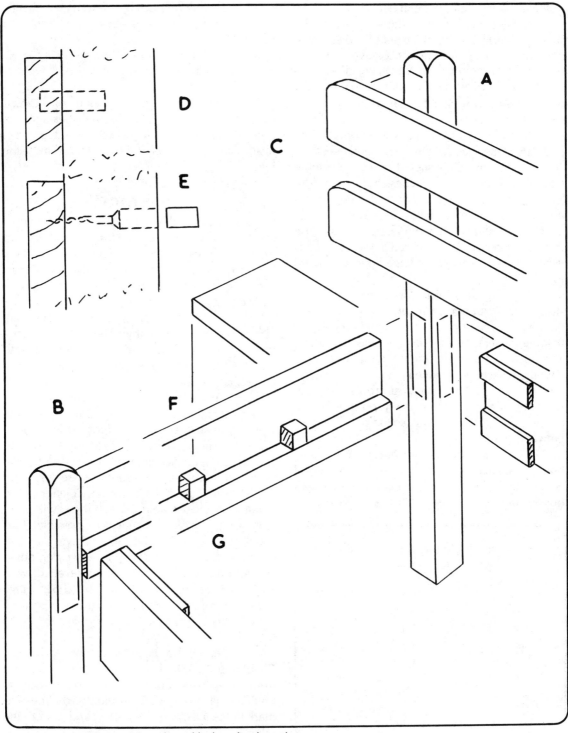

Fig. 7-18. How the parts of the softwood bed are fitted together.

tress with a little clearance at each end.

8. Glue and screw on the supports for the slats (Fig.7-17F), level with the bottom edges. With the 1-inch slats above them this leaves 3 inches of the sides to enclose the mattress, which will project 2 or 3 inches higher. If you intend to use a thinner mattress, you might wish to position the supporting strips higher.

9. The slats rest on the side supports. The end ones come against the bed ends and the others are spaced evenly. Gaps should not be much more than 1 inch, unless the mattress has a very firm base. In this case they could be increased, but not usually more than 2 inches. The gaps provide necessary ventilation. It would be possible to use thick plywood as a base, instead of the slats. If this is chosen, drill a pattern of large holes through it for ventilation.

10. It might be satisfactory to merely lay the slats on their supports, suitably spaced, and rely on them staying in place. It is possible, however, that the movements of sleepers could shift them. You could put a single screw through each end. It would have to be removed when you disassemble the bed, but that is no great problem if occasions are infrequent. Alternatively, position blocks on the supports (Fig. 7-18G), so the slats can drop between them.

11. At the corners prepare to use metal brackets 5 or 6 inches long (Fig. 7-17G). They will go directly on the side parts, but on the ends pack out the rails to the level of the leg surfaces.

Materials List for Softwood Bed

2 legs	2 1/2 × 2 1/2 × 36	
2 legs	2 1/2 × 2 1/2 × 18	
2 rails	1 1/2 × 6 × 36	
2 sides	1 1/2 × 6 × 80	
2 supports	1 × 2 × 80	
2 headboards	1 × 6 × 46	
4 packings	1/2 × 2 × 7	
1 slat	1 × 6 × 37	

---

12. The brackets can be screwed permanently to the bed sides. Use wood screws or bolts through in the other direction.

13. Add the casters, if they are being used, and make a trial assembly of the bed with its mattress.

14. Separate the parts. Round all exposed edges. The top outer edges of the sides and foot rails can be curved well, so there is no hard edge against bare skin. Apply finish and reassemble the bed.

SHOE RACK

If shoes are left on the floor, damp soles may never dry, they can be piled up and lose their shape, and they tend to become scattered and untidy. A rack will provide somewhere to store them where air can circulate and they will be tidy. This rack is intended to stand on the floor or shelf of a closet (Fig. 7-19A). Its length can be made to suit the available space. Shoes have their heels hooked over a bar and the soles supported on a rod. Underneath is a shelf that will hold polishing materials and other shallow things.

For use inside a closet, appearance is not very important and the ends can be 1/2-inch plywood, with any available wood used for the lengthwise parts. If the rack is to be used in a more visible position you could make it of an attractive wood, finished with polish or varnish. Sizes are suggested (Fig. 7-20A), but there could be variations. The length can suit available space, but you will probably want to make it as great as possible. Two shoes need about 7 inches, so that gives a clue to capacity. The rack could be made two-tier, possibly with his and hers on different levels or with closer rails at the top for children's shoes. Have the pieces for the lengthwise parts ready because their sections affect the marking out of the ends.

1. Set out the shapes of the two ends (Figs. 7-19B and 7-20B). First mark the positions of the front rail and rear rod. These give you the centers for curves at the edges. Draw the straight lines and mark in the shelf. Cut the outline and smooth the edges.

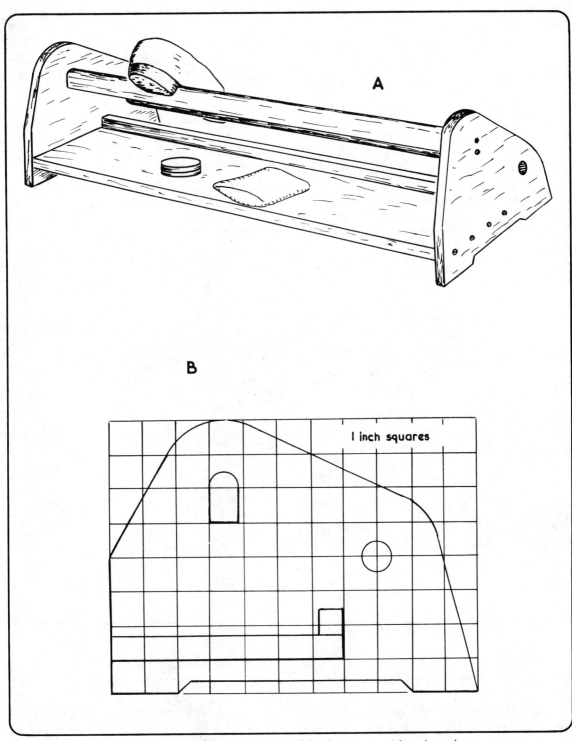

A

B

I inch squares

Fig. 7-19. This shoe rack supports shoes on rails and has a shelf for cleaning materials underneath.

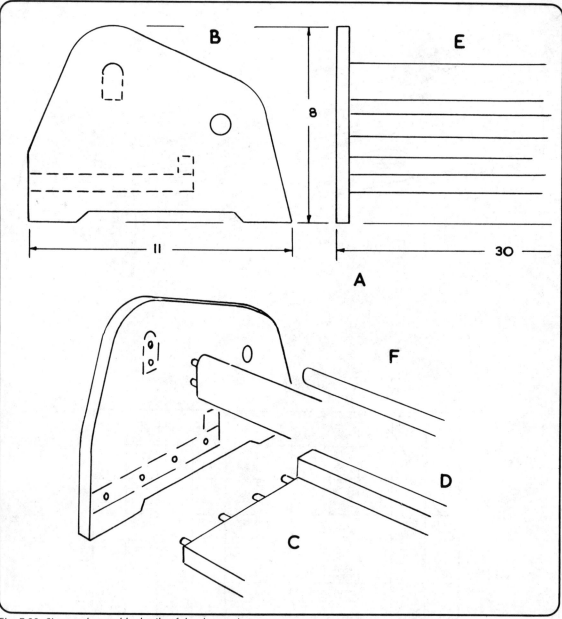

Fig. 7-20. Sizes and assembly details of the shoe rack.

2. Make the shelf (Fig. 7-20C). A strip along the back (Fig. 7-20D) will prevent articles from falling over the edge.

3. Make the front rail (Fig. 7-20E) the same length as the shelf. Shape its top edge to a semi-circular section.

4. The rear rod is 3/4-inch diameter and goes through the ends, so make it that much longer than the shelf (Fig. 7-20F).

5. Use 1/4-inch or 5/8-inch dowels to join the shelf and rail to the ends. Drill right through the ends for the dowels. If the rack is to be used

where the rod ends will be seen and you do not want the dowels to show, drill holes only part way, but take them as deep as you can to get as large a glue area as possible.

6. Assemble the parts. The shelf should ensure squareness, but see that the ends stand upright and level on the floor. Sight along to check that there is no twist. The rod and dowel ends may be allowed to project so you can plane them off after the glue has set.

7. For use in a closet there might be no need of any surface treatment on the wood, but if the rack is to stand in the room, stain and varnish it to match other furniture.

Materials List for Shoe Rack		
2 ends	8	× 11 × 1/2 plywood
1 shelf	3/4	× 7 × 30
1 shelf strip	3/4	× 3/4 × 30
1 front rail	3/4	× 1 1/2 × 30
1 rear rod	31	× 3/4 diameter

Chapter 8

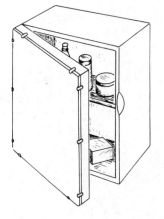

Bathroom and Laundry

Neither bathroom nor laundry are usually very big, so there is not much room for additional furniture and anything added has to justify itself. If the addition will go on the wall, over a tub or above something else, they will be valuable without using up floor space. The items in this chapter are mostly of that type. Stools and tables that could be useful in either place are described in Chapters 4 and 5.

Wood can be chosen for appearance. Any finish applied should be water-resistant. End grain is particularly vulnerable to water penetration and extra finish should be applied there to prevent moisture from creeping along the grain and spoiling the appearance. Screws, nails, and fittings should be corrosion-resistant metal, because even plated steel will often develop rust.

TOWEL HOOKS

One or more wooden hooks are useful in a bathroom to hold towels. They can be large enough to take a towel without it slipping off, even if you

reach for it with soap in your eyes. Similar hooks can be used elsewhere. They could take clothing. There are several things in a kitchen that could hang on them. In a garage or outdoors they will take a coiled rope or similar items, such as electric extension cable. Two, at a suitable spacing, would hold a coiled water hose.

The basic hook is attached to a back, which will screw to a wall (Fig. 8-1). Sizes are suggested (Fig. 8-2A), but these are really a starting point and you can develop the idea to suit your needs.

It is possible to use softwood, but the hooks will be more durable if made of close-grained hardwood. The choice of wood for the back is not so important. An interesting effect could be obtained by using wood of contrasting colors.

1. It is advisable to make all hooks at the same time, so they match. If you expect to make very many, a hardboard template is worth having. Otherwise, cut one hook to the outline and use it to mark the others before rounding it. For maxi-

Fig. 8-1. Wooden hooks are useful for towels in a bathroom or for many other purposes elsewhere.

mum strength, make the hooks with the grain as shown (Fig. 8-3A).

2. Make sure the back of a hook is flat, but the other parts should be well-rounded. A graceful, fully-rounded tip can be very attractive. A thickness of 5/8 inch throughout is satisfactory, but you could taper from 3/4 inch at the back to 1/2 inch at the tip.

3. The basic back for a single hook is shown as a simple piece (Fig. 8-2B). Drill for two screws into the hook and two from the front into the wall (Fig. 8-3B).

4. Many other shapes of back are possible and a few are shown (Fig. 8-2C). A round back is better made on a lathe.

5. If you want two or more hooks close together, it is better to have a single back—which may be horizontal—developed from one of the sin-

gle designs. It could be vertical, with any outline you choose. The hooks could be offset so the towels are kept apart (Fig. 8-2D).

6. A horizontal arrangement could be combined with pegs for clothes (Fig. 8-2E), either with a long back or an arrangement linking single backs. The link can be made with notched joints at the rear (Fig. 8-3C), glued, and with one or two screws which will not show.

7. The clothes hooks could be smaller ver-

Materials List for Towel Hooks (basic design)	
1 peg	5/8 × 2 × 6
1 back	1/2 × 2 × 4

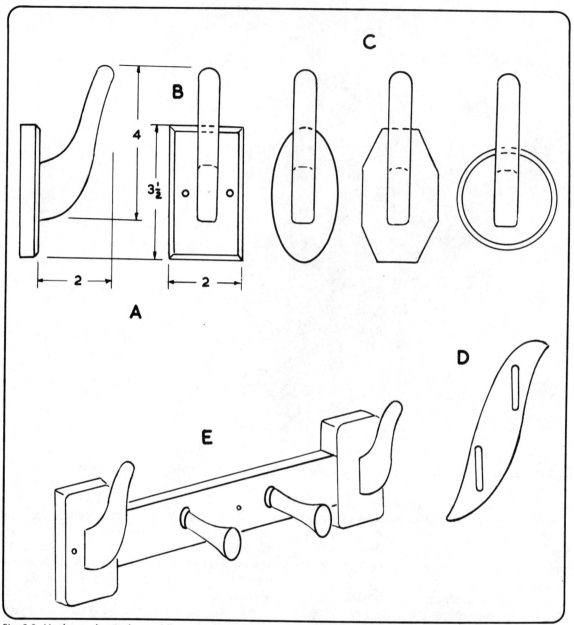

Fig. 8-2. Hooks can be single, on different backs (A-C), or several may be mounted together (D,E).

sions of the towel hooks or turned pegs (Fig. 8-3D) you can make. There are also suitable bought pegs, sometimes sold as "Shaker" pegs.

8. Finish the wood in any way you wish, but for bathroom use the surface should be water-resistant.

TOWEL HORSE

Something on which to hang towels or drying clothing is useful in the bathroom and elsewhere. This stand (Fig. 8-4) has five rails and can be moved to where you need it. The suggested length of rails is 27 inches, but that can be adjusted to suit the place where the towel horse is to stand or the lengths of available dowel rods.

The ends could be almost completely turned, if you wish, but an arrangement of similar turnings between square parts is shown (Fig. 8-5A). Alternatively the wood can be left square and the ends chamfered (Fig. 8-5B). Construction is the same for both types.

1. Mark the two posts together (Fig. 8-5C) with the joint details and location of rail holes.

2. Mark the bases together (Fig. 8-5D) with mortises to suit the posts.

3. Mark the spreaders together (Fig. 8-5E) with the halved joint details.

4. If the parts are to be turned, do this before cutting the joints.

5. Cut the joints and drill the rail holes as deeply as possible. Rigidity of the assembly depends on the fit of the rails, so make sure the drill used gives a good push fit for the dowel rods.

6. If square feet are used (Fig. 8-5F), they can be glued and screwed on. If the feet are turned, they can be attached in the same way or be made with dowels to fit in holes in the bases.

7. Assemble the two ends. Squareness at the bases is important.

8. Add the rails and see that parts fit

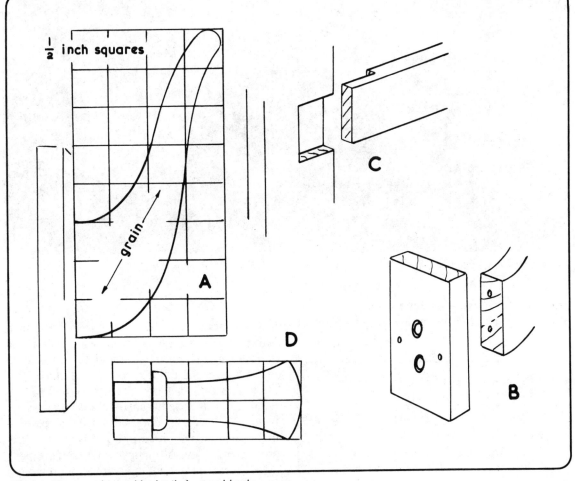

Fig. 8-3. Shapes and assembly details for towel hooks.

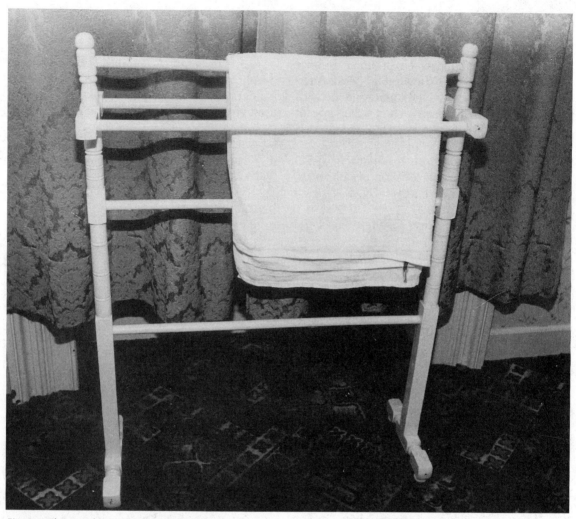

Fig. 8-4. This towel stand, or horse, has five rails and some turned sections in the supports.

squarely. Leave the assembly standing on a level surface for the glue to set. Finish with paint or varnish.

Materials List for Towel Horse					
2 posts	1 1/4	×	1 1/4	×	33
2 bases	1 1/4	×	1 1/4	×	11
2 spreaders	1 1/4	×	1 1/4	×	9
5 rails	27			×	5/8 dowel rods

BATH CLOTHES AIRER

If wet things have to be hung to drip, a tub bath is the obvious place to catch the water. Even if all you want to do is hang near-dry clothes to air them indoors, over the tub is a convenient place. This airer (Fig. 8-6) can be adjusted to suit various widths and its length can be made to suit your needs. As drawn, the airer will suit a tub about 24 inches wide inside the top, but it is equally suitable for tubs several inches wider or narrower.

The two frames are made to pivot on the top rod, so the airer can be folded almost flat when

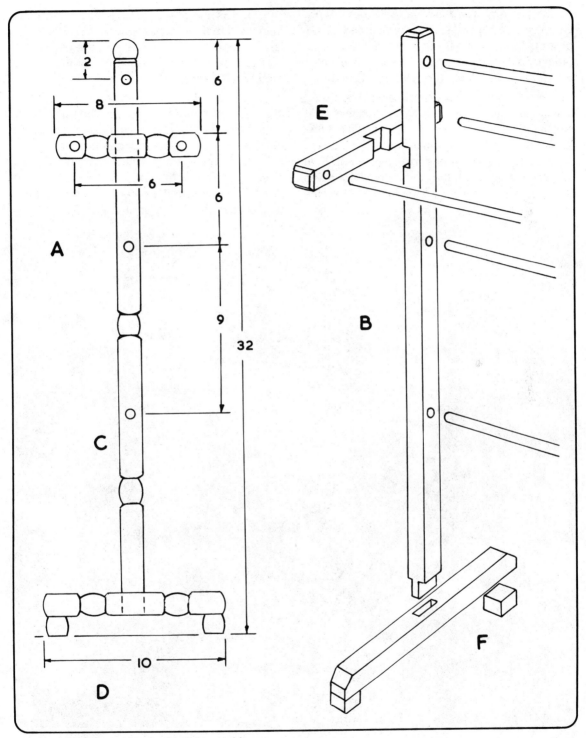

Fig. 8-5. Sizes and assembly details of the towel horse.

173

out of use. Any wood can be used, but the plywood ends should be exterior or marine grade, if possible, to withstand damp conditions. However, ordinary plywood protected with paint should have a long life. Use waterproof glue for assembly.

1. The four arms are the same (Fig. 8-7A). Mark them together and drill to suit the dowel rods. Notch the arm ends to suit the plywood (Fig. 8-8A). Round the tops and take sharpness off the edges.

2. Mark and cut one fork (Fig. 8-8B), then use it as a template for the other three. Round and sand all projecting edges. Glue the forks into the arms.

3. Cut the dowel rods to length. An outer frame width of 24 inches is suggested (Fig. 8-7B). Leave the top hole empty, but fit the other three rods to make the outer frame. Check that the assembly is square.

4. Make the inner frame so the tops of the arms fit easily inside the tops of the arms of the outer frame (Fig. 8-7C). Check squareness and that the frames match when opened or closed.

5. Remove any surplus glue and do any sanding necessary, then pass the top rod through its holes. Glue it to the outer frame holes so the inner frame can swing on it (Fig. 8-7D).

Fig. 8-6. A bath clothes airer may be fitted on a tub bath to dry or air clothes.

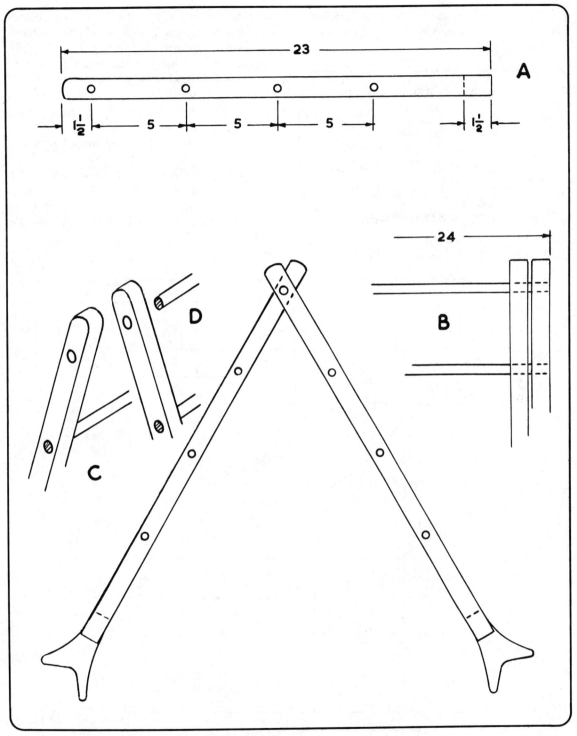

Fig. 8-7. Sizes and assembly details of the bath clothes airer.

6. The wood could be left untreated, but it might be better painted white or to match the bathroom.

Materials List for Bath Clothes Airer

4 arms	1 × 1 × 24
4 forks	5 × 5 × 1/4 plywood
7 rods	25 × 3/8 or 1/2 dowel rods

CLOTHES HANGER ARM

Shirts, blouses, and similar items are best finally dried and aired on clothes hangers, but if there are many they take up a lot of space. This folding arm is intended to allow a large number of clothes hangers to be supported close together (Fig. 8-9). As drawn, 9 or 10 hangers can be put on the arm, but it could be made a length to suit your needs. When out of use the arm folds against the wall. A stop is provided to hold the arm square to the wall, but that could be left out and the arm allowed to swing fully from one side to the other, if you wish.

It is advisable to use a strong hardwood, so the arm does not warp and the bracket has enough strength for the pivot to remain rigid and without excessive play. The pivot pins are hardwood dowels; you could use a metal rod, but that is not really necessary.

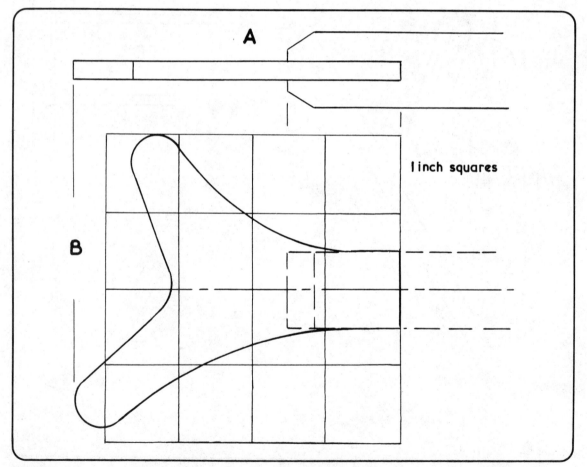

Fig. 8-8. Feet for the bath clothes airer.

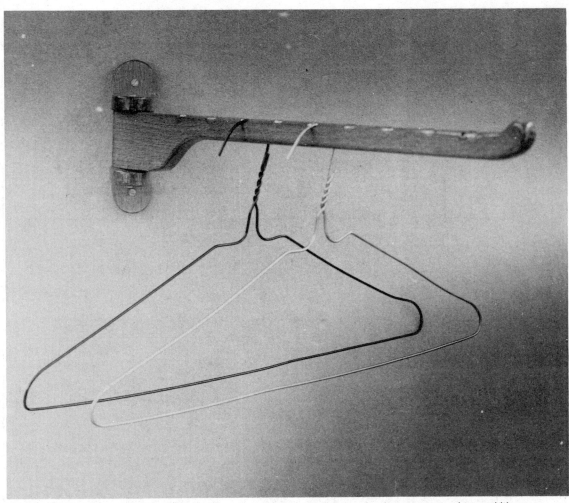

Fig. 8-9. This arm mounts on the wall and will support many clothes hangers for drying or airing shirts and blouses.

Sizes are not critical, but the section of the arm should be enough to maintain stiffness over the length you select.

1. Make the arm first. This starts 1/4 inch wider than its final depth over most of its length (Fig. 8-10A), so the grooves can be made by drilling 3/8-inch holes and cutting through them (Fig. 8-11A). Mark the shape, curving down to a parallel part 1 1/2 inches long at the pivot end (Fig. 8-11B) and with a turned-up part at the other end (Fig. 8-10B). Take the sharpness off the edges of the extending part of the arm, but leave the pivot end with square edges.

2. Mark the pivot centers on the top and bottom edges of the arm. With these as centers for a compass, draw a curved end (Figs. 8-10C and 8-11C). Shape the end. This is necessary to give clearance against the bracket as the arm swings. You can leave final rounding until you fit the parts together.

3. The bracket lugs extend to hold the pivots 3/4 inch in front of the back (Fig. 8-11D). There are several possible ways of attaching the lugs to the back. A tenon could be taken through (Fig. 8-10D). It would be satisfactory to use screws and glue, (Fig. 8-10E) or 1/4-inch dowels (Fig. 8-10F).

4. Make the back (Fig. 8-10G), with end that

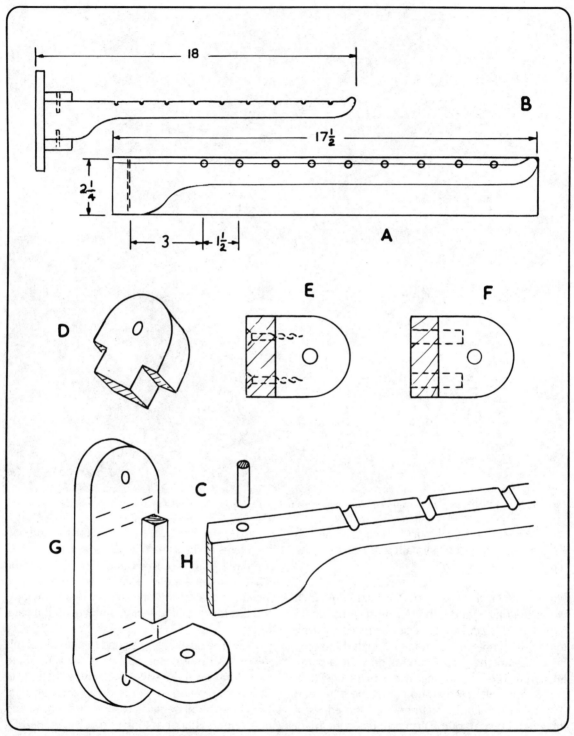

Fig. 8-10. Main sizes and alternative constructions of the clothes hanger arm.

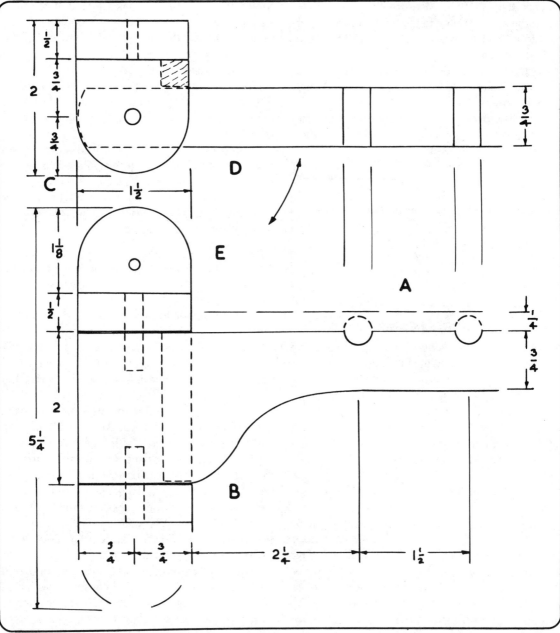

Fig. 8-11. Detailed sizes of parts of the clothes hanger arm.

curve to match the lugs (Fig. 8-11E) and holes for screws to the wall.

5. The arm should be reasonably tight between the lugs at first to allow for a little wear as it settles down.

6. Use temporary pieces of dowel rod as pivots to check the action. When the arm is square to the wall its curved end should only just clear the bracket back.

7. The stop is a square piece attached to the

bracket (Fig. 8-10H). Measure the space there when the arm is square to the wall and when parallel to it. That gives you the section of the stop.

8. When you have checked that this action is satisfactory, separate the parts for finishing. Rubbing with wax would be a suitable finish. A high gloss is unnecessary.

9. The pivot pins will probably be satisfactory as a drive fit, although they could be glued into the lugs, if necessary.

Materials List for Clothes Hanger Arm

1 arm	3/4 × 2 1/4 × 18	
1 bracket	1/2 × 1 1/2 × 12	
2 pivots	3 × 1/4 diameter dowel rod	

BATHROOM CABINET

All of the cosmetics, powders, soaps, and other small items that accumulate in a bathroom may be kept on shelves, but it is neater if they are hidden behind a door. If you keep tablets, medicines, and first-aid materials there as well, these things should certainly be enclosed, away from young prying hands. It might then be advisable to lock the cabinet door. It would be a good idea to make two wall cabinets, one for medications and the other for general bathroom items. Either, or both, could have mirror fronts.

The cabinet shown (Fig. 8-12) has a mirror front, a shelf, and enough depth inside the door for shallow items such as a toothbrush rack (Fig. 8-13A). There could be hooks for keys and other things that do not project far. The inside of the door would be a good place for a card carrying a list of emergency addresses or details of tablets or medicines.

The mirror suggested is bought as a frameless type, with its edges smoothed and rounded. It could then be held to the door with clips (Fig. 8-14A). Although you could get one made to any size, it will be simpler and cheaper to buy a stock size and make the cabinet to match. The sizes

shown (Fig. 8-14B) will make a cabinet of useful size, but one of very different size could be made in the same way to suit an available mirror or the wall space you want to fill.

If you make a door separate from its cabinet carcase, it is difficult to make one fit the other. In this cabinet the door and carcase are made as one, then separated, so a perfect fit is automatically obtained.

Almost any wood can be used and you can choose several corner joints, from nailed or screwed, to rabbets, combs, or dovetails—depending on how much you want to exercise your skill. With a painted finish details of construction will not be very apparent.

1. Prepare the wood to width. Unless your cabinet is very much bigger, a thickness of 1/2 inch should be enough.

2. Using the mirror as a guide, mark out the lengths of the sides, top and bottom.

3. For a nailed or screwed construction, allow for the overlaps. For other joints, cut the wood full length with a little left for trimming after the glue has set.

4. Mark parallel lines on the wood where the cut will come (Fig. 8-14C). Allow just sufficient width for the saw and planing after separating.

5. With comb or finger joints, try to arrange the cut so the finished parts will have sufficient wood in remaining combs each side of the cut. A very thin remainder on one edge would not look right. With dovetails you can mark the tails separately on the lid and carcase (Fig. 8-14D), allowing a wide pin at the cut.

6. Cut the joints and assemble the parts. Add the back and front plywood or hardboard with glue and pins, so you have an enclosed assembly. When the glue has set, plane the corners and edges level.

7. Separate the lid from the carcase. A fine circular saw will make a clean cut if you run the assembly against the fence, but you could use a hand saw. Fine teeth will leave reasonably smooth edges that will not require much planing. Mark adjoining edges as you will not reverse the parts dur-

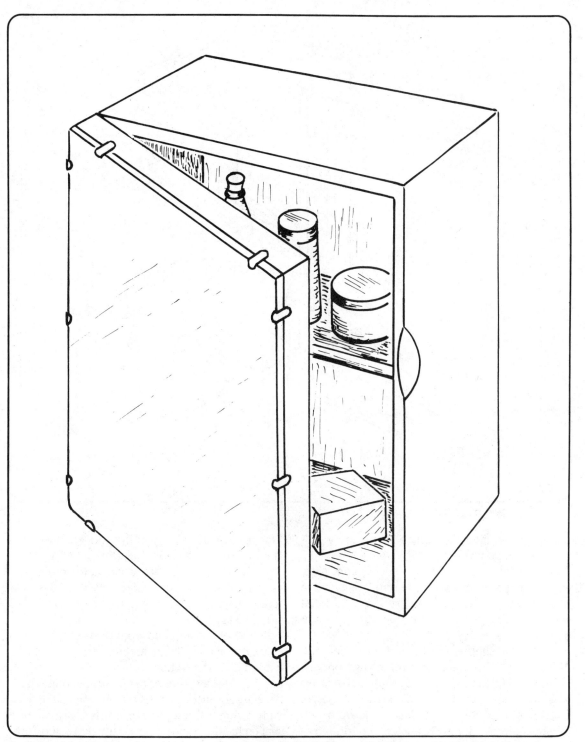

Fig. 8-12. This bathroom cabinet has a mirror mounted on its hinged door, which has a toothbrush rack inside.

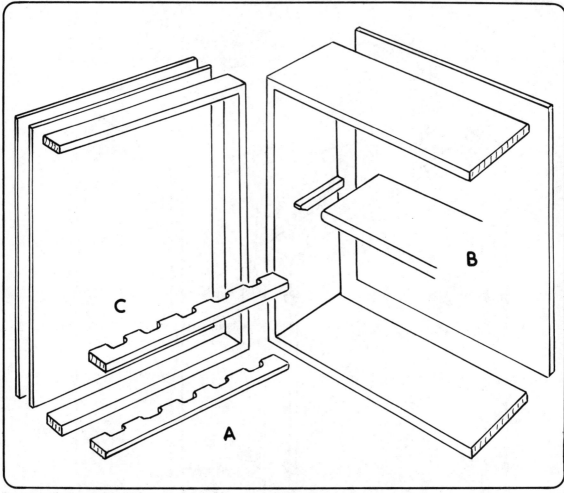

Fig. 8-13. The parts of the bathroom cabinet.

ing assembly, then the parts will match even if there are slight errors.

8. Let two hinges into the edges at one side. Make a trial assembly with one screw in each leg of each hinge, to try the fit and action. When that is satisfactory separate the parts for further treatment.

9. One shelf is shown in the cabinet (Fig. 8-13B), but there could be two. It rests on two cleats screwed to the sides and might be left loose to allow removal for cleaning. Round its front edge.

10. The toothbrush rack is made from two identical pieces (Fig. 8-13C) notched or drilled to suit the brushes or other items that will fit in slots.

One rests on the bottom of the door and the other is glued in at a suitable height (Fig. 8-14E).

11. Mirror clips are obtainable, preferably plated, to suit the glass and attach with single screws (Fig. 8-14A), or they could be made from strip brass about 18 gauge by 3/8 inch. Three each side and two at top and bottom should be sufficient, but glass is heavy and tends to drop, so an extra clip at the bottom is advisable.

12. Use a spring or magnetic catch inside. If the glass is drilled, a knob could be put on the front with a screw through from inside. A small bar-shaped handle could be put on the side of the door, but a simple way of opening is to notch the edge

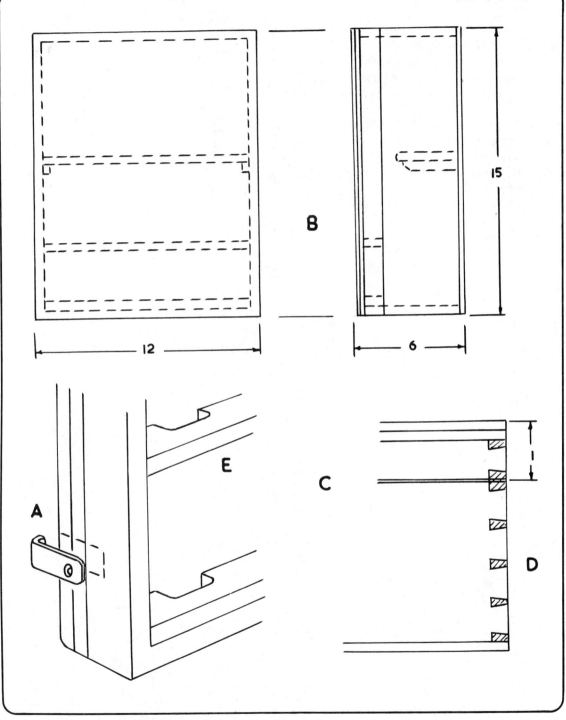

Fig. 8-14. Sizes and construction details of the bathroom cabinet.

so fingers can hook behind the door edge to pull it (Fig. 8-12).

13. Drill the back for screws to the wall. Two fairly high inside should be enough.

14. After a trial assembly remove the glass and metal parts, so the wood can be finished by painting. A different color inside from outside is quite effective. Most modern mirrors have waterproof backs, but if you are doubtful, paint the back of your mirror before assembly. Make sure there are no rough patches, blobs of glue, or nail heads that could damage the mirror back and possibly affect appearance at the front.

Materials List for Bathroom Cabinet

2 sides	1/2 × 5 1/2 × 16	
1 top	1/2 × 5 1/2 × 13	
1 bottom	1/2 × 5 1/2 × 13	
1 back	13 × 16 × 1/4 plywood	
1 door	13 × 16 × 1/4 plywood	
1 shelf	3/8 × 4 × 12	
2 racks	3/8 × 1 × 12	

Chapter 9

Yard and Garden

Many things can be made for use outside the home. There is scope for all grades of woodworking skill; some quite satisfactory pieces of exterior woodwork may be fairly crude, while others call for as much skill as indoor furniture.

Wood, as a natural product which grows out there, is compatible with your garden and yard. It looks like it belongs and is often more appropriate than metal, and certainly more acceptable than plastic to anyone with a feeling for natural things.

Most woods will have a long life outdoors if treated with preservative, while others are durable in any case. If what you make will be stored inside, the choice of wood might not be important, but if you are constructing something that will stay outside, make sure you do not waste time and effort on something made of a wood that will not last.

GARDEN EDGING

If you lay out your garden in plots, some edging helps to mark boundaries, keep soil in place, and improve appearance. If the edging comes alongside a lawn it is convenient if the sections can be lifted and inserted again after the mower has done its work.

This edging (Fig. 9-1A) is made in sections to build up to any length, with uprights that match on the visible parts, but only occasional ones are continued to press or knock into the ground. With comparatively short sections it is possible to use the edging again if you decide to rearrange the garden plots. It is also possible to use the sections to follow a sweeping curve.

The wood chosen should be a durable or naturally resinous type, or the parts should be soaked in preservative before use. A dark green or brown preservative can improve appearance, but be careful to avoid any preservative that could affect anything growing nearby.

Sections need not be made up in the lengths shown, and you can assemble parts to suit your needs. For a long edge let the lengthwise piece only cover half of one upright, but make its other end long enough to overlap the next upright.

185

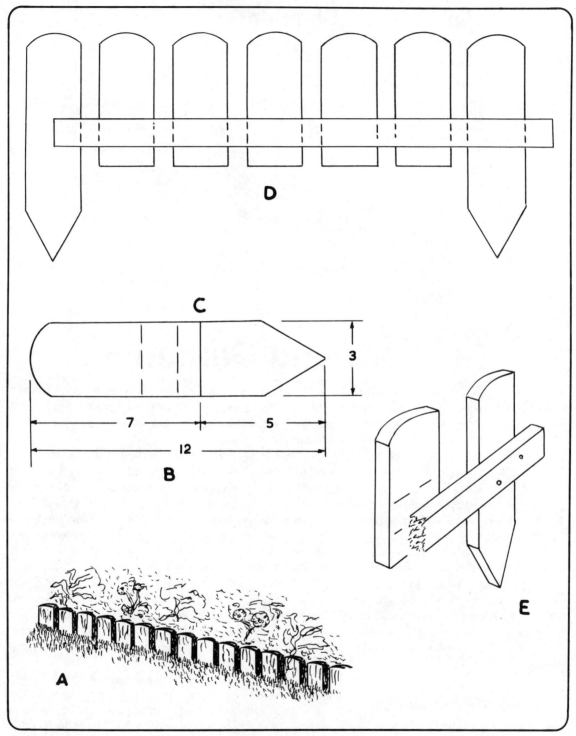

Fig. 9-1. This garden edging is made in sections to be pushed into the ground.

1. All of the uprights should be the same section, so prepare enough wood 3/4 inch by 3 inches.

2. The long uprights are 12 inches (Fig. 9-1B) and the short ones 7 inches (Fig. 9-1C). If yours is very soft soil you might prefer to allow more to go into the ground.

3. Curve the tops—a 2-inch radius will give a neat shape. Point the ends that will enter the ground. Cut the others across squarely. Mark where the lengthwise strip will cross.

4. Make the lengthwise strips. Mark on the upright positions. They are shown 1 inch apart (Fig. 9-1D).

Materials List for Garden Edging (one section)

2 uprights	3/4 × 3 × 13
5 uprights	3/4 × 3 × 8
1 strip	3/4 × 1 1/2 × 28

---

5. Treat the wood with preservative before assembly. Use screws arranged diagonally across each joint (Fig. 9-1E) so they do not come in the same grain lines either way. This reduces the risk of splitting.

SEED BOXES AND SOIL SIFTER

An enthusiastic gardener has plenty of uses for boxes, particularly when sowing seeds to plant out later. If the boxes can be arranged to stack with an air space between they can be kept in a small space, whether full of soil and plants or empty. A similar box could be made with a mesh bottom for use as a soil sifter. You could make two or more with different size meshes. A soil sifter could be converted to a seed box with a loose piece of plywood in the bottom.

Boxes need only be of simple construction (Fig. 9-2), but make them strong enough so that you are not troubled by corners opening or the bottom loosening. A box full of soil can be quite heavy and exert more pressure on joints than you expect.

Fig. 9-2. A box can be completed to hold seeds or act as a soil sifter.

When you sift soil, the shaking action works against corner joints. Nails can be driven at opposing angles so they have a dovetail effect. Put nails closer at the top of the box, where separating pressures may be greatest. Screws, in at least some places, would be stronger.

Boxes can be made of any wood available. This is a chance to use up oddments and it does not matter if you mix woods. The sizes shown (Fig. 9-3A) are about the smallest that would be useful. Assess your needs and make the boxes any size you wish.

If the boxes are to stack, it is advisable to make them all at the same time, cutting parts for all boxes so they match. Six seed boxes and two soil sifters could be made in a weekend.

1. Cut the wood for the sides (Fig. 9-3B) and ends. Nail these parts together for all boxes and see that sizes match. A tolerance up to 1/8 inch is acceptable.

2. Nail on the bottom (Fig. 9-3C) with just enough nails to keep the box in shape. Check squareness and one box against another. Exterior plywood or several strips of thin wood could be used.

3. Add the bottom strips (Fig. 9-3D), nailing through into the sides and ends.

4. For the soil sifters use wire mesh of a suitable size. Hardware cloth with 1/4-inch mesh will suit soil you are preparing for seeds in the boxes, but you might have use for a coarser mesh for other work in the garden. Attach the sifter bottom with the border strips in the same way as the solid bottom.

5. In the corners of each box fit square strips to stand up (Fig. 9-3E). These are to fit inside the bottom strips of the box above. Taper the outer surfaces so they fit in easily. How high they should stand depends on your needs and what you intend to plant and leave in a stack, but for general use a projection of 2 inches should be enough. This means that each box in a stack accounts for 6 inches, so six boxes would reach 36 inches. Is that what you need?

6. The handles are strips across the top edges

of the ends (Fig. 9-3F). Take off sharpness, but there is no need for careful rounding.

7. It will probably be best to leave the wood untreated. If you use paint or preservative, give the boxes a long time to dry before putting in soil, so there is no risk of it being contaminated.

Materials List for Seed Boxes and Soil Sifter (one box)	
2 sides	1/2 × 4 × 17
2 ends	1/2 × 4 × 10
1 bottom	1/4 × 10 × 17
2 bottoms	1/2 × 1/2 × 17
2 bottoms	1/2 × 1/2 × 10
4 corners	3/4 × 3/4 × 7

GARDEN HOSE HANGER

A rubber or plastic garden hose is usually a considerable length and it should be looked after. If it does not have its own reel it should be stored in a way that keeps it free from kinks and tight twists and in such a way that it is in coils that can be run out without the hose tangling. It is less of a problem if the coils are kept fairly large. Many reels and other storage arrangements tend to curl the hose tighter than it wants to go, so it is difficult to pull it reasonably straight when you want to use it.

A rack on a wall or fence allows you to make a coil of large diameter so the hose is not distorted. This rack (Fig. 9-4), consisting of three horns on a board, is designed to suit coils about 36 inches across (Fig 9-5A). You do not have to loop up the hose with precision—anything within 12 inches or so will do—but 36 inches is about the size loops you naturally form when coiling the hose in front of you.

The rack could be made of softwood, preferably treated with preservative. A durable hardwood would be better, particularly if there is a risk of knocking and damaging the horns. How good a finish you give the rack depends on your needs. You could screw the parts together and leave the

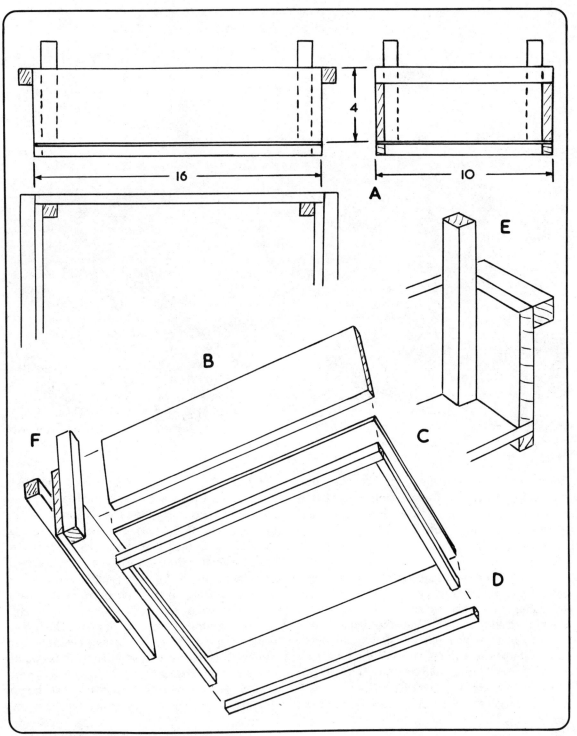

Fig. 9-3. Sizes and construction of a seed box.

Fig. 9-4. This garden hose hanger has three hooks to take the coiled hose.

horns without rounding them. This would support a hose just as well, but good joints and a better finish would be more satisfying. The instructions assume the horns will be tenoned to the backboard.

1. The three horns are the same. For strength they should be cut a full 1 inch thick and could be slightly thicker, although the projecting part will be thinned and rounded. Draw the shape on one (Fig. 9-5B), preferably with the grain in the direction of the arrow. Cut this out and use it to mark the shape of the other two, or make a hardboard template and use it to mark all three.

2. Mark out the backboard with the positions of the horns. The two outer horns are at 60 degrees (Fig. 9-5C). Mark the shapes of the tenons on the

horns and the shapes of the mortises on the backboard. Square tenons with a 1/2-inch gap between them should be satisfactory. The section is the central one (Fig. 9-5D). Arrange the others at the marked angles, near the bottom edge of the board.

3. Well round the extended part of each horn, reducing the thickness slightly towards the rounded points. There is no need to produce a sanded finish for outdoor use.

4. Cut the tenons and mortises. The tenons may be slightly too long for planing level later. Saw diagonally across the tenons for about three-fourths of their depth (Fig. 9-5E).

5. Finish the outline of the backboard. Round its corners and edges. Drill for fixing screws or bolts.

6. Glue the tenons in the mortises. If you

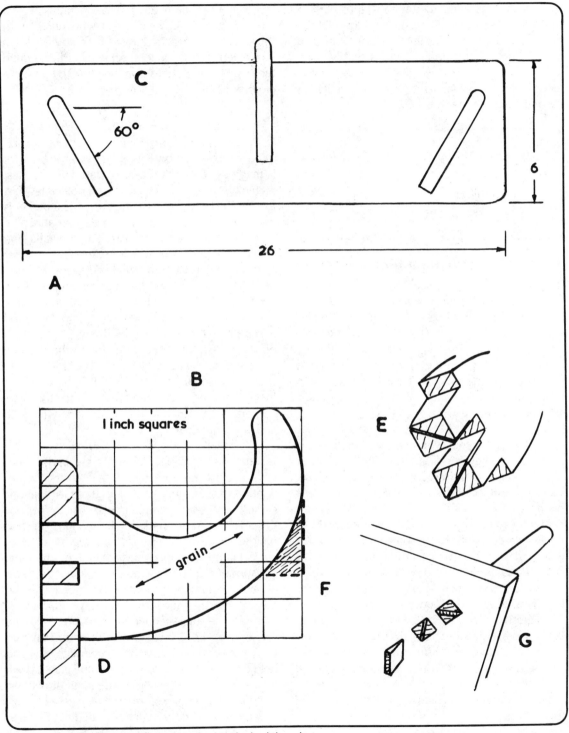

Fig. 9-5. The hooks have their tenons wedged in the back board.

want to pull the joints tight with clamps, it helps to leave a projection on each horn (Fig. 9-5F) for the clamp to squeeze against, then it can be cut off and the wood rounded after assembly.

7. At the back, drive glued wedges into the tenons (Fig. 9-5G). When the glue has set, cut them off and plane the tenons level.

Materials List for Garden Hose Hanger

1 backboard	1 × 6 × 27
3 horns	1 × 5 × 10

GARDEN BASKET

A wooden basket with a central handle can have many uses, either practical or decorative or both. If made a reasonable size and given a painted finish it will carry many small things during the planting season and be used for carrying fruit, flowers, or vegetables later in the year. If made of attractive wood and varnished, a small basket could be used as a table decoration, filled with fruit or containing a plant.

This basket (Fig. 9-6) is square with a laminated loop handle. Some woodworkers are hesitant about laminating wood, but this handle is simple and can serve as an introduction to the process if you have not tackled it before. Most woods will bend in thin sections (in this case 1/8 inch), except if they are excessively dry—as they might be if over-seasoned or kept for some time in very hot, dry conditions. The basket could be made of the same wood throughout, or you might have to use a flexible wood—such as ash or hickory—for the handle and another wood for the other parts.

The sizes shown (Fig. 9-7A) will make a basket of average size, but other sizes are equally suitable without altering construction. The shape need not be square, but it would not be advisable to make the basket too narrow in the direction of the handle because this would tighten the curve and might make the handle more difficult to bend. There are two shaped ends, with side strips at-

tached over a bottom and the handle fitting against the ends (Fig. 9-8). The main parts are all 1/2 inch thick. They may be solid wood or could be 1/2 inch exterior plywood for a painted finish, although the exposed ply edges may be attractive under a clear finish if smoothly finished.

1. Make the two ends (Figs. 9-8A and 9-7B) to suit the chosen corner joints. The strips may be nailed or screwed on (Fig. 9-7C). A stronger joint is made by letting the rails overlap with notches, then nails or screws may be driven both ways (Fig. 9-7D). The best joints—particularly if the basket is intended for display and is made in an attractive wood and given a clear finish—are dovetails (Fig. 9-7E). Although there is a slope, the angles of the sides of the tails should be related to the width of the end pieces and not tilted to the angles of the cut ends, which would result in a weak short grain.

2. Make the four side strips (Figs. 9-8B and 9-7F). Bevel the bottom ones. Take the sharpness off all edges. Assemble the strips to the ends so the assembly is square when viewed from above.

3. Make the bottom (Fig. 9-8C) to extend 1/2 inch all around. Take sharpness off the edges and corners, then join it to the other parts with glue and nails or screws.

4. Make a former for bending the handle laminations (Fig. 9-9A). Allow for the handle width to fit against the ends (Fig. 9-8D), so the former width is this less the thickness of three laminations each side. The top is semi-circular. The former and the strips could be a little longer than the finished handle because it is easier to get the handle size correct if there is enough at each end for trimming. The former can be any scrap wood, about the thickness of the handle. It could be made up of several pieces held together with temporary strips across.

5. The suggested laminations (Fig. 9-9B) are 1/8 inch by 1 1/2 inches, with three to make up the handle. They have to be coated with glue and held close around the former until the glue has set. It is possible to merely tie tightly in all directions, but you have better control with separate clamps. You can use cord through holes, tied tightly, then further tightened with wedges (Fig. 9-9C). Small

strip steel clamps can be used through holes (Fig. 9-9D). Put wood pads against the laminations. At the end of the former you can put a bar clamp across (Fig. 9-10). Another way of applying pressure is to fasten the former to a large board, then mount blocks with single stout screws so they will turn to match wedges driven against the laminations (Fig. 9-9E). This is probably worth setting up if you intend to make several baskets. It is difficult to do the laminating without getting glue where you do not want it. Newspaper under the laminations or anywhere that setting glue might stick them to other things, can be pulled away and easily cleaned off.

6. When the glue has set, plane the edges of the handle level and round the curved top. Trim the ends to length and join the handle to the basket ends vertically, with glue and screws.

Materials List for Garden Basket	
2 ends	1/2 × 4 × 13
4 sides	1/2 × 2 × 13
1 bottom	1/2 × 10 × 13
3 laminations	1/8 × 1 1/2 × 33

Fig. 9-6. This garden basket could be made large enough to carry things around the garden, or a small one could be used as a table decoration to hold flowers or a plant in a pot.

193

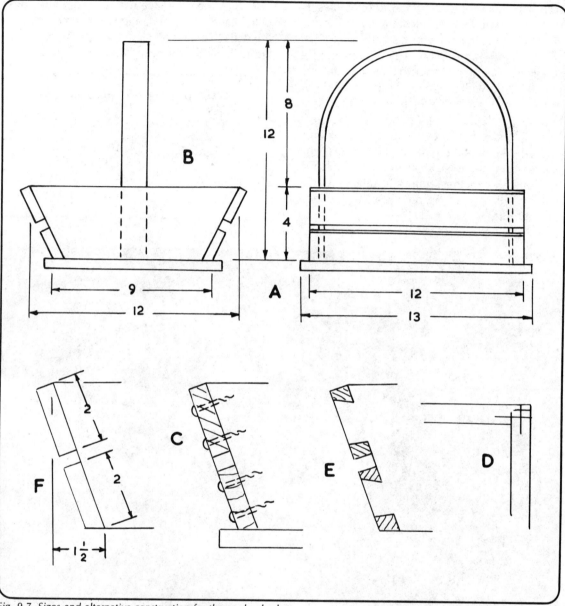

Fig. 9-7. Sizes and alternative construction for the garden basket.

7. Check that all excess glue has been removed, sand all surfaces, and make sure there are no sharp or rough edges. Finish with paint or varnish.

GARDEN TOOL CARRIER

In the days when the main means of transport was horses there was a constant demand for new shoes and farriers had regular employment. Either horses were brought to them or they visited stables, taking along a portable forge. The farrier traditionally carried his horse-shoeing tools in a long box with a fairly tall handle. The box was usually made by a carpenter who wanted it to be a good example

194

of his skill, so he might get other commissions as a result of the farrier's customers seeing it.

Although there are fewer farriers today, a box of the type they used could make a useful carrier for a gardener's small tools and other items. It also makes a good project on which to exercise your weekend skill. Although a simple nailed box might suit your needs, a well-made farrier's box had

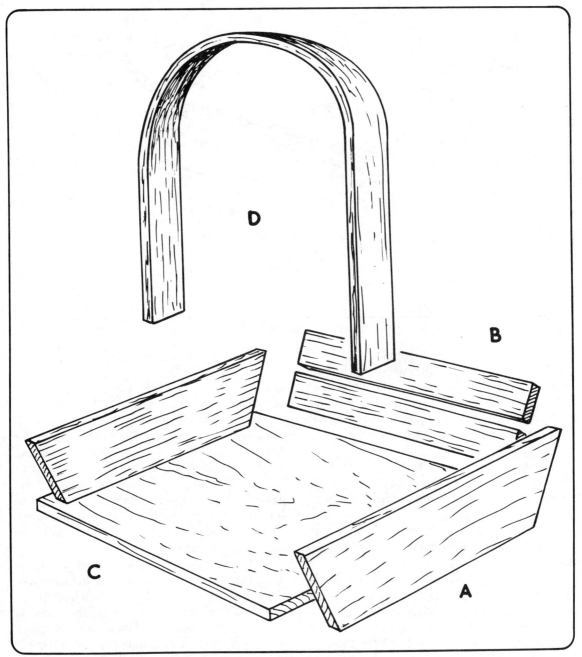

Fig. 9-8. How the parts of the garden basket are fitted together.

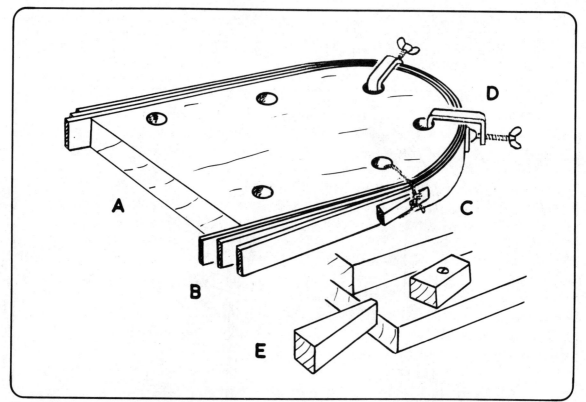

Fig. 9-9. The laminated handle has to be shaped around a former (A). Three strips are shown (B), held with clamps and wedges (C-E).

dovetailed corners and the bottom let in. This box (Fig. 9-11) has a loop handle, which might have been made from unseasoned flexible wood in an original box. The old-time carpenter, however, did not have reliable glue as we do; it would be better to laminate the handle in a modern carrier (Fig. 9-12A).

Any wood can be used, but if the box is to be stood on damp soil, a durable hardwood would be best. Ash or hickory would make the handle.

1. Prepare the wood for the sides and ends. Plow a groove for the bottom in each piece (Fig. 9-12B).

2. Mark out these pieces, using the inside measurements and allowing enough for the joints and a little left over for trimming after joining.

3. From these inside measurements make the bottom, with rabbets to match them. Close fitting will be easier if the tongues around the edges do not quite reach the bottoms of the grooves.

4. The dovetails are complicated by the need to hide the inset bottom. This can be done by mitering as high as the first tail (Figs. 9-12C and 9-12D). The joint is shown with a narrow tail, for extra strength, at the top (Fig. 9-12E). Except for the miters at the bottom corners the joints are simple through dovetails.

5. With the parts of the joints cut, check the size of the bottom against the sides and ends. Once you start assembly, you cannot make adjustments.

6. Let the glue set, then plane the joints level and round all edges.

7. The handle is made of three 3/16-inch strips, laminated around a former in the same way as the handle of the garden basket (Fig. 9-9). Allow some extra length for trimming after shaping.

8. Prepare the handle for gluing and screwing or bolting to the box. Bolts are only advisable if you want to carry heavy loads. Round the edges

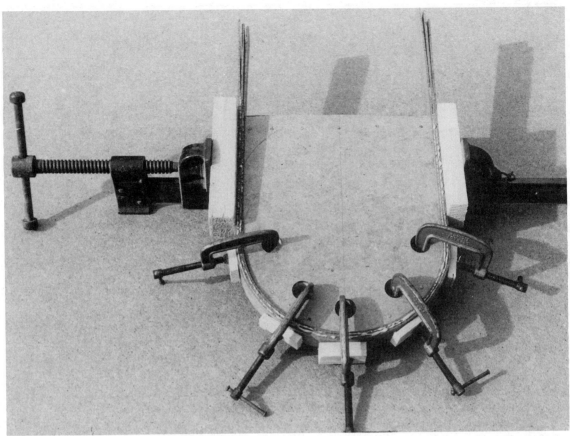

Fig. 9-10. These handle strips are held to the former with clamps, using blocks of scrap wood to spread the pressure.

of the upper part of the handle. Bevel the outer edges of the parts against the box.

9. Attach the handle. The wood could be left untreated or you could soak it in preservative, but if you have made a good job of its construction, the joint details will look good under exterior or boat varnish.

Materials List for Garden Tool Carrier	
2 sides	5/8 × 6 × 19
2 ends	5/8 × 6 × 10
1 bottom	5/8 × 9 × 18
3 laminations	3/16 × 2 × 32

BIRD HOUSE OR NESTING BOX

Houses for birds in your garden or yard will be welcomed by some birds and will add interest for you. However, you do not just throw something together and wait for the birds to move in. You might wait a long time; birds are often very fussy about where they build their nests.

The general construction of a nesting box can be quite simple, but it is getting the details right to suit the intended species that might be difficult. Birds need insulation from heat and cold. Wood is a good insulator, but it should be 3/4 inch, or preferably 1 inch thick. Birds can get through surprisingly small holes and prefer the hole to be no bigger than their minimum limit. A small bird will not make a home in a box where the entrance hole is too big, no matter how desirable other features

Fig. 9-11. This garden tool carrier is modeled on a traditional farrier's box.

are. A perch outside is not considered necessary—in fact it might help predators waiting for the bird to emerge. The floor area and the height of the entrance are also considerations when a bird is thinking of setting up a home. Many birds will be attracted by a vertical box (Fig. 9-13) if the sizes suit them. Obviously, extreme precision is unnecessary, but for the box shown, these are suggested sizes.

	a	b	c	d
Smallest birds, such as wren	4	8	1 1/4	5
Small birds, such as bluebirds	4	11	1 1/2	9
Medium birds, such as swallow	5	8	1 1/2	5
Medium birds, such as martin	6	6	2 1/4	1

A useful publication giving information on the house needs of particular birds is the booklet *Homes for Birds* (Conservation Bulletin 14, Revised 1979) published by the U.S. Department of the Interior. The box described here conforms to their recommendations.

Any wood can be used, even offcuts from a lumber yard. Boards with a certain roughness might be better than planed boards, to fit in better with surroundings. The house may be painted, but the smell should be given a long time to disappear before you expect birds to nest. Nails should be galvanized or made from a corrosion-resistant metal. Parts could also be glued. Proof against the entry of rain is important. A sloping roof is better than a flat one. You should be able to clean the box after use. The roof could be hinged, but the box shown here has a side opening. You want to look in the box while it is occupied, but much interference might frighten a bird away.

1. Draw a side view to suit the size needed and the wood you have (Fig. 9-14B). Allow for the back extending up and down about 2 inches, for attaching to a tree or post (Fig. 9-14B).

2. Cut the back and front. Drill the access hole. It should not be excessively ragged, but do not round its edges.

3. Make the bottom to fit inside the other parts and raise it 1/4 inch (Fig. 9-14C). That prevents water seeping back from the sides.

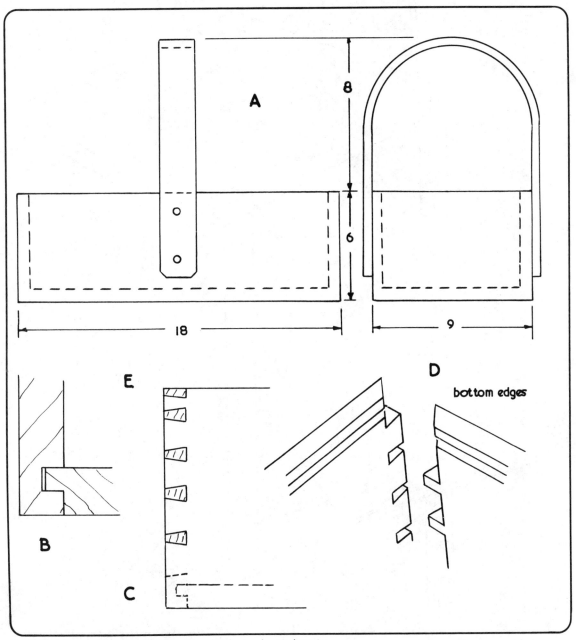

Fig. 9-12. Sizes and suggested construction for the garden tool carrier.

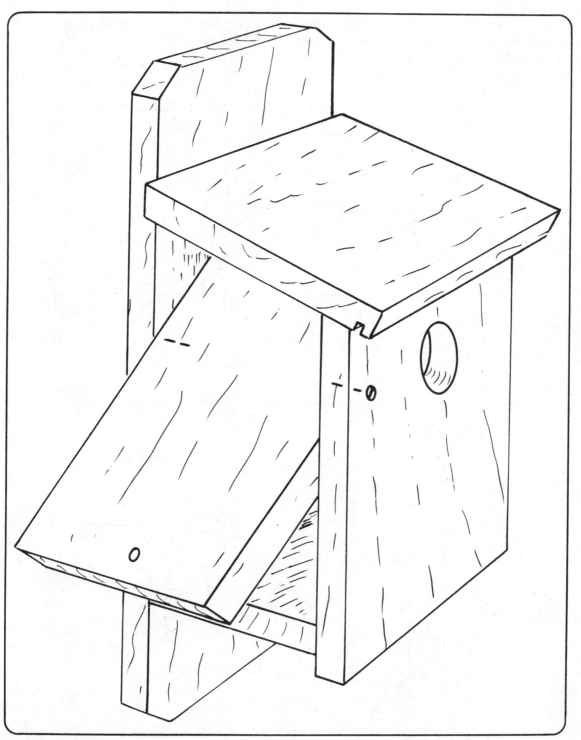

Fig. 9-13. This bird house can have one side pivoted to give access to the inside.

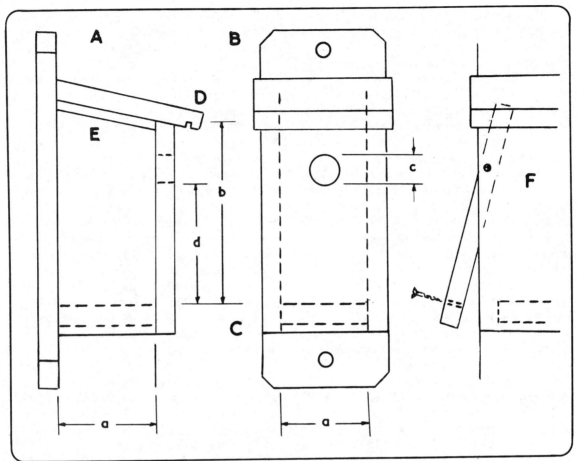

Fig. 9-14. Bird house details. Sizes have to be adapted to suit the birds you wish to attract.

4. Make the top to overhang slightly in the width and about 1 inch at the front. To prevent water running back underneath there can be a small groove (Fig. 9-14D), either plowed or just a saw cut. Make a close glued fit at the back to keep out rain.

5. The sides overlap the bottom, but should be kept down 1/4 inch at the top (Fig. 9-14E) to provide ventilation. If more ventilation is considered necessary in hot weather, some small holes could be drilled high in the sides.

6. The two sides are the same. One is permanently built in. The other can be pivoted on two screws or nails (Fig. 9-14F), arranged fairly high up, then the side can be swung out for access. When closed, it is secured with a screw.

7. Some roughness inside the box is desirable so the birds can climb to the hole. There could be a few saw cuts across or dents punched in the wood. Hardware cloth could be nailed in.

8. Where you mount the box depends on several things. No bird will be attracted if it is less than 48 inches from the ground and most prefer it two or three times this height. The box could be on a post or tree, or attached to a fence or a house wall. Consider predators. Determined animals will climb almost anything, but try to make it difficult.

BIRD FEEDING TABLE

Birds prefer to feed in a position where they are free from predators. A high place is safer than feeding on the ground. If you want to watch the birds you attract, it will also be advisable to arrange a feeder about eye level. A central post and a table with a good overhang will make it impossible for cats and squirrels to get at the birds.

This feeding table (Fig. 9-15) should blend in with other things in the yard or garden so it looks attractive. It has a reasonable area for food, with a roofed central area and a swinging perch. Some birds chase away other birds while feeding. The roofed part will let some smaller birds feed there, while larger birds keep to the outer edges. Many birds scatter food and the table is given a rim to prevent some of it being pushed over the edge. At the corners of the rim there are extensions with holes, which can be used to hang food, such as nuts in nets.

Paint and preservative hold their smell for a very long time and birds find this objectionable, so it is better to choose a wood which is reasonably durable without treatment. As it weathers it will blend better into its background than if it had been painted.

This is not the sort of woodworking that calls for elaborate cut joints. Many parts can be merely nailed together. Perhaps the wood won't need to be planed, except that some wood bought as sawn is of irregular section, so parts might not fit very well if you do not plane the surfaces.

The feeding table is shown on a base (Fig. 9-16A). On a hard surface this might be adequate. Weights could be put on the ends of the base. On a suitable surface the feet could be drilled and spikes driven through. In soft ground you need not bother with the base, but could point the post and drive it in. Elsewhere it might be better to concrete the bottom of the post.

1. Make the main platform (Fig. 9-16B) from a square of exterior or marine plywood.

2. The border is shown with extensions in turn, so all parts are the same. Drill and round the ends (Fig. 9-16C). Nail through the plywood into the border.

3. Mark the position of the post centrally underneath the platform. This will be held by four

6-inch metal shelf brackets (Fig. 9-16D). You could make a temporary assembly to locate screw holes, then remove the post and brackets until final assembly.

4. Make the ends of the covered part with a slope of about 30 degrees (Fig. 9-17A). Nail them to four uprights. Drill for a 1/2-inch dowel rod that will extend to form end perches and support the swinging perch inside (Fig. 9-17B). The roof could be two pieces of plywood (Fig. 9-17C) or you could use overlapping strips of wood to give a clapboard effect. You might even put a few strips across and thatch the roof.

5. Locate the four uprights on the platform and drill through so screws can be driven upwards. For the sake of appearance, get the four posts upright.

6. The main parts of the base are two pieces crossing (Fig. 9-17D). Notch them together so they will stand level. If you are doubtful about the surface they will stand on, put square blocks under the ends to form feet.

7. The post fits into a square or octagonal block over the crossing pieces. It could have a square cut out to take the full size of the end post, but it will be better if the post is given a tenon—made by reducing it 1/4 inch all round, then the block is cut out to fit (Fig. 9-17E).

8. The post is held upright by four struts (Fig. 9-16E). They are drawn at 45 degrees, but they could be more upright. It would help in maintaining accuracy if you draw two lines square to each other and in them draw a strut. If you cut all four struts to this drawing, accurate assembly should be easy.

9. Join the post to its base and add the struts, nailing through the tapered ends. Check squareness. It might be advisable to drive nails first only partly into opposite sides of the post. Then check that the post appears upright when you stand it, before driving the nails fully. Do the same the other way and you should finish with a satisfactory upright bird feeding table.

10. Join on the top assembly with its brackets.

11. The swinging perch is a piece of dowel rod (Fig. 9-17F). Use wire—preferably copper or

Fig. 9-15. A bird feeding table with a large feeding area at a height to attract birds.

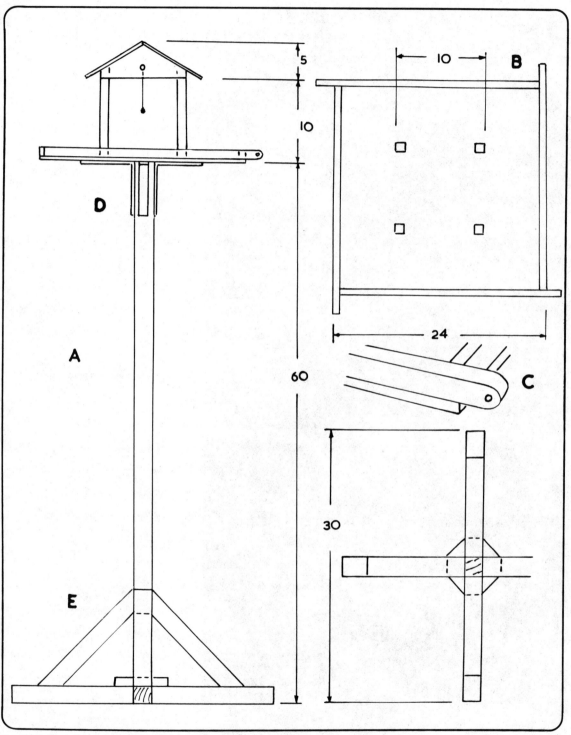

Fig. 9-16. Sizes and layout of the bird feeding table.

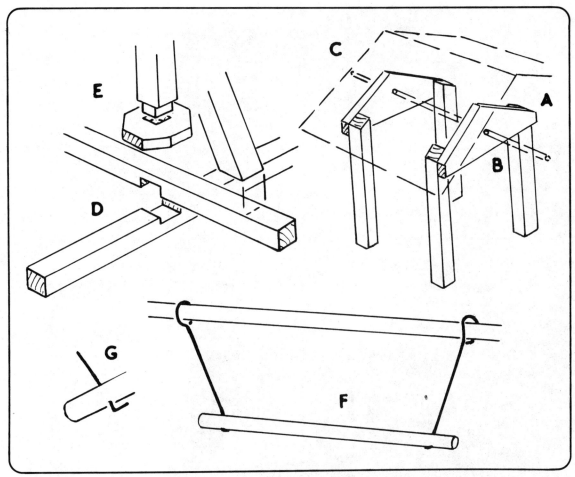

Fig. 9-17. Details of the house (A-C), feet (D,E), and swing (F,G).

Materials List for Bird Feeding Table

2 bases	2 × 2 × 31
4 struts	2 × 2 × 20
1 pad	1 × 7 × 7
1 post	2 × 2 × 60
1 platform	24 × 24 × 1/2 plywood
4 platform edges	3/4 × 1 1/2 × 27
4 roof ends	1/2 × 6 × 11
4 roof legs	1 × 1 × 12
2 roofs	9 × 14 × 1/4 plywood
1 perch	20 × 1/2 dowel rod
1 swing	9 × 1/2 dowel rod

other non-corrosive type—loosely around the main perch, and with the other ends taken through holes in the swinging perch and turned over (Fig. 9-17G).

OUTDOOR BULLETIN BOARD

If you want to pin notices, bulletins, and similar things to a board outdoors it is helpful if the board can be protected from the weather. Even if your area is mainly dry, there is a risk of wind ripping paper off. If you suffer from rain and snow, exposed paper will soon deteriorate. There is also the problem of exposed papers being handled. The answer is a bulletin board with an opening glass front.

This bulletin board (Fig. 9-18) has a rear assembly on which there can be a name board. This

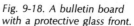

Fig. 9-18. A bulletin board with a protective glass front.

is capped by a roof to prevent rain water or snow running inside. Hinged to this is a framed glass front, which can be held with a catch and may be locked.

Because the board is intended to withstand exposure to anything the weather can bring, a durable hardwood is best. Painting will protect other woods and given them a reasonable life, providing repainting is done when needed.

Although the bulletin board might seem a large

undertaking, it is not as complicated if you consider it as two picture frames with a wood block roof above (Fig. 9-19). Anyone with power tools should have no difficulty in making the whole project in a weekend. If you have to cut rabbets and do other work by hand, the job could be divided into two weekends, with the rear part first and the framed door as the second weekend project.

This is a project that could be any reasonable size, depending on the space where it is to be mounted or the size and quantity of papers you expect to pin on at any one time. In any case, it is best to make the framed board first, then the roof, followed by the door, because the door sizes should be matched to the board framing.

1. Settle on the overall sizes. Those shown (Fig. 9-20) are offered as a guide and the instructions and drawing details are related to them. In the front view the door is shown with dashed lines.

2. The section and its accompanying scale (Fig. 9-21A) show the sizes of parts and the arrangement of rabbets. The back has exterior plywood let into the frame (Fig. 9-20A). The actual surface to take pins or push tacks is a piece of softboard

inside the frame (Fig. 9-21B). If you want to have the name of the organization displayed at the top (Fig. 9-20B), that is best painted on a board that extends far enough for the lettering to be seen through the glass door (Fig. 9-21C). It might be on a board outside, but including it inside will protect painted or decal lettering so it lasts longer.

3. Prepare the back framing with rabbets to suit the plywood. The plywood will provide stiffness in the mitered corners, so let it in at least 3/8 inch for a good overlap.

4. Miter the corners. With the additional strength provided by the plywood, it might be sufficient to supplement glue with a thin nail each way.

Fig. 9-19. The outdoor bulletin board is made as two frames; one for the board and one for the glass.

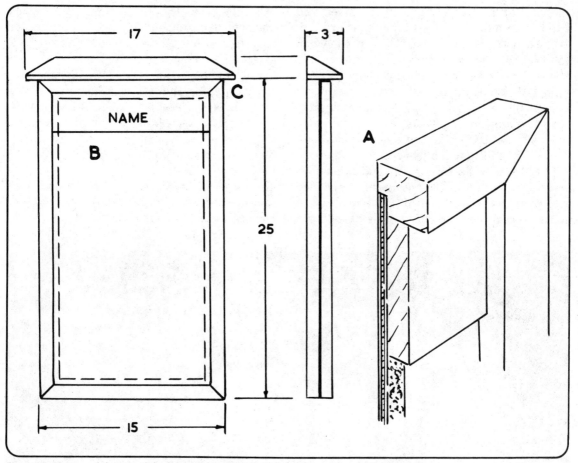

Fig. 9-20. Section of the top of the back and suggested sizes for the outdoor bulletin board.

For a better corner, however, drill diagonally for a 1/4-inch dowel (Fig. 9-21D), which can be made too long, then planed level after the glue has set. Drill the hole so it comes close to the rabbet, without breaking into it, for maximum strength.

5. Fit the plywood with glue and nails or fine screws at fairly close intervals—3-inch spacing should hold the parts tight.

6. Make the roof (Fig. 9-20C). Give it a good overhang. You can cut it from a 2-inch-by-3-inch section (Fig. 9-21E). The slope is about 30 degrees. The ends extend 1 inch and have similar bevels.

7. Running water will creep back under an overhang. To prevent this plow a small groove (Fig. 9-21F)—even a saw cut might be enough.

8. Attach the roof with glue and screws

driven upwards through the top of the back frame. Make sure all the rear surfaces are level.

9. If there is to be a name board inside at the top, prepare it now and check that it fits. It should be kept out for lettering, and you will probably want to varnish it or paint it a different color from the surrounding frame.

10. Cut the piece of softboard to fit below the name board, but do not fix it until all the parts have been painted.

11. Prepare the door framing. This should be reasonably straight-grained to resist any tendency to warp in use. The section allows for the glass being set in 3/8 inch, where it is held in the rabbets by fillets nailed to the framing. The front surface is shown with a simple bevel (Fig. 9-21G). You

could mold the edge or the whole from surface, but do not cut in too deeply because there must be some bulk in the wood to provide stiffness.

12. Make the frame the same overall width as the back. Have its bottom edge level, but allow about 1/8-inch clearance under the roof.

13. Miter the corners, but strengthen with two 1/4-inch dowels at each corner (Fig. 9-21H), keeping the holes well spaced and crossing close to the rabbets (Fig. 9-21J).

14. Make the fillets that will hold the glass a size that comes level with the inner surface of the

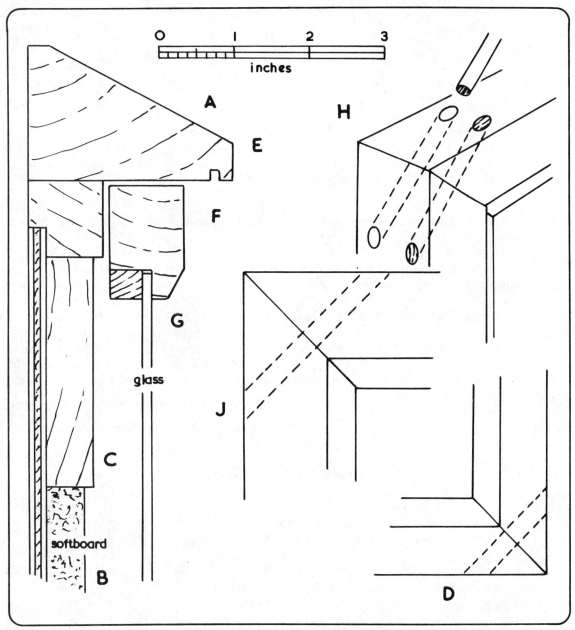

Fig. 9-21. Section showing the main parts. Corner miters can be strengthened with dowels.

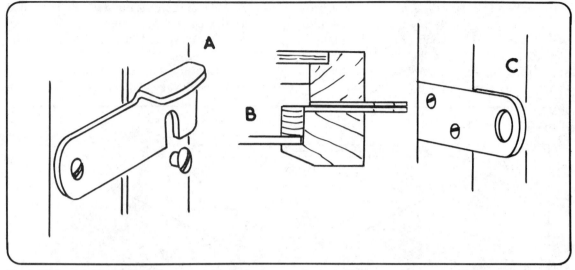

Fig. 9-22. A catch is made from sheet metal (A). Lock plates can be let in (B,C).

frame, for a neat appearance through the glass, and with the other surface level with the inside of the frame. This could also be left slightly too thick for planing back level after fitting. Do not make the glass too tight a fit in its frame, or it could crack in use. Leave assembling the glass and fillets in the door until after all parts have been painted. Paint inside the rabbets will prevent trapped water from soaking in and rotting the wood.

15. Two 3-inch hinges will join the parts. They should be brass or other corrosion-resistant metal. Keep the hinge knuckles clear of the edges so the door will swing clear, but let the hinges into both surfaces so there is minimum clearance between the closed surfaces.

16. At the other side there must be a catch to keep the door closed. Several types of hook or other catches are suitable. You can make one from sheet brass about 1/16 inch thick (Fig. 9-22A). A turned-over grip makes operating easy. The slot closes over a stout round-head screw (gauge 8 or 10). Put a washer under the catch on the pivot screw.

17. If you want to lock the bulletin board, it might be possible to find a box or door lock to fit inside the parts, with a keyhole through one of them, but there is not much space to fit it and you might have to use a padlock. That can go through

holes in two extending plates, let into both parts and screwed to them (Fig. 9-22B). Make the plates from 1/16-inch brass sheet (Fig. 9-22C). The hole should be large enough to take the padlock, but do not let the plates extend excessively.

18. Use good exterior paint on all outside parts, including the back of the plywood and inside the rabbets. Paint the fillets to match before nailing them in. Paint or varnish the name board and add the lettering. Fit it in with glue and screws driven from the back through the plywood. The softboard could be left untreated, but paint on it

Materials List for Outdoor Bulletin Board	
2 back frames	1 × 1 × 26
2 back frames	1 × 1 × 16
1 back	14 × 24 × 1/4 plywood
1 roof	2 × 3 × 18
1 name board	5/8 × 3 × 14
1 pin board	14 × 24 × 1/2 softboard
2 door frames	1 × 1 1/2 × 26
2 door frames	1 × 1 1/2 × 16
2 door fillets	3/8 × 3/8 × 24
2 door fillets	3/8 × 3/8 × 14

will show up paper pinned on. Paint will also strengthen the surface and prevent deterioration, that takes place after frequent driving of tacks over a long period. Green is a good choice, whatever other colors are used on the frame. Glue the softboard to the plywood.

19. Put the glass in the door. Fit the fillet strips tight to it, with pins or fine nails driven into the frame at about 3-inch intervals. It helps to put a piece of card on the glass and slide the hammer on it. There could be a thin layer of jointing compound around the edge of the glass, especially at the bottom, to keep out water.

KNEELER/STOOL

Anyone who has difficulty kneeling or in getting up again afterwards will appreciate something to kneel on when gardening and something to press down on with their hands when straightening up again. They will also be glad of something to sit on between bouts of gardening, or when they just want to contemplate the next job or admire what they have done. This kneeler/stool (Fig. 9-23) is reversible and is intended to serve both purposes. With the shelf at the lower position the knees will be about 5 inches above the ground and the hand grips about 12 inches above that. When reversed there is a seat 14 inches above the ground. Padding could be provided and arranged to strap on with two tapes to tie around the shelf. It could then be put on either side of the shelf. Feet are provided both ways to prevent the kneeler from sinking into soft ground. If you do not think that would be a problem, the blocks could be left off or only put on the outside surfaces.

Any wood could be used. If weight is a consideration, use softwood. Hardwood will give greater rigidity in the joints, which have to resist possible sideways loads in case the user slips. The main parts are 1-by-9-inch boards. It would be unwise to reduce the section much.

1. Mark out the two sides (Fig. 9-24A). At both ends there is a notch 1/2 inch deep, then a hand hole (Fig. 9-24B). Drill 1-inch holes and cut between them to make the slots. Round the notch

and the hand hole in each place to make comfortable grips, but do not take off so much as to weaken the wood.

2. Mark out the shelf (Fig. 9-24C). Allow for tenons through the sides (Fig.9-24D), which should be stronger than any other form of joint. Allow for the tenons being a little too long so they can be planed level later.

3. To reduce the risk of grain breaking out, mark the mortises on both surfaces of the sides and cut them partially each way.

4. Make the blocks for the feet (Fig. 9-24E). You may trust waterproof glue to hold them. They could also be screwed, or a neat way of strengthening is to put two 3/8-inch dowels right through each pair of feet. Round all outer corners.

5. It might be sufficient to glue the mortise and tenon joints, but you could strengthen them by sawing across their ends before fitting so you can drive and glue in wedges, and cut off level after the glue has set.

6. If you consider it necessary, particularly with softwood, triangular fillets (Fig. 9-24F) could be glued above and below the joints. With the bevelled sections they will not affect the fit of a pad.

7. The wood could be treated with preservative, although if it is to be stored dry, a painted finish might be better. A bright color, such as red, will make it easier to find if you cannot remember where you left the kneeler in a large garden.

Materials List for Kneeler/Stool	
2 sides	1 × 9 × 18
1 shelf	1 × 9 × 19
16 feet	3/4 × 3/4 × 2 1/2

PLANT POT STAND

Plants in pots may be grown indoors or outdoors, or moved in and out according to the weather. They form decorations along an inside wall or around the edge of a deck or patio. A group of

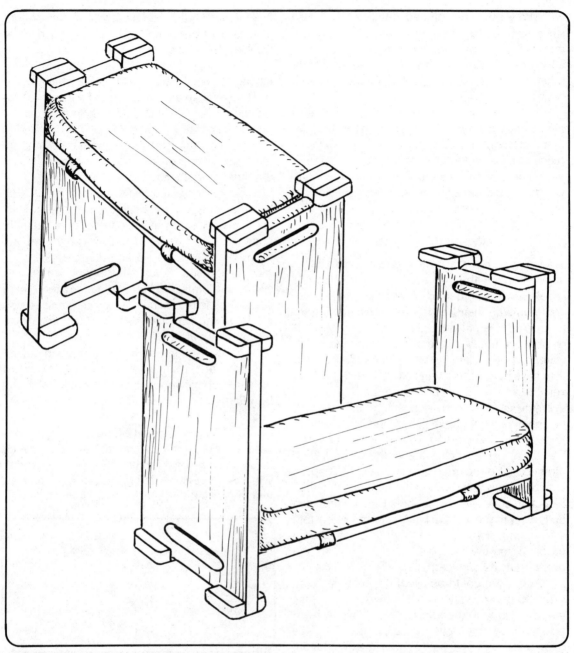

Fig. 9-23. This garden helper can be turned over to make a seat one way or a kneeler with hand holds the other way. Widened ends prevent sinking in soft soil.

plants in pots look best if they are brought together in a stand.

This plant pot stand (Fig. 9-25) is intended to hold three 9-inch pots with their bases 15 inches off the floor. The drawings suit those sizes, but the design could be adapted to suit other sizes of pots and other numbers. Pots full of soil can be quite heavy and very long stands are inadvisable, due

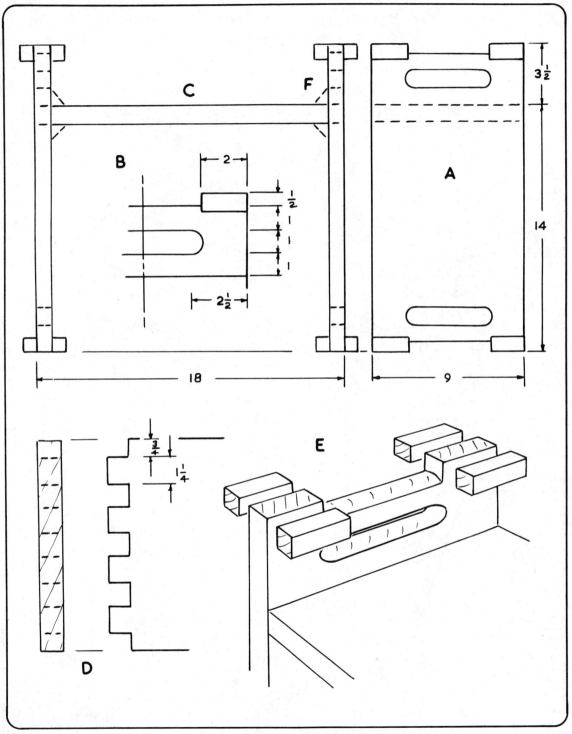

Fig. 9-24. Sizes of the kneeler/stool and details of joints.

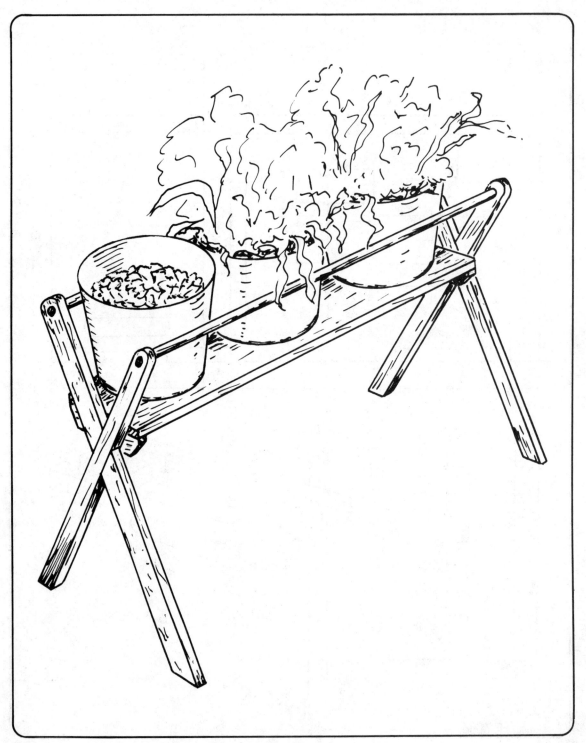

Fig. 9-25. *This plant pot stand is of light and simple construction.*

to the risk of sagging. It would be better, for instance, to support six pots in two stands than to make one long one. This gives you an opportunity for rearrangement when you want to try a new layout.

Any wood could be used. Softwood may be painted. Hardwood might be treated with oil or varnished. If the stand is to be permanently outside, it should be treated with preservative. For regular indoor use a furniture-quality stain and polish would be appropriate.

1. Measure the pots (the largest if they vary). Allow for the rods coming at about two-thirds of the pot height. In the example (Fig. 9-26) the pots are 9 inches high and 9 inches diameter, tapering to 7-inch diameter bases. The feet spread to 15 inches, which should be ample for stability (Fig. 9-26A). The legs cross with halving joints and the supports for the shelf cross these joints to provide mutual support (Fig. 9-26B). If sizes are altered, try to arrange the leg crossing and the shelf in these relative positions.

2. Start by setting out the centerlines of the legs (Fig. 9-27A), with a line across at the shelf height. Draw the widths of the legs each side of these centerlines. From this layout mark the wood for the legs, showing the angles of the feet and the curves of the top with the rod holes as centers. The crossings give you the outlines of the halving joints (Fig. 9-27B). Mark and cut these joints so the surfaces finish level.

3. Drill for the rods and cut both ends to shape.

4. Join the pairs of legs. If the joints are a good fit, it should be sufficient to use glue only. If advisable, you can also screw from inside because the screw heads will be hidden by the shelf supports.

5. Mark on the crossed legs the positions of the shelf and its supports.

6. Make the supports with tapered ends to fit under the shelf.

7. Glue and screw the supports to the legs. Check that the opposite assemblies match as a pair.

8. Make the shelf (Fig. 9-27C) to the length

required between the legs. The rods (Fig. 9-27D) go through the legs, so allow this extra length.

9. Rigidity lengthwise depends on the strength of the rod and shelf joints. Screw the shelf securely to its supports. If you want to provide additional stiffness there could be two more rods between the lower parts of the legs (Fig. 9-26C).

10. Check that the four feet stand firmly and trim bottoms, if necessary, before applying a finish.

Materials List for Plant Pot Stand	
4 legs	1 × 2 × 28
1 shelf	1 × 7 × 28
2 shelf supports	1 × 2 × 8
2 rods	30 × 3/4 diameter

LADDER

A ladder long enough to reach higher than you can manager from the ground or on short folding steps is useful if you want to clean windows, repair gutters, or pick fruit. A plain ladder might be suitable, but some people don't like to be more than a short distance from the ground unless their ladder is secured. This ladder (Fig. 9-28) is just over 8 feet long and could be made as a plain one. It could have the base shown. This is bolted on and will fold against the sides when out of use. On soft ground it prevents the ladder sides from sinking in and it can be secured with stakes pushed through holes. On a hard surface it makes a steady base and can be held by a weight, such as a rock or a bag of sand. The top could be left plain, but if a regular use is against something soft or easily damaged, the top shown will spread the load. The base may be unbolted if you do not need it, but the top is not intended to be removable. The ladder could be turned end-for-end without the base.

The sides may be hard or softwood, but it is important that their grain is fairly straight and there are no knots or other flaws. The rungs ought to be a hardwood, such as oak, if heavy use is expected. For occasional use, softwood might have a reasonable life.

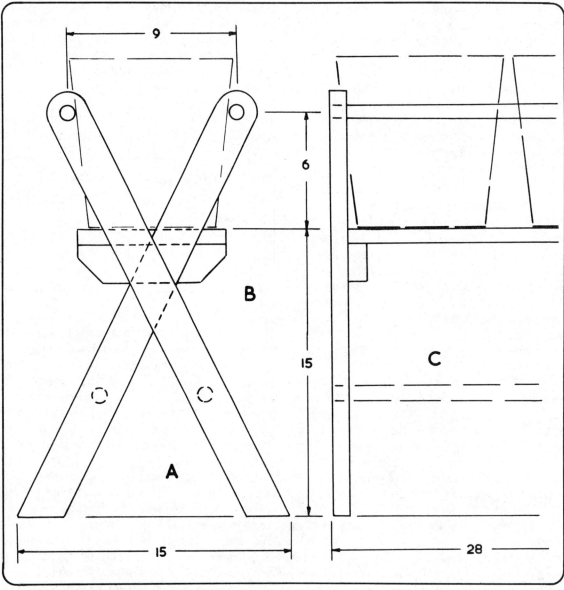

Fig. 9-26. Suggested sizes of the plant pot stand.

The rungs are shown spaced 11 inches from step to step. You could make it more or less, but keep the steps all the same from the ground to the top. A width of 15 inches gives a tread width of 12 inches, but you could increase this slightly, particularly if you make the ladder longer.

1. For a plain ladder, mark out the pair of sides (Fig. 9-29A) with the positions of the rungs.

2. Cut the wood for the rungs. They should be tenoned through the sides. Dowels would not be strong enough. There is no need to reduce the ends very much. If the wood is a 1-by-2-inch section, the tenons could be 3/4 inch thick (Fig. 9-29B).

3. Mark out all the rungs together. It is the

length between shoulders that is important. Allow enough length on the tenons to go through the sides a short distance and make saw cuts across so they can be tightened with wedges. Take sharpness off the rung edges.

4. Cut the mortises as accurately as possible. If working by hand, it helps to mark out and work from both surfaces. Round the ends of the sides.

5. Drive the glued tenons into all the mortises in one side, then glue the other ends and drive on the other side. Tighten with wedges, then check squareness and leave the assembly for the glue to set. Plane the wedges and ends of tenons level.

6. If a base is to be used, its suggested sizes are shown (Fig. 9-29C). For regular use on very soft ground you might want it bigger, but too big makes it bulky for storage.

7. Strengthen the end of the ladder with blocks glued inside (Fig. 9-29D). These should preferably be hardwood with the grain across, to provide reinforcement of the lengthwise grain in the sides.

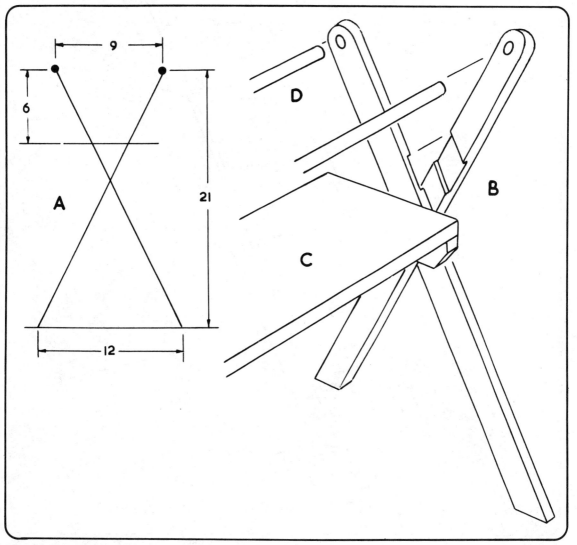

Fig. 9-27. Layout of an end and the method of assembly.

Fig. 9-28. This ladder has base and top attached to prevent slipping.

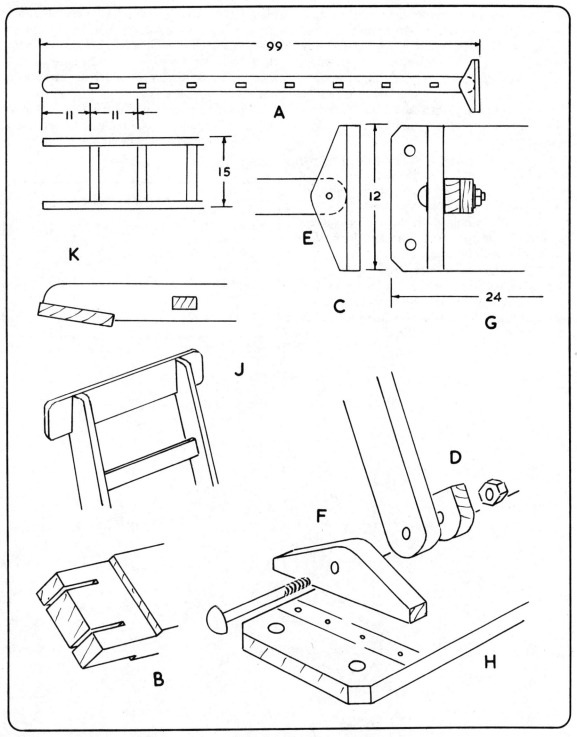

Fig. 9-29. Sizes and the method of assembly of the ladder with a base and top.

8. Make the two base supports (Figs. 9-29E and 9-29F). The hole centers should be high enough to allow the ladder end to turn with no more clearance than necessary for full movement.

9. Because the base might be in frequent contact with damp ground, the large part and the supports are best made of a durable hardwood and joined with waterproof glue and corrosion-resistant screws.

10. Make the base (Figs. 9-29G and 9-29H). Mark on it the positions of the supports, to fit outside the ladder sides and drill for screws. Also drill four or more 1-inch holes for stakes.

11. Drill for bolts, which may be galvanized steel, not less than 1/2-inch diameter. Use washers under the heads and nuts.

12. If a top is to be made (Fig. 9-29J), its sizes depends on your needs, but it is shown 6 inches wide and extending 3 inches each side of the ladder. Cut notches so the top fits into each side (Fig. 9-29K) and does not just depend on screws on a plain bevel. The angle could be found by experimenting with the ladder in its most common position, but allow for it being not too far from upright. A ladder should not have its base any further from a vertical line under its top than is necessary for ease of use.

13. The ladder may be painted, but it is usual to leave the centers of the rungs untreated. Paint from the sides may extend neatly about 1 inch onto each rung.

Materials List for Ladder	
2 sides	1 1/2 × 3 × 100
8 rungs	1 × 2 × 18
1 base	1 × 12 × 25
2 base supports	1 1/2 × 3 × 13
2 reinforcements	1 × 3 × 3
1 top	1 × 6 × 22

Chapter 10

Office Aids

Even if we do not work elsewhere in an office, most of us have to reserve a place in the home for dealing with bills and other household business affairs. There are many aids to tidiness and efficiency that can be made, from a complete desk to small things to use on it. Several of the racks described in Chapter 6 will have office uses. Most of the small items described here can be used anywhere in the home you tackle your business affairs.

Things have become more electronic, even in home affairs, so computers and business machines have to be accommodated. Wood stands and storage items help to avoid too clinical a look in what is still part of your home. You will also have the satisfaction of sitting and using things you have made yourself.

UNIT DESK

A desk with a flat top has the advantage of also serving as a table for other purposes, if required. It provides a good working area for a typewriter and other business machines, and space for the

papers and books you need, either for domestic or occupational affairs. It is a good place for the student to spread his work and it also serves as a place for many hobbies.

Some desks are quite complicated and could not be regarded as weekend projects, but this one (Fig. 10-1) is made entirely of veneered particleboard, with all joints dowelled. A skilled woodworker with ample equipment might make the whole desk in a weekend, but it is conveniently divided into three units, each of which could be regarded as the work for one weekend: the bookcase pedestal, the cabinet pedestal, followed by the top and assembly.

The material should be particleboard about 3/4 inch thick, bought with veneer on surfaces and edges. The veneer could be natural wood or a plastic with a plain or grained surface. You also need strips of similar veneer to put on exposed cut edges. If you check what stock widths are available you might be able to adjust some sizes to keep cutting to width and subsequent veneering of edges to a minimum. However, some cutting to size can-

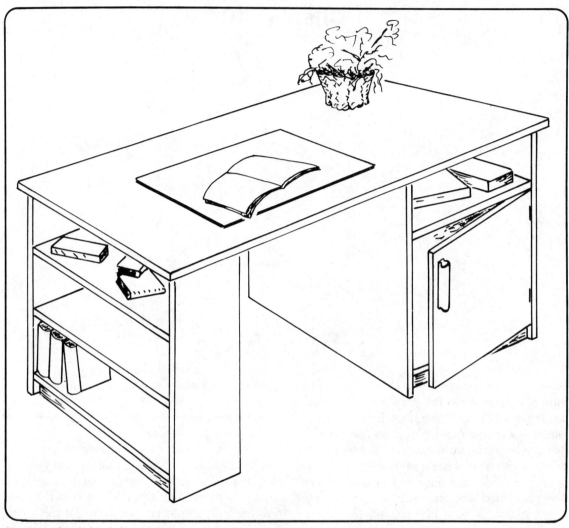

Fig. 10-1. This desk is built in three parts: the bookcase, a pedestal, and a top.

not be avoided. For instance, if you use 24-inch width for the top, some of the uprights will have to be cut down from that width, while if you make the uprights 24 inches, the top will have to be cut from a wider piece.

The design could be used for making the pedestals as independent pieces of furniture. In that case the only alterations will be to make them with their tops overlapping instead of between the sides. If they are made the same height you could build them into a desk later, or keep a separate top to put on for temporary use.

Joints can be standardized as far as possible, with 3/8-inch or 5/16-inch dowels taken about 1 inch into ends and as deep as can be drilled without breaking through into thicknesses (Fig. 10-2A). There should be one within 1 1/2 inches of an edge (Fig. 10-2B). If an edge is supported by a piece the other way the nearest dowel could then be 3 inches (Fig. 10-2C). In most of the assemblies other dowels should be spaced 3 inches to 4 inches apart. For less important joints, like the plinth to its shelf or shelves to the back, it would be sufficient to have them about 6 inches apart. One of the dowelling guides or a depth stop on the drill will be a help in maintaining accuracy. The considerable number of dowels needed can be cut in advance. Take any raggedness off the ends. Allow for the dowels being slightly shorter than the combined depths of holes, so joints will pull tight.

Suggested sizes are shown (Fig. 10-3A). The key parts, which control other sizes, are the bookcase pedestal side (Fig. 10-3B) and the cabinet pedestal side (Fig. 10-3C). Check these sizes in relation to your needs and the available material. Adjust them if necessary.

Bookcase Pedestal

1. Mark out and cut a pair of sides (Fig. 10-3B and 4A). The back will fit between the sides (Fig. 10-2D), so the shelves will be cut back to allow for this. The plinth is set back about 3/4 inch (Fig. 10-2E). The shelves could come level with the front edges.

2. Make the back (Fig. 10-4B) to fit between the sides and give a width of 23 inches over them. Make it the same height as the sides. If the pedestal is not to be used independently there is no need to veneer the cut top ends of sides and back, but if the sides have been cut from wider pieces, veneer the edges.

3. Make the four shelves (Fig. 10-4C) the same length as the width of the back and wide enough to be level with the front edges of the sides when tight against the back.

4. Make the plinth (Fig. 10-4D) the same

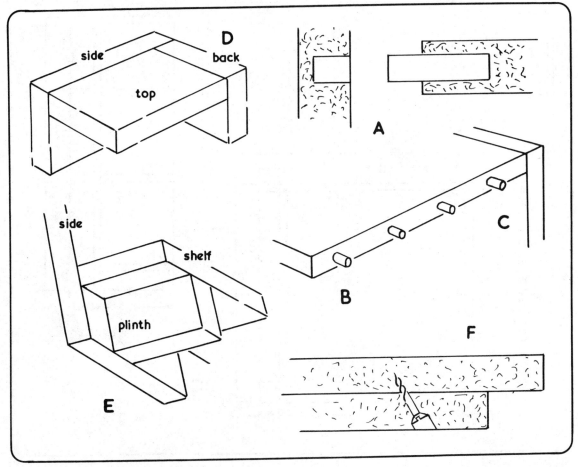

Fig. 10-2. Joint details of the pedestal desk.

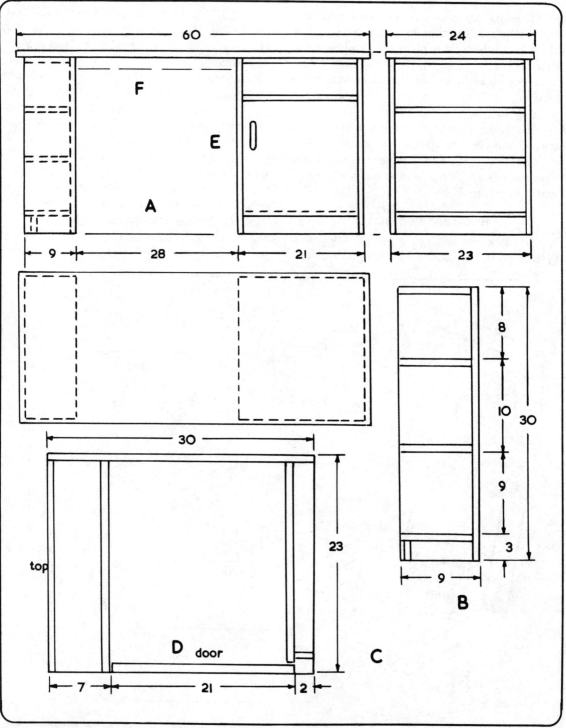

Fig. 10-3. Suggested sizes for the unit desk.

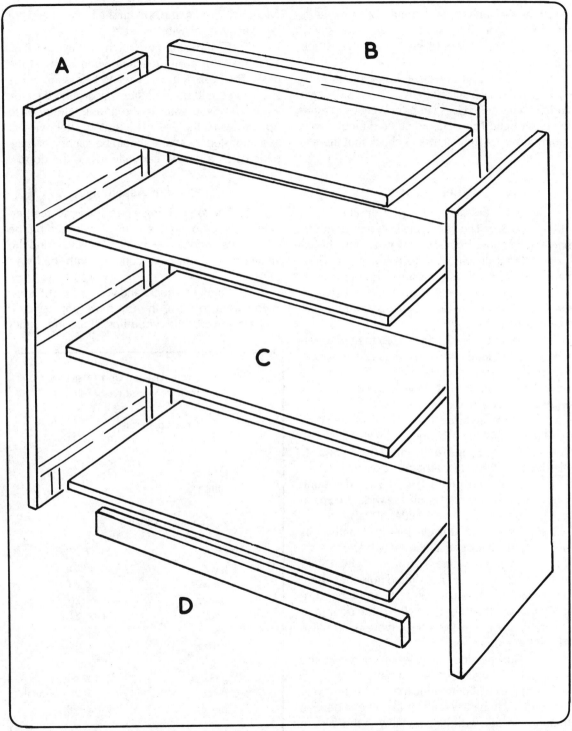

Fig. 10-4. The parts of the bookcase end of the desk.

length as the shelves. Be careful not to make its lower edge beneath the sides, or it will affect standing on a floor. It would be better slightly too narrow.

5. Drill for all dowels. Join the plinth to its shelf. Join the back and all shelves to one side, then add the other side. Use clamps or weights to force the joints tight. There should be no difficulty with squareness, but sight across to check that there is no twist.

Cabinet Pedestal

1. Mark out and cut a pair of sides (Figs. 10-3C and 5A). The back, shelves, and plinth fit between the sides in the same way as in the bookcase pedestal. If you want to use a stock width panel for the depth of the door, allow for this in positioning the shelves. The door comes between the sides, under the middle shelf, and over the bottom shelf (Fig. 10-3D).

2. Make the back (Fig. 10-5B) to fit between the sides. The final overall width is not as critical as in the bookcase pedestal, which fits across the other way, so you might be able to use a near stock width. Veneer any exposed edges.

3. Make the three shelves. The top two (Fig. 10-5C) fit against the back and are level at the front. The bottom shelf (Fig. 10-5D) must be cut back at the front to clear the overlapping door.

4. Make the plinth (Fig. 10-5E) the same length as the shelves and a suitable width (see paragraph 4 under "Bookcase Pedestal" above).

5. Drill for all dowels. Join the plinth to its shelf. Join the back and all the shelves to one side, then add the other side. Clamp or tighten with weights. Although the back should hold the assembly square, check squareness at the front, because it is important that the space allows the door to fit squarely. Sight across to check there is no twist. Allow the glue to set.

6. Cut the door to fit easily between the sides. If thin hinges that do not have to be let in are used, they will determine the clearance at one side and it can be the same at the other side. See that the top edge will be parallel with the middle shelf. The bottom edge of the door should be deep

enough to overlap the bottom shelf, but it need not be exactly level with its edge.

7. Fit a handle fairly high on the door (Fig. 10-3E), so it is easily reached when sitting at the desk. The desk does not have to be assembled as shown. It could be the other way around. Decide which way you want it and arrange the door to open towards the user. The bottom shelf will act as a door stop, but there should be a spring or magnetic catch arranged centrally inside the door.

Top and Assembly

1. The top is a single panel of veneered particleboard, probably the same as that used on the other parts. It could be thicker, however, and the veneer may be one that contrasts with the lower parts.

2. Carefully square and veneer the cut ends. If you want to make the top more impressive it could be given solid wood lips all around, either

---

**Materials List for Unit Desk
(all 3/4-inch veneered particleboard)**

Bookcase pedestal

2 sides	9	× 31
1 back	22	× 31
4 shelves	9	× 22
1 plinth	3	× 22

Cabinet pedestal

2 sides	23	× 31
1 back	20	× 31
3 shelves	20	× 23
1 plinth	3	× 20
1 door	21	× 21

Top

1 piece	24	× 61
2 pieces	2	× 29 optional
1 piece	3/4	× 20

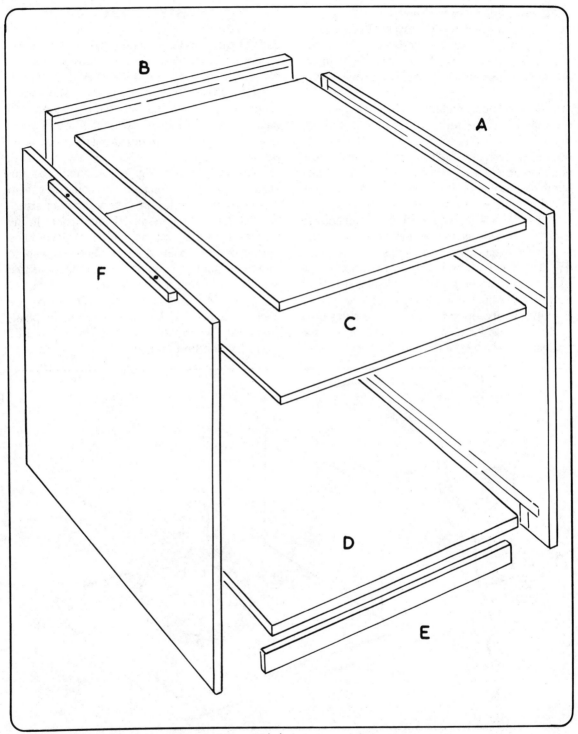

Fig. 10-5. The parts of the cabinet pedestal of the unit desk.

227

narrow strips or wider pieces with molded edges.

3. If you want the desk to take down, the top could merely rest on the pedestals, but it will usually be better to use screws, even if you might want to disassemble for transport only occasionally.

4. Drill up through the tops of the pedestals for screws into the desk top. For ease of driving, the holes can be angled (Fig. 10-2F). You will not be able to reach very far inside the top of the cabinet, and the screws driven there can be supplemented with some driven through a strip of wood along the inner top edge (Fig. 10-5F).

5. The desk top will probably be stiff enough over the gap between the pedestals, but if you want to provide extra stiffness add strips 2 inches wide (Fig. 10-3F) at back and front. In a permanent assembly they can be dowelled into the pedestals as well as the top. If you want to be able to remove the top from its supports, dowel these strips only to the top and let them merely rest against the pedestals.

STRING BOX

Balls of string and cord tend to get mislaid if you do not use them very often and have no regular place for storing them. A string box (Fig. 10-6) will keep string ready for use and the type shown will accommodate two sizes. It could be extended to have a box at each end, if you often use different sizes of string for parcels, gardening, or other purposes.

The sizes shown (Fig. 10-7A) should be ample for most balls of string, but you could alter them if your usual supplies are a very different size.

The main parts are all 1/2-inch wood. In the simplest form the joints are nailed. This would be satisfactory for a painted finish, but if you want to show your skill you could cut and glue joints that will show through a clear finish.

Any wood can be used, but for cut joints a good hardwood will look best. It would be possible to use plywood for some or all parts, but solid wood has the best appearance.

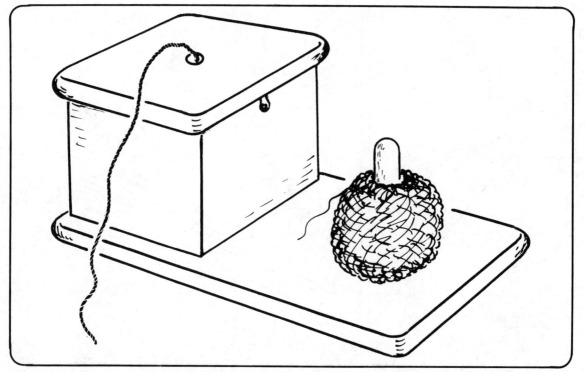

Fig. 10-6. This string box has some in the box, with the end through a hole and more string can go on the peg.

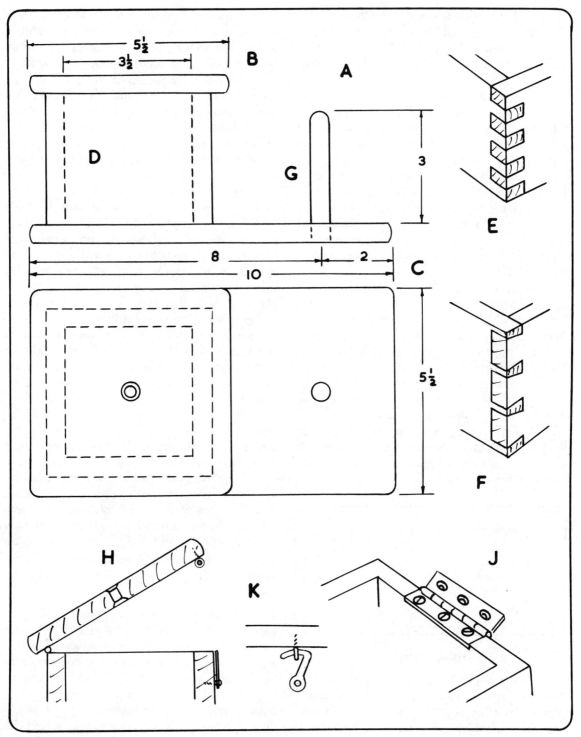

Fig. 10-7. Sizes and alternative constructions of the string box.

1. Prepare all the wood to width and thickness. The top (Fig. 10-7B) is a square the same width as the base (Fig. 10-7C). The box height is enough to form a cube inside, but slight variations will not matter.

2. Make and join the box sides (Fig. 10-7D). Have the grain horizontal. Allow for an overlap if the corners are to be screwed or nailed. A better joint uses fingers (Fig. 10-7E) or you could cut dovetails (Fig. 10-7F).

3. Make the top and base to match and overlap the box sides by 1/2 inch. The appearance will be improved if the corners and edges are rounded.

4. Drill the base for a 1/2-inch dowel rod (Fig. 10-7G), which should have its top rounded. Make sure it is upright when glued in, because an error will be obvious to everyone.

5. Drill the center of the lid (Fig. 10-7H) and countersink the hole slightly both sides. The size hole depends on your string, which should pass through easily—1/4 inch should be satisfactory.

6. One 2-inch hinge can be used (Fig. 10-7J). Two smaller ones that are let into the box, but on the surface of the lid can also be used.

7. At the opposite side a small hook and eye (Fig. 10-7K) will be a suitable fastener.

8. Finish in any way you wish. To prevent the box from sliding, there could be cloth or rubber glued underneath, either all over the bottom or just at the corners.

Materials List for String Box		
1 base	1/2 × 5 1/2 × 11	
1 top	1/2 × 5 1/2 × 6	
4 sides	1/2 × 3 1/2 × 5	
1 peg	4 × 1/2 diameter rod	

DESK TIDY

Anyone who uses a table as a desk will welcome a unit to keep together the accumulation of papers, books, and other items needed to deal with correspondence, studying, journalism, and other writing activities. This desk tidy (Fig. 10-8) is intended to be a free-standing unit to place across the rear of a table, so it could be removed if the table is needed for other purposes. For permanent installation it could be screwed down. A similar arrangement could be used at the back of a bench or table used for a hobby. Knitting and sewing equipment, fabric and paper for book covering, albums and folders for pictures, wood and metal for models, or cane and cords for basketry are all things that could be kept in this or a similar arrangement of shelves and compartments.

Sizes can be adapted to suit your table and the things you want to store. Make sure there are shelves large enough to take standard sheets of paper. As shown (Fig. 10-9A) the central part takes sheets of paper and other oddments. At one side there is space for books. At the other side there are compartments for envelopes and other items that can store vertically. The top gives extra storage space or it can be used for flowers or plants.

Solid wood 1/2 inch thick could be used. It would be possible to use 1/2-inch plywood, if the exposed ply edges are acceptable. The slightly thicker veneered particleboard would also be suitable.

The corners of the main parts could be dovetailed, but notching the corners is simpler and makes a neat assembly. The internal parts could fit into stopped dadoes or they may be merely positioned and fixed with glue and pins, set below the surface, and covered with stopping. The back is a piece of hardboard or thin plywood fitted into rabbets. The top rails can be screwed from below or fitted with glue and dowels. Much depends on the quality of construction and appearance that will fit your needs.

1. Cut rabbets in the pieces for the top, bottom, and ends (Fig. 10-9B). Make the rabbet about three-fourths of the thickness of the wood, to give a good bearing for the back and to coincide with the amount to be cut out for the notched corners.

2. Mark out the top and bottom together with the positions of the divisions (Fig. 10-9C). If there are to be stopped dadoes, cut them. The envelope divisions are set back from the front edge,

so the stopped dadoes there will be for their full width.

3. Make the two ends to fit into notches in the top and bottom (Fig. 10-9D), cut to the same depth as the back rabbets.

4. Make the two main divisions (Fig. 10-9E) either to fit dado grooves or to fit between top and bottom surfaces for pinning.

5. Make the central shelf (Fig. 10-9F). Even if other compartment joints are only pinned, the shelf joints would be better if stopped dadoes.

6. The envelope divisions could have straight fronts, but hollowing them (Fig. 10-9G) im- proves appearance and lets you get fingers in easier.

7. The height of the top rails could be ar- ranged to suit your needs. If they only have to pre- vent a few things from sliding off they can be about 2 inches, as shown (Fig. 10-9H). If you expect to stack books or other bulky items they could be deeper. Set the rails in a short distance from the ends of the top, but have the back one level.

8. The corners of the top rails may be dovetailed or notched. The end pieces are shown curved down to the front, but they could be left level or bevelled.

Fig. 10-8. A desk tidy stands on a table to hold office requirements. It could also be used for hobby or shop items.

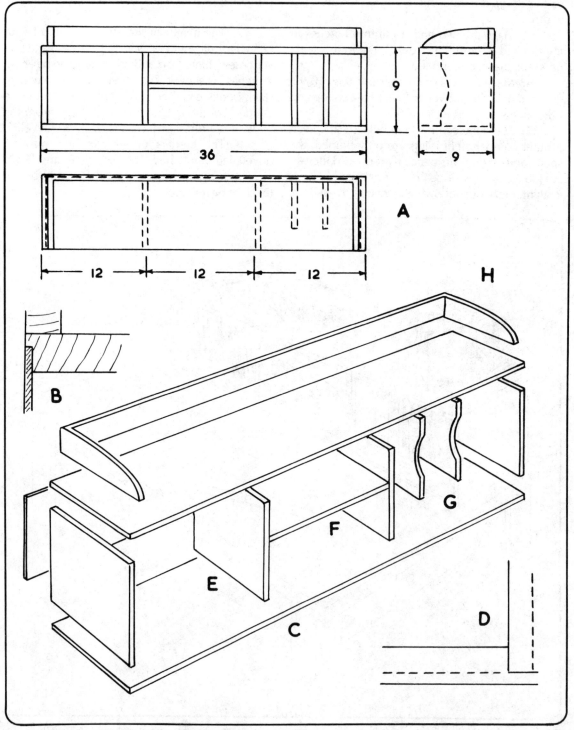

Fig. 10-9. Sizes and details of the desk tidy.

9. With all of the parts prepared, join the central shelf to its upright divisions, then fit these and all other upright parts to the top and bottom. At the notched corner joints use pins or fine nails both ways.

10. Square this assembly and glue in the back to hold it in shape. Supplement the glue with pins or small screws through the back.

11. Drill holes for screws upwards into the top rails or drill for dowels, then attach the rails to the top.

12. Finish the wood with stain and polish or varnish. Any tendency of the desk tidy to slide on the table top can be reduced by gluing cloth underneath, either all over or at the corners.

Materials List for Desk Tidy

1 top	1/2 × 9 × 37
1 bottom	1/2 × 9 × 37
2 ends	1/2 × 9 × 9
2 divisions	1/2 × 8 7/8 × 9
2 divisions	1/2 × 6 × 9
1 shelf	1/2 × 8 7/8 × 13
1 back	9 × 36 × 1/8 hardboard
1 top rail	1/2 × 2 × 36
2 top rails	1/2 × 2 × 9

BUSINESS MACHINE STAND

Most of us use small business machines, and if you use a desk-top machine you might wish to turn it about to the best direction, particularly if you change your position. If there are other people who want to use the machine from the other side of the table, an easy way of turning the machine around will be welcomed.

The stand illustrated includes a turntable, so the machine can be altered to any direction with minimum effort, This is a stand for a calculator (Fig. 10-10), but a stand for any other small business machine could be made in the same way, with sizes adjusted to suit.

The stand consists of a tray to take the machine and a square base, joined with a "lazy susan" bear-ing. The base and the bottom of the tray could be solid wood or 1/2-inch plywood. The rim of the tray is more prominent and might be an attractive hardwood with a clear finish. Lazy susan bearings are made in several sizes. For the tray shown, the 3-inch size should be adequate, but for bigger stands there are other sizes up to 12 inches.

1. Measure the machine and decide how high the rim should stand to keep it in place. An excessive height looks ugly, but some machine edges vary and there must be enough rim all round to prevent the machine from slipping out. You might have to allow for notching around a switch or an electric cable.

2. Cut the bottom of the tray (Fig. 10-11A) about 1/4 inch bigger than the machine.

3. Cut the border strips with rounded tops (Fig. 10-11B). Make them to fit around the tray bottom with mitered corners (Fig. 10-11C).

4. If there have to be any notches, shape them with rounded edges (Fig. 10-11D).

5. Attach the rim strips with glue and a few pins, which can be punched below the surface and covered with stopping.

6. The base (Fig. 10-11E) is a simple square block. Its edges and corners could be chamfered or rounded, but because it is almost hidden that is not important.

7. Details for fitting a lazy susan bearing are given in the instructions for making the television turntable in Chapter 2. This bearing is fitted in exactly the same way.

8. After you have drilled for screws and made a trial assembly, separate the parts and fin-

Materials List for Business Machine Stand

1 tray	1/2 × 9 × 11
2 tray borders	1/4 × 1 1/8 × 12
2 tray borders	1/4 × 1 1/8 × 10
1 base	1/2 × 7 × 7
1 lazy susan bearing,	
3-inch size	

Fig. 10-10. This stand for a calculator can be moved in any direction on a turntable.

ish the wood with stain and polish. Reassemble with the lazy susan bearing permanently screwed on. Glue cloth to the underside of the base to prevent slipping or marking a polished surface.

FLOPPY DISC CABINET

The computer user needs somewhere to store and protect an ever-increasing accumulation of floppy discs. This cabinet (Fig. 10-12) should hold up to one hundred 5 1/4-inch floppy discs in a way that protects them and keeps them accessible. They can be gathered in up to nine groups, which makes sorting easy. This cabinet, or another made in the same way to different sizes, could be used to file cards or hobby items.

The cabinet could be made of solid wood with dovetailed corners, but it might follow the design of scientific instrument cases and be made of mahogany or similar wood, with all the joints made with brass screws that have their heads exposed. Plywood could be used in the same way. Edges cut to avoid splintering and all external angles rounded would, under a polished or varnished finish, give the traditional scientific instrument-case appearance.

The line between the lid and base slopes, with a hinge at the rear end. An accurate fit between the two parts is achieved by making up as a box in one piece, then cutting along the sloping line.

1. Make the sides and ends 6 inches wide, but mark on the lines to be cut to separate the parts later (Fig. 10-13A). For screwed joints, allow for

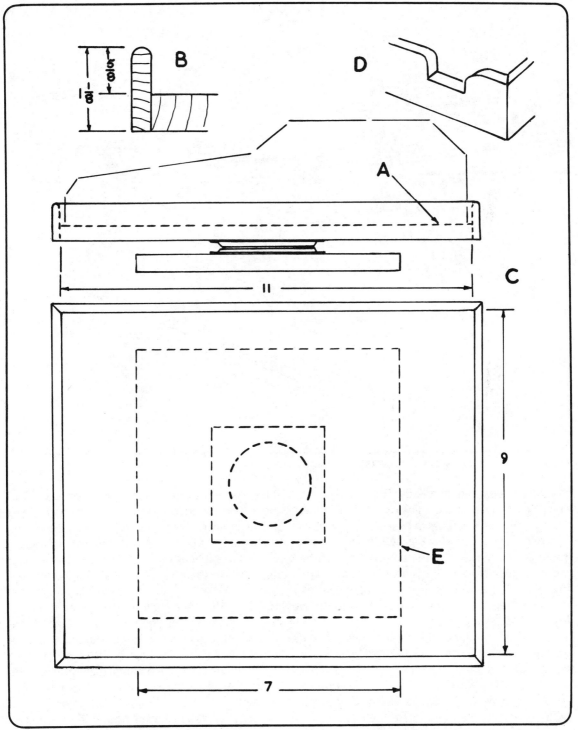

Fig. 10-11. Typical sizes of a business machine stand.

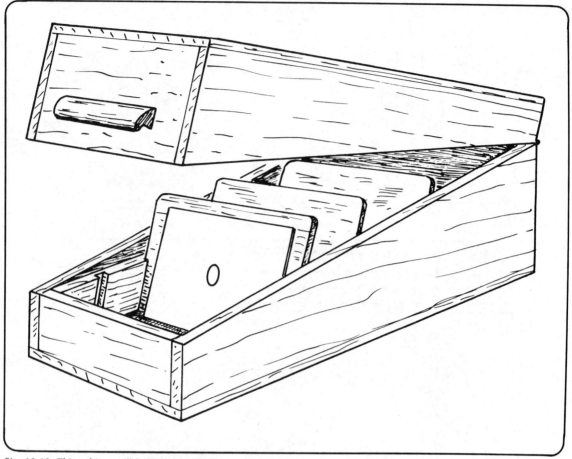

Fig. 10-12. This cabinet will hold about 100 floppy discs.

the sides overlapping the ends. For dovetails the ends must be marked the full width of the cabinet.

2. Mark screw holes in the sides in positions to avoid the cut. Screws 6-gauge by 1 1/4-inch could be located two on the narrow sides of the cut and three or four on the other sides. Drill carefully so as not to break out end grain, and countersink just enough for the screw heads to finish level.

3. Screw and glue these parts, then add the top and bottom. Glue and screw them in the same way. True and sand the outside surfaces, then round all edges and corners. The exterior surfaces should be in as good shape as you require them, before you separate the parts of the cabinet.

4. Although it would be possible to separate the parts with a power saw, it is wiser to work at the slower pace of hand sawing, which gives greater control of accuracy. A fine tenon saw, used at a flat angle all around to gradually cut through, will leave surfaces that only require a little planing to make them close together smoothly.

5. Make the slotted strips (Figs. 10-13B and 10-13C). They are parallel and cut at about 10 degrees, but you can experiment and make the angles to suit your needs. The slots should be an easy fit on the dividers. If you wish, the strips could be shortened by being cut off immediately behind the last slots, to leave space at the back for storing spare dividers.

6. Make the dividers from thin plywood or hardboard. Cut them to drop easily into the slots

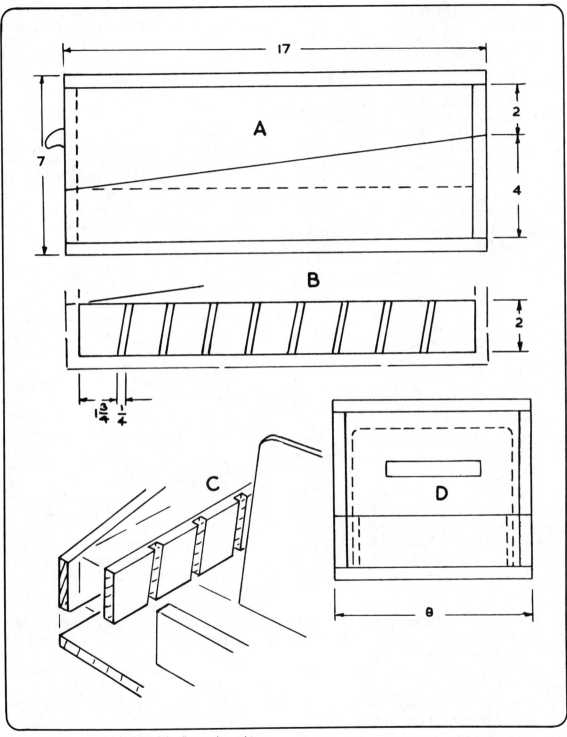

Fig. 10-13. Sizes and assembly of the floppy disc cabinet.

and high enough to support the discs. Round the upper corners. The slots are intended to give alternative positions for a few dividers, depending on how you wish to group your discs. Make whatever number of dividers you require, although you might eventually want a full set of eight.

7. You can lift the lid by gripping its sides, but a handle (Fig. 10-13D) at the front is worth having. It could be a bought metal or plastic handle, or you could shape a block of wood and screw it on from inside. At the rear you could fit a full-width piece of piano hinge, or let in two 1 1/2-inch hinges, preferably brass.

8. Finish with several coats of polish or varnish. Squares of cloth glued under the corners will prevent slipping.

Materials List for Floppy Disc Cabinet	
2 sides	1/2 × 6 × 18
2 ends	1/2 × 6 × 9
1 top	1/2 × 8 × 18
1 bottom	1/2 × 8 × 18
2 strips	1/2 × 2 × 17
1 handle	3/4 × 3/4 × 5
Dividers	1/8 or 3/16 × 5 1/2 × 7 as required

STATIONERY RACK

It is convenient to have writing and typing paper, plus envelopes and cards, within reach on a desk or table. The rack looks best if made of fairly thin wood, preferably of a type that will match the table it stands on. This rack (Fig. 10-14) is made of oak, with the ends 3/8 inch thick and the other parts only 1/4 inch thick. You might have to modify thicknesses to suit the wood you use. If utility is more important than appearance, the design could be used with plywood. Plywood with well-finished, rounded edges can have a beauty of its own under varnish.

The sizes shown (Fig. 10-15) will take the usual size of typing paper, as well as other papers, cards, and envelopes. If you will only want to fit in writing paper, the sizes can probably be reduced. If desk space is limited, you could make the rack narrower and higher so the larger papers stand on end. However, there is less risk of them curling over when a compartment is not full if the narrow width of large papers is vertical.

1. Prepare all the wood to thickness and width, as far as possible. A regular thickness is necessary if the assembled rack is to look neat.

2. Draw the outline of an end (Fig. 10-15A), marking on it the actual thickness of the wood you are using for the other parts. The back will fit into rabbets (Fig. 10-15B), but the ends extend so the front fits into grooves (Fig. 10-15C).

3. Cut the grooves to half the thickness of the ends, or slightly less (Fig. 10-15D) and the rabbet for the back to the same depth (Fig. 10-16A).

4. All the divisions are intended to stand 1/2 inch above the sloping ends. Measure the grooves so you get the same projection on all of them (Fig. 10-15E). Round the corners, so they will blend in (Fig. 10-16B). Also round the front corners of the ends, and all edges of ends and divisions that will be upwards.

5. Make the back (Fig. 10-15F) in the same way as the divisions. Its top edge could be straight, but it would look better with a curve.

6. A divider in the front compartment is not essential, but it will separate cards and envelopes. It need not slope (Fig. 10-16C). Letting it into rabbets in this thin wood is not advised, so it can be located with glue and pins.

7. When you assemble, it should be sufficient to use glue only for the intermediate divisions. The back and front may also have a few pins driven from outside, then set below the surface and covered with stopping.

8. Square this assembly, then leave it for the glue to set. Remove any surplus glue and level the bottom edges, if necessary.

9. Make the bottom (Fig. 10-16D) 1/4 inch bigger all around than the bottom of the assembled other parts. Round its corners and upper edges. Attach it with glue and a few pins.

10. Polish or varnish the wood. There could

Fig. 10-14. This stationery cabinet has divisions for paper and envelopes.

be cloth stuck on the bottom, either all over or just at the corners, to prevent slipping or marking a polished surface.

Materials List for Stationery Rack

2 ends	3/8 × 6 × 9
1 bottom	3/8 × 6 1/2 × 14
1 back	1/4 × 8 × 13
1 division	1/4 × 7 1/4 × 13
1 division	1/4 × 5 3/4 × 13
1 front	1/4 × 4 1/4 × 13
1 divider	1/4 × 3 × 2

CORNER DESK

If you cannot spare the space for a desk along one wall or further out in a room, a corner may be a good place to put it, where it does not interfere with other furniture. It can be inconspicuous when out of use if it is covered with a cloth and a vase of flowers stood on top. If a normal desk is stood in a corner, you either sit facing one wall and the corner projects into the room, or if it is put across the corner it takes up even more space and there is an unused triangle behind it. The solution is to use all the space and make a desk to fit into the corner with its working edge diagonal to the walls.

Such a desk must extend from the corner a reasonable distance along each wall so that the

239

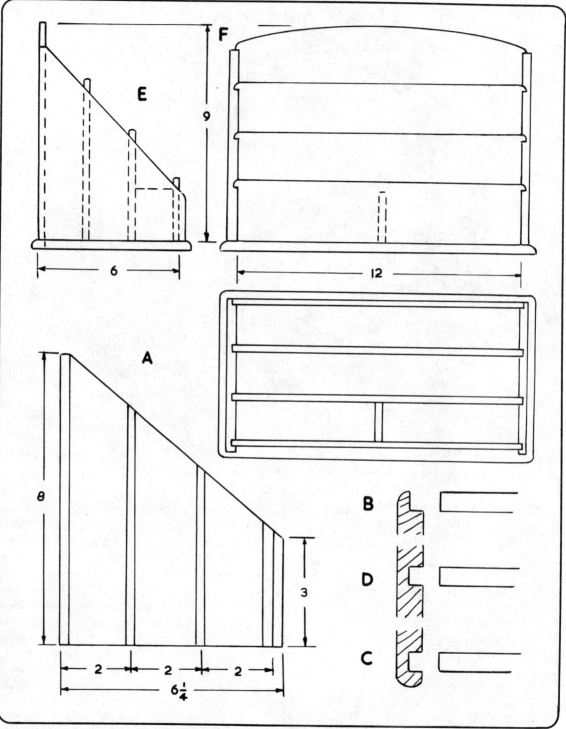

Fig. 10-15. Sizes of the parts of the stationery cabinet.

length of the working front edge and the space for your legs are adequate. This desk (Fig. 10-17) is 36 inches along each wall and projections square from that are 18 inches, leaving space across the front of about 25 inches (Fig. 10-18).

The top could be a single piece of veneered particleboard, or it could be veneered plywood with solid wood lips on the three exposed edges. The other parts are plywood framed with 1-inch square strips. There is an L-shaped shelf underneath framed in the same way.

1. Corners of rooms are supposed to be 90 degrees, but quite often they are a few degrees out. That does not matter for normal living, but if you made the desk 90 degrees and it did not fit, the gaps would be rather obvious. Strips on the top (Fig. 10-18A) could be made to conform to the wall rather than the desk, if there is an error, but it would be better to make the desk to fit. Measure 36 inches from the corner along each wall at desk top level, then measure the distance between these points. Mark lines to match the top and use this

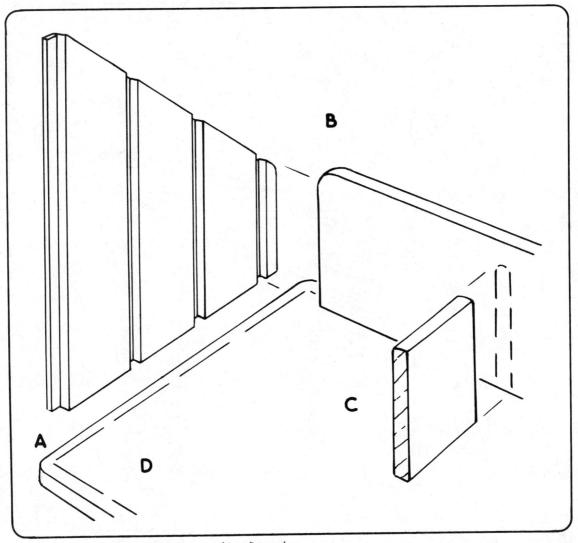

Fig. 10-16. How the parts of the stationary cabinet fit together.

corner angle instead of 90 degrees, if there is any difference.

2. Cut the plywood for the fronts (Figs. 10-18B and 10-19A). It will be 16 1/2 inches wide and 30 inches less the top thickness high. Attach two uprights—one set back by the thickness of the back plywood (Figs. 10-18C and 10-19C) so the front will hide its edge, and the other level, to be covered by a 1/2-inch lip (Figs. 10-18D and 10-19B). Join the strips and the lip with glue and enough pins to hold the parts while the glue sets.

Put other strips across top and bottom edges and a support for the plywood shelf at the height you want it. Slightly above halfway should suit most needs. Notch the support for the shelf, which will extend 15 inches from the corner (Figs. 10-19D and 10-19E).

3. Make the two backs (Figs. 10-19F and 10-19G). They are almost the same, but one will overlap the other in the corner, with a similar joint to that at the front corners (Fig. 10-18C). Put an upright at the corner edge of one piece. Put strips

Fig. 10-17. A corner desk makes maximum use of the space without interfering with furniture in other parts of a room.

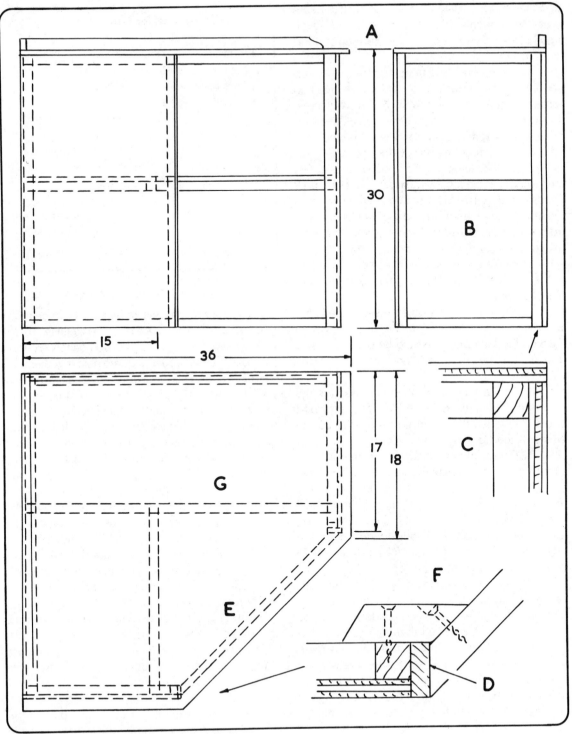

Fig. 10-18. Sizes and details of the corner desk.

along the top and bottom edges, cut back to fit between the uprights and other strips at shelf level. Notch one of these strips to take the shelf support (Fig. 10-19H).

4. Try the back and fronts together in the corner. If they are satisfactory join them with glue and screws. It does not matter which way you screw through the plywood in the corner, but at the fronts drive screws from the back plywood into the front parts so the screw heads will not show.

5. Get the length of the strip that goes across the front under the top, by measuring with the desk in position (Fig. 10-18E). Cut it to fit where it meets the fronts and secure it with glued blocks screwed from inside (Fig. 10-18F). This will lock the assembly in shape to match the room walls.

6. Make a shelf strip with notched ends to fit the notches in one back and the opposite front (Fig. 10-18G).

7. Make another strip to meet it the other way (Fig. 10-19J). Notching the two together would weaken the long one. It would be better to use a dowel. The plywood will add strength to the corner.

8. Fit the shelf strips, then cut and glue the plywood shelf in place. The edges of the plywood could be hidden by lips in the same way as the edges of the front.

9. Check all parts made so far, remove any surplus glue, and prepare the surfaces for finishing.

10. Cut the top to size. It should overlap the three front edges by 1 inch. If you have used veneered particleboard, veneer the edges. If you have used plywood, add solid wood lips to the edges. Drill the underframing for a few screws to be driven upwards into the top.

11. It will be easiest to apply finish to the parts before screwing into the top. The inside might be given a lighter finish than the outside so it will be easier to see things stored there.

12. If you want to fit top strips (Fig. 10-18A), screw upwards through the top before screwing the frame strips to the top. Alternatively, screw the strips to the wall and not to the desk. This would be advisable if the desk top edges do not make a good fit with the walls.

Materials List for Corner Desk		
2 fronts	17	× 30 × 1/2 plywood
4 front frames	1	× 1 × 30
6 front frames	1	× 1 × 17
2 front lips	1/2	× 1 × 30
2 backs	30	× 35 × 1/2 plywood
6 back frames	1	× 1 × 36
1 shelf	36	× 36 × 1/2 plywood
1 shelf strip	1	× 1 × 36
1 shelf strip	1	× 1 × 22
2 shelf lips	1/2	× 1 1/2 × 22
1 top	36	× 36 × 3/4 veneered particleboard
2 top strips	1	× 2 × 34

WASTE PAPER BASKET

A wooden basket for waste paper should be more than just a box. This waste paper basket (Fig. 10-20) is octagonal with tapered plywood panels screwed to a base, but the upper parts are held together with a cord or rope. This has a decorative effect and simplifies construction, because there is no need for the precision that would be entailed if all the joints had to be closely fitted. The result is a light, attractive container. The same method of construction could be used for other purposes. A plant in a plain pot could stand in a similar wooden basket, tailored to a fairly close fit.

The base could be 1/2-inch plywood, but solid wood 5/8 inch thick would take screws better. The eight sides are best made of 1/4-inch plywood. For careful use they could be a good-quality hardboard. There are some attractive synthetic cords and ropes available in several colors, although a white rope against stained wood will look good.

The suggested sizes will make a basket 12 inches across and 14 inches high (Fig. 10-21). Other sizes can be made in the same way. A base 3 inches less than the top will give a reasonable flare to the sides.

1. Mark out the octagonal base (Fig. 10-21A). On a 9-inch square draw diagonals and

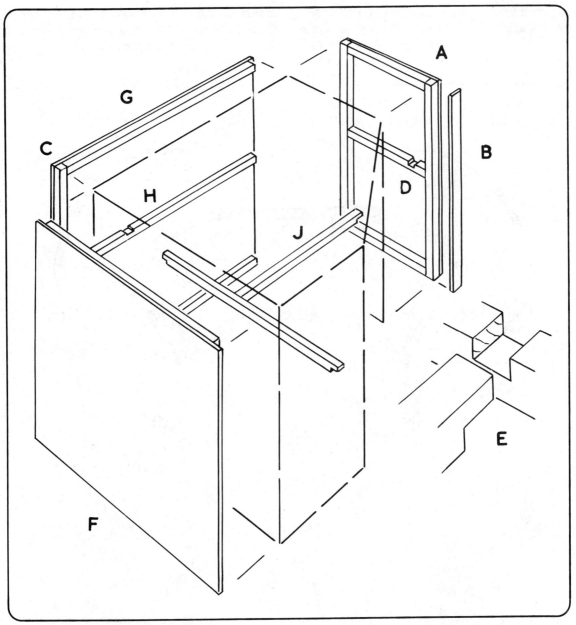

Fig. 10-19. Assembly of the parts of a corner desk.

measure half of one (Fig. 10-21B). Measure that distance from each corner along each side and join these marks. Check the lengths obtained. There should be eight equal edges. Cut this shape.

2. With the small amount of flare in the sides you might decide to leave the bottom edges square, but the sides will make a better fit if you bevel them slightly. If you measure the angle, 82 degrees will make a close fit (Fig. 10-21C).

3. Mark out the eight panels symmetrically around their centerlines (Fig. 10-21D). The bottom is shown 3 1/2 inches wide, but check the actual

length of an edge of the base. The long edges could be left square, but they will pull closer and look better if they are bevelled. A slight bevelling without measuring should be sufficient, but if you want to measure the angle it is one-fourth of 90 degrees, or 22 1/2 degrees. The width across the inside of the bottom of each piece should match an edge of the base.

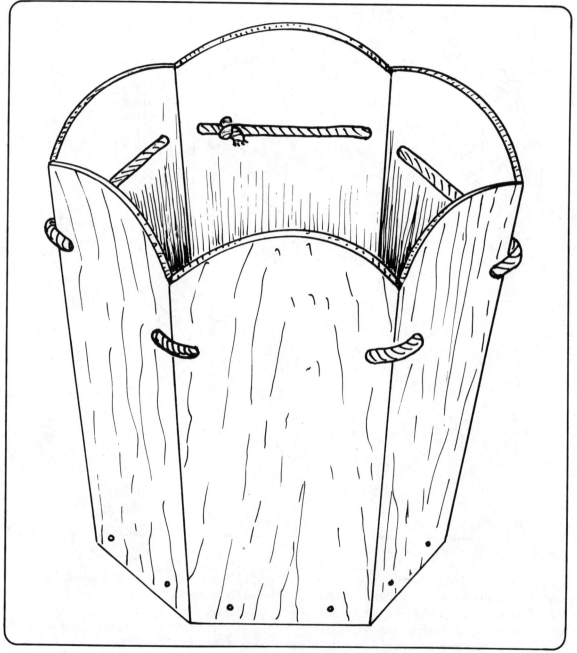

Fig. 10-20. This wooden waste paper basket uses a rope to secure the tops of the panels.

246

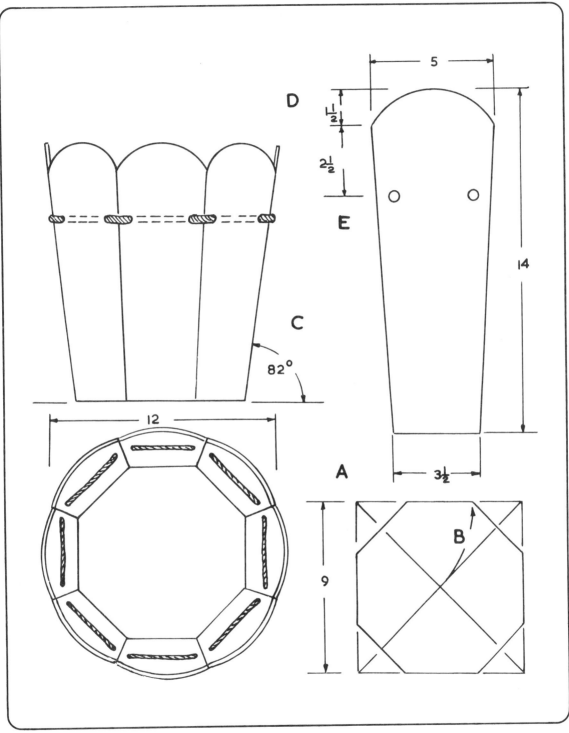

Fig. 10-21. Sizes and layout of the waste paper basket and its parts.

247

4. Drill holes for the cord (Fig. 10-21E) about 3/4 inch in from the edges. The size should allow the cord to pass through easily. Lightly countersink the holes both sides.

5. Well-round the top curved edges. Try two panels in position to check their fit. If this is satisfactory, sand all wood. It will probably be most convenient to stain and polish the wood before assembly.

6. Drill for screws through the panels for attaching the base. Two round-head brass or plated screws, 6-gauge by 3/4-inch, would be suitable.

7. Screw all panels to the base. Thread the cord through the holes and pull it tight with a knot inside.

8. The waste paper basket could stand on the floor as it is, or there could be four small square blocks or metal glides spread evenly underneath, if you wish.

Materials List for Waste Paper Basket

1 base	$5/8 \times 9 \times 9$
8 panels	$5 \times 15 \times 1/4$ plywood

Chapter 11

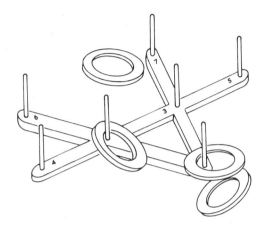

Toys, Games, and Puzzles

If there are children in the home there are many toys that can be made, so much so that whole books cover the making of toys and children's furniture. In this chapter there are just a few suggestions and you can develop your own ideas for more projects. Games and puzzles will appeal to adults as well as children and can provide many combined activities.

Wood is a good material to use for things handled by children, but you should avoid types that may split or splinter, and all edges and corners should be well-rounded. As children tend to put things in their mouths; be careful in the choice of finish and avoid making the parts so small that they could be jammed in the mouth or swallowed. Fine detail in toys, games, and puzzles is usually unnecessary and a bold treatment is stronger and just as satisfying. If you need to justify the time spent in your shop, in your family's eyes, produce things for the younger members!

SWINGING DOLL CRADLE

A little girl needs to be able to put her doll to bed,

so a cradle is necessary. A static one may serve, but a swinging or rocking one is more enjoyable. This cradle (Fig. 11-1) swings, but can be locked with a catch by the child, so it remains level. The suggested sizes (Fig. 11-2A) should suit any doll that a young child might have.

Most of the parts are solid wood, but the cradle ends could be 1/2-inch plywood. The cradle sides and bottom could also be plywood, but they would be better of slightly thicker solid wood. Because a painted finish, possibly decorated with decals, will probably be used, it does not matter much what woods are chosen and they could be mixed. The uprights, feet, and stretcher should be straight-grained and free from large knots, so there will be no problem of strength or warping. The key parts are uprights and cradle ends. They should be made to match, then the sizes of most other parts chosen.

Some shaping of edges is shown. The curves blend into each other and there are no angular parts that might harm a young user. Many edges could be left straight, if you wish, but the curves

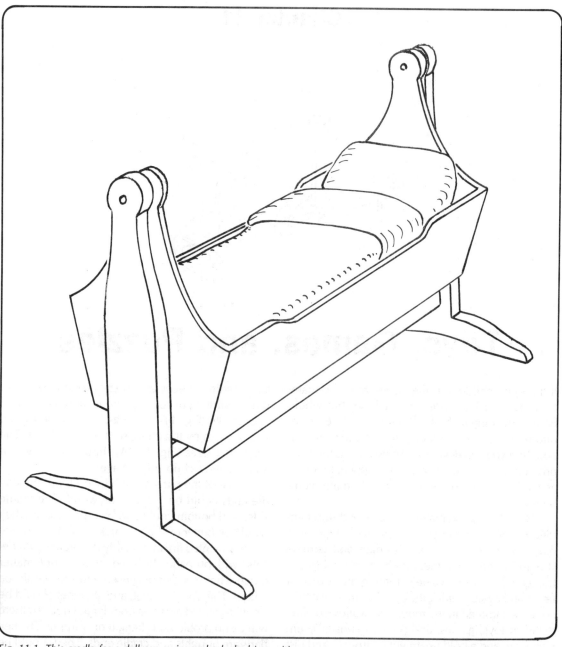

Fig. 11-1. This cradle for a doll can swing or be locked in position.

lighten appearance and make the cradle more attractive.

1. Make the two cradle ends, using the squared drawing as a guide (Fig. 11-3A). Mark the holes, but do not drill them yet. Round all edges that will not be joined to other parts.

2. Make the two uprights (Fig. 11-2B). The upper ends are shaped to match the cradle ends (Fig. 11-3B). The lower ends are shown cut square

for dowels into the feet, but if you prefer tenons allow extra length for them.

3. So the swinging cradle does not touch the uprights, there have to be washers between (Fig. 11-4A). They are best made from 3/8-inch or 1/2-inch plywood.

4. The pivots will be 1/2-inch dowels (Fig. 11-4B), glued into the uprights, but loose in the washers and cot ends. Drill all parts for the dowels.

5. Make the two feet (Fig. 11-4C). It is easier to drill for dowels or cut mortises while the wood still has straight edges. Mark the curves from the squared drawing (Fig. 11-3C) and cut them.

6. The bottom and sides of the cradle fit between the ends (Fig. 11-4D). Hollow the top edges of the sides (Fig. 11-2C), if you wish. Get the ends of these parts square so the assembled cradle swings accurately between the uprights. Join the sides to the bottom and all three parts to the ends with glue and nails or screws.

7. Measure the distance over the ends and the two wood washers. Add 1/8 inch for clearance

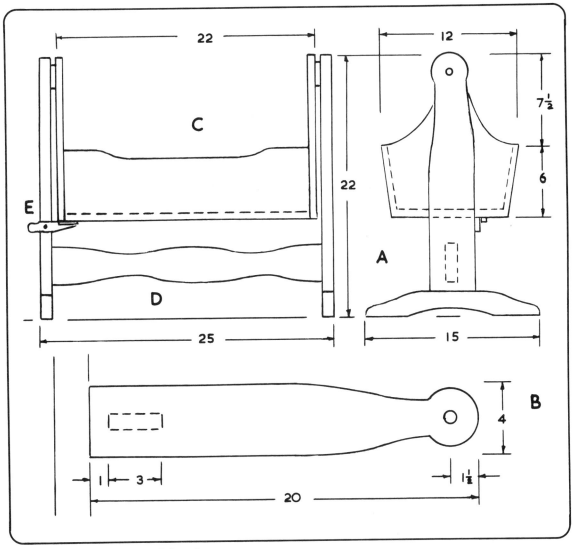

Fig. 11-2. Sizes of the swinging doll cradle.

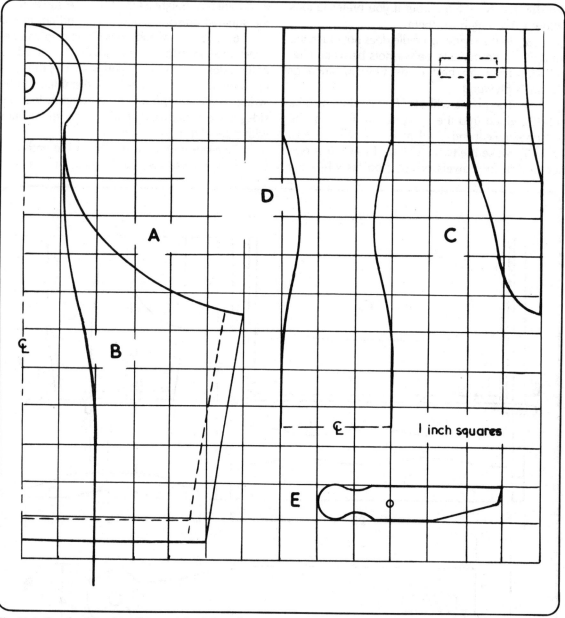

Fig. 11-3. Details of the shaped parts of the doll cradle.

and this will be the length of the stretcher (Fig. 11-2D)—if it is dowelled or between shoulders—if you cut tenons.

8. Make the stretcher, using the squared drawing as a guide to shaping (Fig. 11-3D).

9. Drill the main parts for dowels or complete cutting mortise and tenon joints. Round all edges that will be handled and sand all parts before assembly.

10. Join the uprights to the feet squarely and check that they match as a pair.

11. Join the stretcher to the uprights (Fig.

11-4E). Besides checking squareness, make sure the distance apart is the same at the top as the bottom.

12. Put in temporary dowel pivots to test the swinging action. It will be best to delay gluing in the dowels until after you have completed painting.

13. The catch for locking the cradle level is a lever at the side of one upright (Fig. 11-2E). It has a shaped handle for the child to swing up or down.

14. Make the lever from 1/2-inch wood (Fig. 11-3E). Even if the rest of the cradle is softwood,

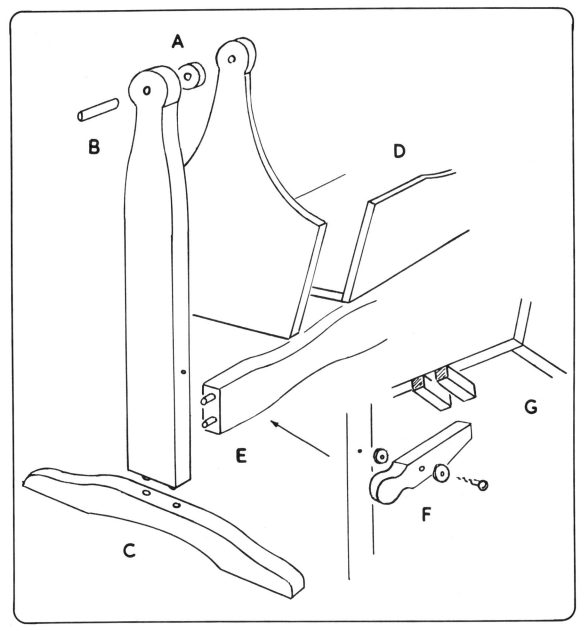

Fig. 11-4. Assembly of the cradle (A-E) and the method of locking (F,G).

this would be better made of hardwood, to resist splitting in use. Well round the handle end.

15. Drill for a roundhead screw, which can pass through two washers. If the inner washer is fiber, that will provide friction to hold the lever where it is set (Fig. 11-4F).

16. Locate the lever on the side of an upright so when it is in the locking position it rests under the cradle. Put two small blocks under the cradle, so it will fit easily between them (Fig. 11-4G).

17. If the parts fit and move as desired, make sure there are no sharp edges and angles, then sand everything before painting.

18. Glue in the pivot dowels. If you think you might want to take the cradle apart, the dowels could have screws driven across them in the uprights instead of being glued.

Materials List for Swinging Doll Cradle

2 cot ends	1/2 × 12 × 14
1 cot bottom	5/8 × 10 × 23
2 cot sides	5/8 × 6 × 23
2 uprights	1 × 4 × 21
2 feet	1 × 2 × 16
1 stretcher	1 × 3 × 24
2 washers	1/2 × 2 × 2
1 catch	1/2 × 1 × 6

BALL GAME

This is a competitive game where the object is to get the highest or exact score by sending balls through holes in a target. It would be possible to arrange a table-top game for quite small balls, such as balls from bearings, but the sizes shown (Fig. 11-5A) are for balls about 1 inch in diameter. They could be soft rubber or hard plastic or wood. The target board is given holes with ample clearance, so a young child should be able to get a satisfying number of successes. Adding the scores would provide good practice in simple arithmetic. The balls could be rolled by hand, but a chute is suggested. This can be used at the marked distance and directed towards the target hole.

Any wood could be used. The toy might get rough treatment and could benefit from weight, so a close-grained hardwood is advisable. Except for the rounding of the front corners the two parts of the target are the same.

1. Prepare a sufficient 1-by-3 1/2-inch section of wood. Cut the two pieces and mark them out together with the hole positions on their centerlines (Fig. 11-5B). Drill 1 1/2-inch holes at each position.

2. Mark the sides of the slots and saw into the holes to remove the waste. Smooth the edges of the slots. Round the corners of the front and take the sharpness off all edges that will be exposed. Glue and nail or screw the parts together.

3. The chute is shown with a moderate slope (Fig. 11-5C). For very light balls it could be steeper. Even with heavier balls at a long distance it might be better steeper. The slope shown should suit the usual child's playing distance. Make the block wide enough to give easy clearance to the balls. Add raised sides to control the ball. An alternative would be a chute with a deep groove and no sides.

4. A bright color of paint would be the best finish for a child's toy. Paint the numbers.

Materials List for Ball Game

2 pieces	1 × 3 1/2 × 18
1 piece	1 1/2 × 2 × 11
2 pieces	1/4 × 3 × 11

NUMBER PUZZLE

This is a puzzle in which eight numbered "tiles" have to be moved around a case with nine spaces (Fig. 11-6) so as to get them in sequence, after starting with a haphazard arrangement. Obviously the pieces must not be lifted out of the frame while attempting a solution. The number of moves necessary depends on the starting pattern, but the technique is to use the vacant space and three adjoining pieces to move around each other to get the numbers right, but complications come as the avail-

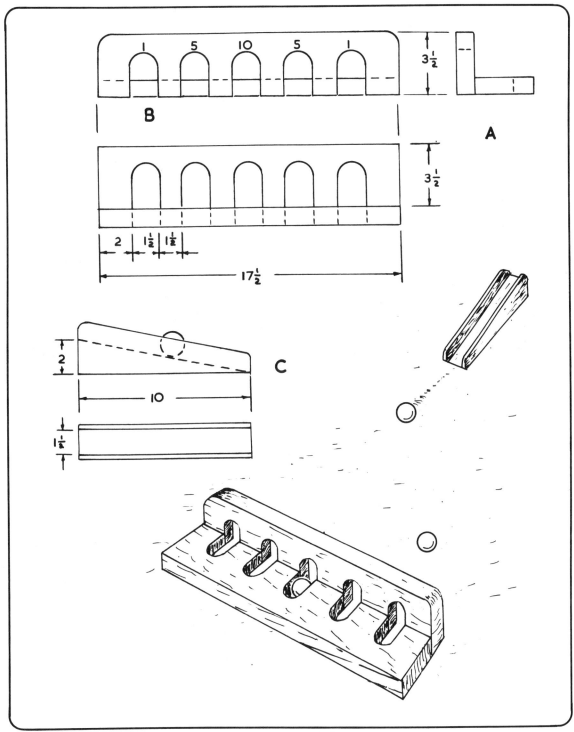

Fig. 11-5. The ball game has a target and a chute for directing the balls.

255

able moves overlap. A similar puzzle can be made with 24 tiles in 25 spaces.

The puzzle can be made of any wood and to any size. It could all be solid wood, or you could use a solid wood frame around a plywood base and tiles. The size suggested (Fig. 11-7A) is a reasonable size for a child or an adult to handle. A pocket version could be made down to half this size. It will probably be simplest to make the eight tiles first and make the case when you have been able to measure the tiles after they have been sanded. Accuracy is easier to obtain than if you work the other way around.

1. Cut a piece of wood for all tiles that is at least 13 inches long. Make sure it is parallel, then mark across squares with gaps for saw cuts (Fig. 11-7B).

2. A very fine back saw can be used for hand sawing. With a fine table saw it will be possible to cut the squares to size both ways, by using the fence.

3. Sand the edges and lightly round the corners of the tiles. They should all be the same

Fig. 11-6. In this number game the numbered tiles have to be moved from a random arrangement to consecutive order, by sliding about a framed base.

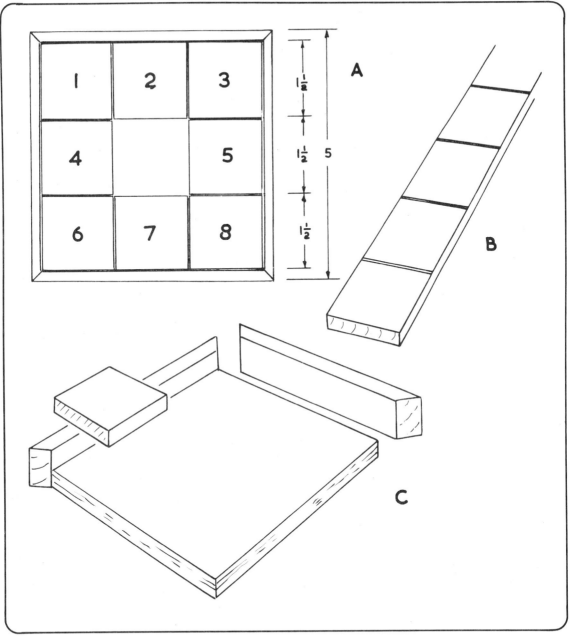

Fig. 11-7. Suggested sizes (A) and the method of construction (B,C) of the number puzzle.

size and have all angles lightly rounded, so they will slide smoothly against each other.

4. Measure across the grouped tile and make the base not more than 1/8 inch bigger. How much clearance you allow depends on the accuracy of the tile shapes, but they have to move without restriction.

5. Frame the base with mitered strips (Fig. 11-7C), to stand slightly higher than the thickness of the tiles.

6. Number the tiles. All of the parts are best finished with wax so the tiles slide easily. The case could be stained first so the tiles are more prominent.

```
         Materials List for Number Puzzle

    8 tiles       1/4  × 1 1/2 × 1 1/2
    1 base        3/8  × 4 1/2 × 4 1/2
    4 frames      1/4  × 3/4  × 6
```

GEOMETRIC PUZZLE

A pattern of straight lines can make a geometric type of jigsaw puzzle that will mystify and test the skill of adults as well as children. If marked and cut as shown (Fig. 11-8A), the parts can be reformed into at least five other geometric shapes. You could just cut a scrap of plywood into parts and challenge your friends to make other shapes, but if you provide a marked board, a child will be able to see what shapes are possible and attempt to fit the pieces in, which will still be a challenge.

Sizes are not important, but variations should be in proportion to those given. Do not settle for too small a size or piece 1 will be small enough to be easily lost. Plywood is suitable, but some of the finished angles are acute, so do not choose open-grained plywood, which might be too fragile on thin points. If you use solid wood have the grain lines as shown (Fig. 11-8B) for maximum strength at the narrow points. If the shapes are 3/8 inch or 1/2 inch thick, the marked board could be made from two thicknesses of 1/4-inch plywood, so the assembled shapes stand above their cut-out.

1. Plane a corner of the wood exactly square, then mark out the shape. Cut and plane the outline.

2. Separate the parts with the finest saw you have. Sand the edges, but do not take off any more wood than that, so the parts fit easily in the various patterns without any excess clearance.

3. Although the parts are shown with num- bers it will probably be advisable to leave the parts blank, so competitors do not know which side up to put the pieces together. The numbers on the drawing are to show you the various rearrange- ments (Fig. 11-8C).

4. If you make a marked board, it could have cut-outs for every shape, but it is simpler and ade- quate to have a cut-out in the basic shape for stor- ing the pieces and just draw the other shapes that can be made (Fig. 11-8D). Other layouts are pos- sible. Try the various assemblies and mark where you will draw them on your board. The outlines could overlap.

5. Cut out one piece for the basic shape to fit easily. Glue the panels together. For con- venience in storage the shapes of the parts could be marked in the bottom of the recess.

6. Finish the parts with paint or varnish, but a waxed finish will seal the grain and allow easy movement.

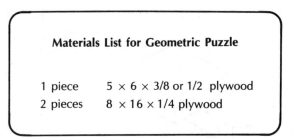

```
       Materials List for Geometric Puzzle

    1 piece       5 × 6 × 3/8 or 1/2  plywood
    2 pieces      8 × 16 × 1/4 plywood
```

RING GAME

Children of all ages like games where rings have to be thrown over pegs to score points. There are many ring games, but this one is unusual. The tar- get is made of three strips forming a pattern (Fig. 11-9), with posts at crossings and a set of rings to be thrown over them. The frame goes flat on the floor and the distance the thrower stands can be adjusted to suit age. There are seven pegs, each marked with a number. If seven rings are made, the rules can allow double score if all seven rings are put over pegs, or even higher scores if all seven pegs are ringed—make your own rules.

The target is made of three pieces of 1-by-2-inch section, which could be hard or soft- wood. The pegs are pieces of 3/4- or 5/8-inch dowel rod. The rings are made from 1/2-inch ply-

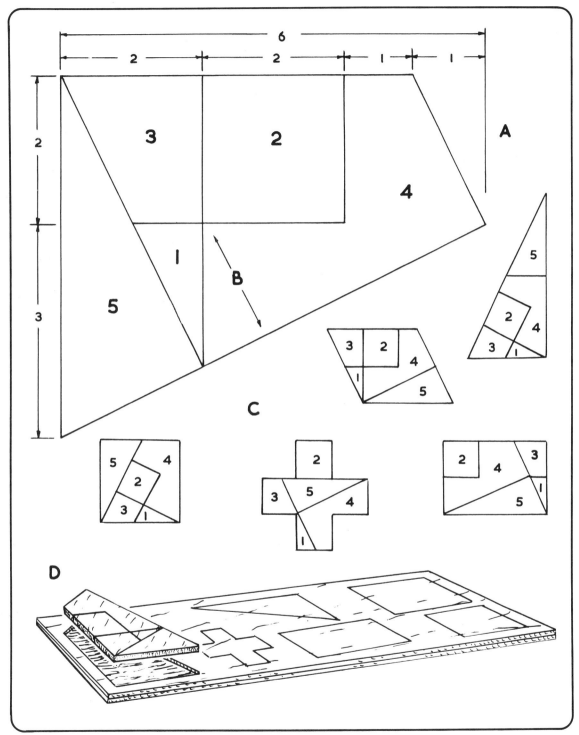

Fig. 11-8. The parts of this geometric puzzle can be rearranged into various patterns.

wood, a bright color paint is probably the best finish.

1. Prepare three straight pieces of wood, longer than the finished sizes. Two 24 inches and one 30 inches will do, if the sizes suggested (Fig. 11-10) are to be used.

2. Set out the centerlines of the strips (Fig. 11-10A). Draw two lines at 60 degrees to each other. Measure 9 inches along each line from the point and draw another across. With 60 degrees at the point this should give 9 inches between the crossings. Measure a further 9 inches outwards from the crossings along each line. The points are the centers of the pegs and the angles of the lines

crossing are those of the joints you will cut.

3. With the peg positions as centers for your compass, draw the curved ends of all pieces.

4. Halving joints have to be cut at the three crossings so the lower edges of the target will be level on the floor. Gauge half the thickness at each crossing. Mark the widths of each piece at the angle it will cross the other piece. Square this down to the half thickness line.

5. Pencil on the waste wood that has to be cut out and check from this that you will be cutting away the correct side. At peg 1 position leave the ends square, to be rounded after joining the parts.

6. Cut the joints (Fig. 11-11A). Pare out the

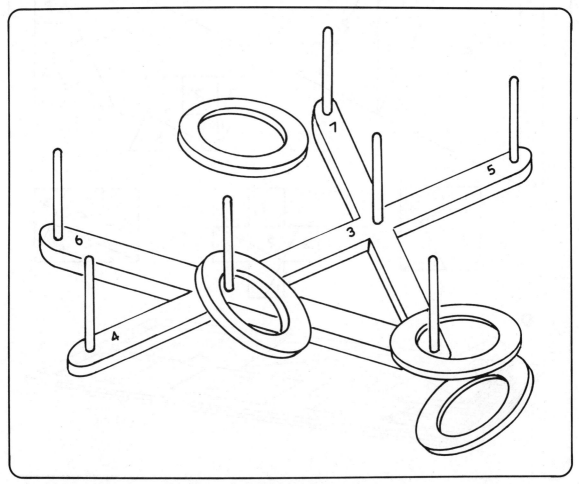

Fig. 11-9. This ring game has seven pegs at the crossings of three strips.

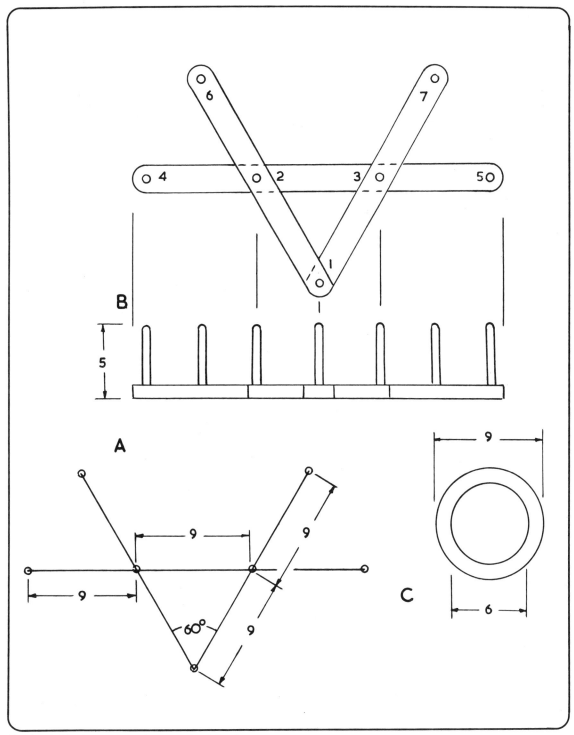

Fig. 11-10. The layout (A) and sizes (B,C) of the ring game parts.

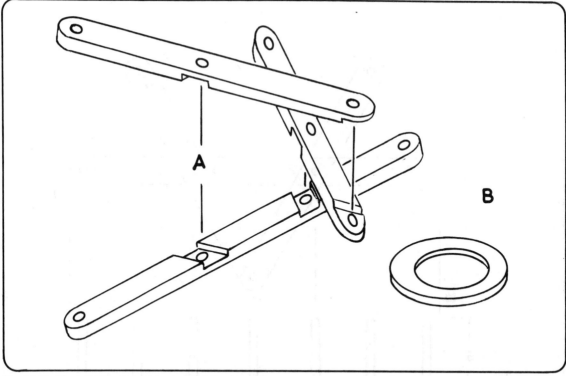

Fig. 11-11. The strips for the ring game are halved together.

bottom of each joint so surfaces will come level during assembly.

7. Round all ends, except at peg 1. Glue the joints.

8. Drill for the dowel pegs. If they are a good fit it will be sufficient to glue them in. If there is any slackness, saw across their ends so wedges can be driven in. A suitable height is 5 inches (Fig. 11-10B). Taller pegs make scoring easier. Short pegs tend to let the pegs jump off. Round the tops of the pegs before gluing them in.

9. The rings may be jigsawn from 1/2-inch plywood (Fig. 11-11B). If possible, choose plywood made from five or more veneers rather than that made from only three thick ones; it will be stronger in a comparatively narrow ring (Fig. 11-10C). If you have a lathe, it might be possible to turn the rings on a faceplate. In any case, round the edges inside and out for comfortable handling. Seven rings are needed for a set, but it will be worthwhile making a few spares.

10. Paint the wood. The pegs could be in a color contrasting with the base. Paint on the numbers or use decals. Clear varnish over the numbers will prevent damage by the rings.

Materials List for Ring Game

2 strips	1 × 2 × 24
1 strip	1 × 2 × 30
7 pegs	6 × 3/4 or 5/8 diameter dowel rod
7 rings	9 × 9 × 1/2 plywood

PUSH TRUCK

When a child is beginning to walk, a box on wheels that can be pushed along provides interest because toys and blocks can be loaded into it and the handle provides something to hold, steadying uncertain legs.

This truck (Fig. 11-12) is a simple box on four wheels with a bar handle at a suitable height. The drawing (Fig. 11-13) shows a possible load of assorted bricks, but they are extras. A reasonable width is advisable to provide steadiness. If the truck is for a particular child, you might wish to adjust the handle height to suit. Wheels of 4-inch diameter are shown. If you intend to buy wheels, do so first, in case you have to make adjustments to suit their size. They should not project past the end of the box. The forward wheels are then arranged conveniently for tipping the load.

Any wood could be used, but the truck might get some rough treatment, so avoid anything that could crack or splinter. Round all edges and corners thoroughly. Bright colors are appropriate, but avoid paint that could be dangerous if bitten.

1. Make the box first. Corners should be dovetailed or you could make comb joints, but it should be sufficient to overlap the sides on the ends and screw them. The sides (Fig. 11-14A) are given some shaping, for ease in loading. Round the upper edges of all parts.

2. Glue and nail on the plywood bottom and round its edges.

3. Position the axle strips (Figs. 11-13A and 11-14B) so the wheel rims come about level with the ends of the box. Let them extend 1/4 inch each side. Use glue and nails through the bottom.

4. The handle sides (Fig. 11-13B) are shown at 60 degrees, which should be satisfactory, but

Fig. 11-12. A push truck helps a child just learning to walk, and is somewhere to store and move toys.

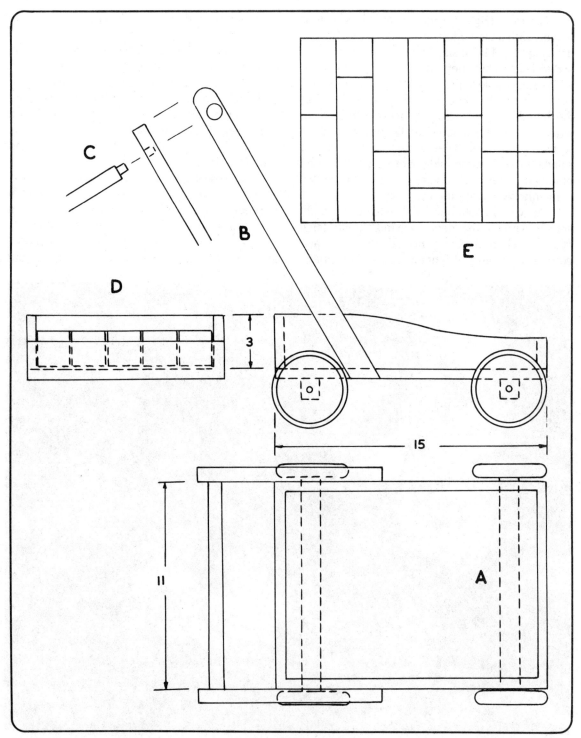

Fig. 11-13. Suggested sizes for the push truck and an arrangement of wood blocks.

you might wish to experiment with the young user. The top is taken far enough to avoid end grain breaking out at the handle (Fig. 11-14C).

5. The handle is a piece of dowel rod. It is shown reduced at its ends (Fig. 11-13C), but a lathe is needed to do that successfully. Alternatively, drill the sides for the full diameter of the dowel. A pin across each joint will supplement the glue.

6. Screw the handles to the box sides in a position that will clear the wheels.

7. Metal or plastic wheels might not have very large holes. They can be attached with large wood screws (Fig. 11-14D). Arrange a washer each side of the wheel and choose a screw long enough

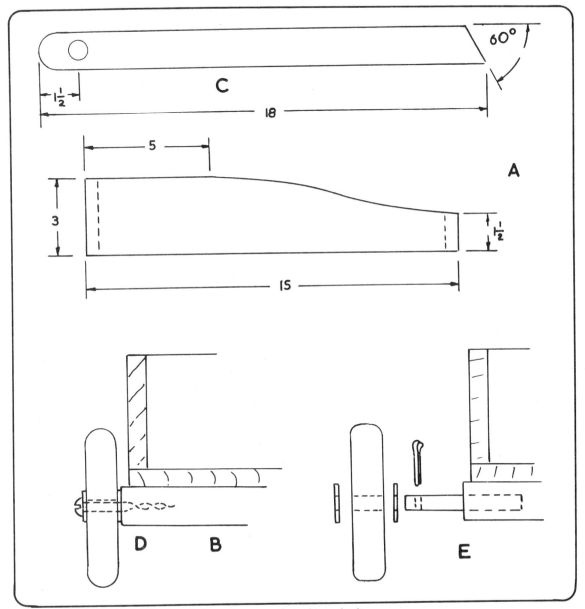

Fig. 11-14. Sizes of the push truck and alternative ways of attaching wheels.

for its plain neck to be in the wheel and all of the threaded part in the wood. The screw should penetrate the wood at least 1 inch for adequate strength in end grain.

8. If you make wheels on a lathe a suitable size is 4 inches diameter and 3/4 inch thick. You could drill them for wood screw axles, but a larger hole will allow you to use pieces of dowel rod into the axle strips so it projects far enough to take the wheel, its washers, and a split pin through a hole (Fig. 11-14E).

9. The size of the inside of the box is in multiples of 2 inches both ways (Fig. 11-13D), so if you make a load of blocks, they should be based on 2-inch cubes. You could make 35 cubes, but mother might find these rather more than she wants to see scattered around a room. It might be better to make up a pattern of mostly longer blocks (Fig. 11-13E), which can still be built into walls and should prove educational when packing into the truck.

10. Finish in the desired colors, but make sure the paint is absolutely hard before letting a child play with the toy.

Materials List for Push Truck		
2 sides	1/2 × 3 × 16	
1 end	1/2 × 3 × 12	
1 end	1/2 × 1 1/2 × 12	
1 bottom	12 × 16 × 1/4 plywood	
2 handle sides	3/4 × 1 1/2 × 19	
1 handle	13 × 3/4 diameter dowel rod	
Bricks from	2 × 2 × 75	

FOLD-FLAT PLAY HOUSE

Young children delight in having a house of their own that is large enough to play inside. Its bulk, however, particularly if it is to be used indoors, makes it almost impossible to consider if it has to remain full-size—unless you are one of those rare families with more rooms than you can find use for. Even if the play house is to be used outside, it might have to be brought in for the winter, which presents a difficult storage problem.

The answer for most homes is to make the play house to fold. Its reduced size may then make storage possible in the garage or elsewhere.

This play house (Fig. 11-15) is designed to be cut economically from standard plywood sheets. It covers a floor area about 38 inches wide and 44 inches long. Total height is 48 inches. When folded the height and length remain the same, but the thickness reduces to 5 or 6 inches. Then there is a folded roof 24 by 48 inches and 3 inches thick, plus two pieces of floor plywood about 19 by 48 inches. If the folded parts have to be stored together, the total thickness is about 9 inches.

The front and back are similar pieces. The ends are each in two parts, hinged at the center. They are also hinged inside to the back and front, so they can be folded between them (Fig. 11-16A) until the package is flat. Two pieces of plywood form the floor and they drop inside to lock the bottoms of the ends in the open position (Fig. 11-16B). The back and front of the roof are hinged along the ridge and their framing is arranged to drop into the walls and lock the tops in the open position (Fig. 11-16C).

There is a choice of materials. The skin could be hardboard, but plywood would be stronger—1/4 inch should be adequate, but you could use thicker if you wish. This is framed all around inside with softwood strips. In most places these could be a 1-inch-square section, but where some hinges come or the edge has to be bevelled they should be of a 1-by-2-inch section. There is no need for cut joints between the framing parts. The strips get their stiffness by being glued and pinned through the plywood.

The drawings show a door and window opening in the front only. There could be windows in other walls and a back door if you wish. The window could be glazed with clear plastic and many additions are possible so long as they do not interfere with folding.

If you decide to alter the size there is only one important consideration. When the ends fold inwards they must be narrow enough to avoid each other. Keep the width of the house about 6 inches less than the length.

Fig. 11-15. This play house is large enough for a large child to get in, but it will fold flat for storage.

1. Start by making the ends (Fig. 11-17A). You need two matching pairs. Frame all around with 1-inch-square strips. Although there will be hinges on the sides, there is no need for 2-inch strips on them. Glue the strips on and use enough fine pins to keep the surfaces close—probably 3-inch spacing.

2. The framing for the openings in the front (Fig. 11-17B) will provide enough stiffness. If the back is not cut open and appears to need stiffen-

ing take strips across its center. The outlines of front and back are the same. Use 2-inch strips on the vertical edges. At the top use 2-inch strips and cut the plywood and the strip to match the slope of the roof (Fig. 11-17C). Use the edge of an end panel as a guide to height and angle. Cut the door and window openings and frame around them.

3. The ends and sides could be joined with hinges on the surface, but the joints will be closer if they are let in (Fig. 11-16D) the ends. Where the

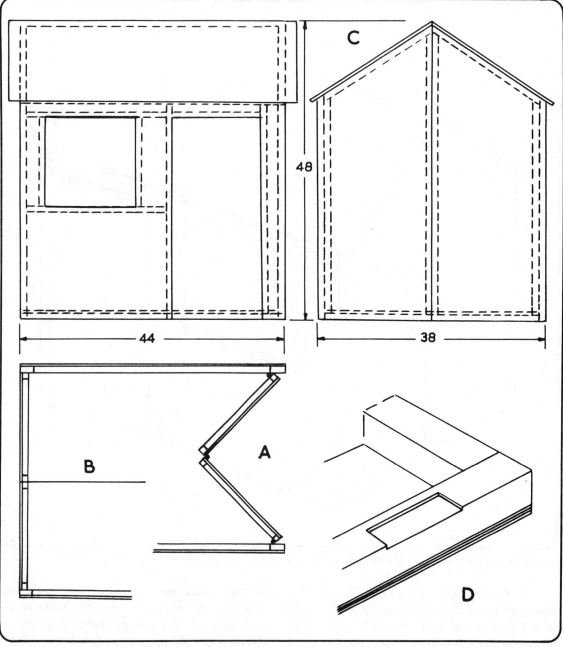

Fig. 11-16. Sizes and method of folding the play house.

long edges of the ends have to be joined, the hinges could be on the surface of the plywood. Hinges come outside of the center joint and inside the others (Fig. 11-16A). Joints should be satisfactory with 2-inch hinges about 18 inches apart.

4. Hinge the walls and check their opening and closing actions. Use the opened assembly as a guide when making the roof and floor.

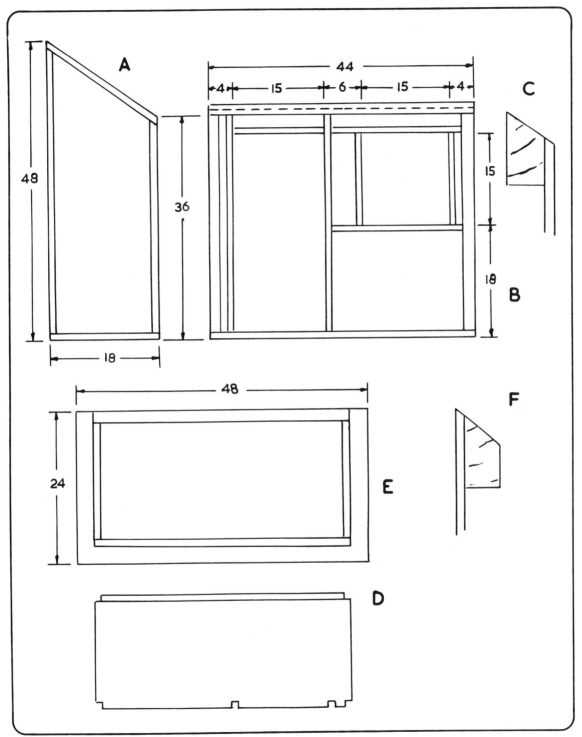

Fig. 11-17. Sizes of the parts of a fold-flat play house.

5. The floor is plywood. If 1/2 inch is used, there should be no need for framing underneath except where the two edges meet along the center (Fig. 11-17D). Cut the plywood to rest on all the bottom framing around the walls with notches at all upright parts. You cannot make the floor in one piece because that would be almost impossible to put in and out, unless it is made very slack.

6. The roof overhangs the walls by about 2 inches all around (Fig. 11-17E). With the walls as a guide, mark the positions of framing strips that will drop inside. They keep the walls in shape, but you need to be able to attach the roof without undue force.

7. Use 1-inch strips except at the ridge, where 2-inch strips have to be bevelled to meet (Fig. 11-17F). They are hinged together along this edge.

8. Put all the parts together and check assembly and disassembly.

9. The door is a piece of plywood that is framed around, to make an easy fit in the opening. Hinge it at one side. A triangle of plywood in the top corner can act as a stop. Fit a spring catch. Any fastener that needs a positive action to open or close might be too much for a young user. Fit a knob at a suitable height. A handle inside will be needed for closing, but put it inside the framing so it does not interfere with folding the house.

10. There are a lot of edges that need sharpness taken off. Round all corners. Children grow rapidly, so corners—such as the roof, which might be out of reach now—could be hazardous in a few months.

11. You will spend a considerable time finishing the house. There can be overall "house" colors outside. Light colors are better inside. Walls could be papered. There could be pictures. It would be possible to provide shelves, but they would have to be taken down for folding. Clothes hooks could be added without interfering with folding. Curtains might hang inside the window, whether that is an open space or covered with clear plastic.

Materials List for Fold-Flat Play House			
4 ends	18 × 48 ×	1/4 plywood
4 strips	1 × 1 × 48	
4 strips	1 × 1 × 36	
8 strips	1 × 1 × 24	
1 back	36 × 44 ×	1/4 plywood
1 strip	1 × 2 × 45	
1 strip	1 × 1 × 45	
2 strips	1 × 2 × 36	
1 front	36 × 44 ×	1/4 plywood
1 strip	1 × 2 × 45	
2 strips	1 × 1 × 45	
2 strips	1 × 1 × 36	
2 strips	1 × 2 × 36	
5 strips	1 × 1 × 24	
2 roofs	24 × 48 ×	1/4 plywood
2 strips	1 × 2 × 44	
2 strips	1 × 1 × 44	
4 strips	1 × 1 × 20	
2 floors	19 × 44 ×	1/2 plywood
2 strips	1 × 1 × 44	
1 door	15 × 33 ×	1/4 plywood
2 strips	1 × 1 × 33	
2 strips	1 × 1 × 15	

PERISCOPE

A toy that allows a child to look over walls or around corners will have enormous appeal. Whatever his age he can discover many ways of amusing himself with a periscope. It can also be useful when he wants to see something higher that his present stature allows. Adults can use it also, if they want to look onto a shelf above eye level or watch an event over the heads of a crowd.

A periscope contains two mirrors facing each other and at 45 degrees to their container. If you look into one you will see the other mirror and whatever is reflected in that. Because there are two mirrors involved, what you see will be the right way around and not reversed as it is when you look into a single mirror.

A periscope can be almost any size or length. A submarine has a very long one, but it works in the same way. How much you can see with a simple periscope depends on the size of the mirrors, particularly the top viewing one. You could manage with a smaller sighting mirror, but that complicates construction, so it is easier to use two mirrors of the same size.

The size of the periscope depends on the available mirrors. Large mirrors give a greater coverage, but the resulting periscope might be too heavy for a child to use. This periscope (Fig. 11-18) is designed around two vanity mirrors 2 1/2 inches by 3 1/2 inches, such as might be carried in a lady's purse (Fig. 11-19). Any two identical mirrors about this size could be used and the wood sections altered to suit.

It might be possible to make most of the parts from plywood, but softwood will make the lightest periscope. Decide on the length you want. That shown lifts the view about 12 inches, but it could be more or less. Prepare wood to suit.

1. The key parts are the pair of sides (Fig. 11-19A). Measure the size of a mirror and mark that at 45 degrees across the wood (Fig. 11-19B). That gives you the width to plane the wood.

2. Mark and cut the slots to take the mirrors (Fig. 11-19C). The angles of these slots are the important considerations if the view through it is to be correct (Fig. 11-19D). Make the mirrors a push fit in the slots. If necessary you can pack paper behind the mirror during assembly.

3. Make the back and front to overlap the sides. The width will be controlled by the sizes of the mirrors in the slots. Length is the same as the sides.

4. Cut away opposite the mirrors (Fig. 11-19E). The top hole should be as large as the area of view covered by the top mirror. Take the sharpness off the edges. Getting the maximum size is not quite so critical at the bottom, but the edge of the hole should be rounded because it might be pushed close to the face.

5. The ends (Fig. 11-19F) cover the edges of the other parts. Although a very young user might grasp the box with both hands, others will be glad for a handle to hold the periscope up to eye level. The simple handle shown is a piece of 5/8-inch dowel rod 4 inches long, held with a screw through

the bottom (Fig. 11-19G). With a lathe you can make a better handle, including a piece to go through a hole in the bottom.

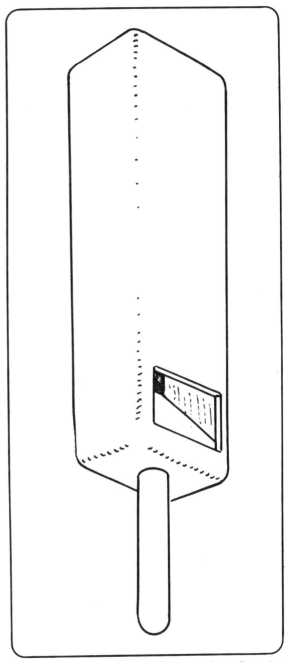

Fig. 11-18. A periscope is a toy with practical uses for seeing around obstructions.

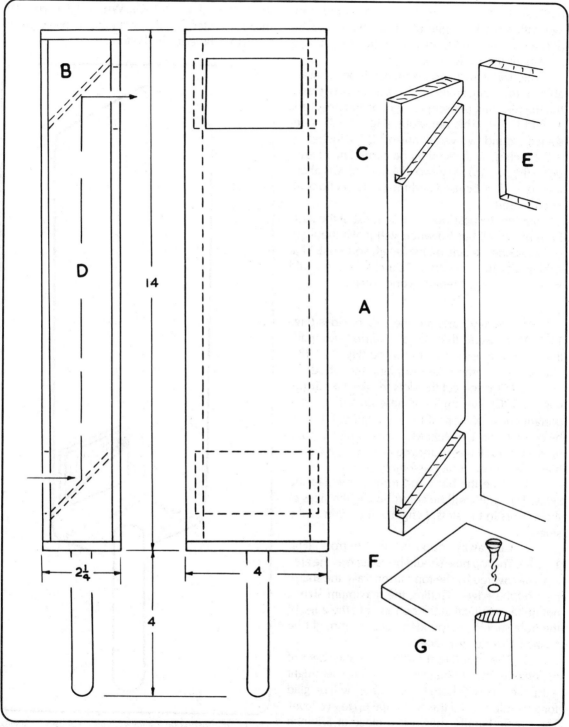

Fig. 11-19. Sizes and construction of the periscope.

6. The inside of the box could be left untreated, but you can avoid unwanted reflections by painting the inner surfaces with a dull black paint.

7. Assemble the parts with glue and thin nails or screws. Round all edges and corners. Finish the outside in any way you wish.

Materials List for Periscope	
2 sides	1/2 × 2 × 14
2 sides	1/4 × 4 × 14
2 ends	1/4 × 2 1/4 × 5
1 handle	4 × 5/8 diameter

TOY BOX

A chest to contain toys helps to encourage tidiness and is useful if toys have to be moved from place to place. If it is a height to sit on, it becomes a spare seat. A similar chest can have other uses. A larger version would become a blanket box. There could be casters underneath so the young user might tow his treasures about.

This box (Fig. 11-20) can have a skin of hardboard or thin plywood. If it is only to be used for a few years, hardboard would be suitable, but for longer life or use as part of the furniture of a room, veneered plywood and matching hardwood strips would make an attractive chest. The method of construction can be the same for either material. Nearly all parts are joined with glue and fine nails

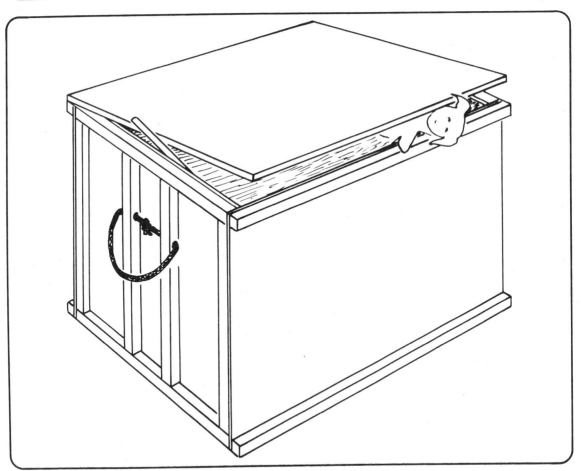

Fig. 11-20. A toy box keeps toys together, can be carried about, and may be used as a seat.

or pins. The design has all the framing outside, so there is nothing projecting to interfere with removing any of the contents. Rope loop handles are suggested on the ends, but there could be wood or metal handles.

All of the framing is 3/4-inch-square wood. For the lightest box and a painted finish this could be softwood. For a clear finish it would be better of hardwood matching the plywood.

1. Make the two ends first because they control other sizes (Fig. 11-21A). Cut the plywood panels to size and frame around the edges with strips, letting the horizontal strips cover the ends of the vertical ones (Fig. 11-22A). Glue the strips on and use fine nails at about 3-inch intervals, driven through the plywood into the strips.

2. If rope handles are to be fitted, prepare two strips for each end (Fig. 11-21B). Drill them to take the rope and fit them in place (Fig. 11-22B).

3. The side panels (Fig. 11-22C) have strips along top and bottom edges and overlap the ends. At the corners use glue and nails through the plywood, but where the strips overlap, drill for dowels (Fig. 11-21C).

4. Cut the bottom (Fig. 11-22D) to overlap the other parts. It could be fitted without framing, but it is shown with strips across the ends. You could frame all around or there could be square blocks under the corners, which would be suitable for attaching casters.

5. The lid (Fig. 11-22E) is a piece of plywood, 1/2 inch or more thick.

6. Two 2- or 3-inch hinges should be used. For a close-fitting lid, fix the hinges on the surface of the plywood, but let most of the total thickness into the strip (Fig. 11-21D). Because the plywood is not thick enough to give screws a good grip, it is better to use rivets with countersunk heads outside and the ends hammered into the countersunk holes of the hinge (Fig. 11-21E). Choose copper or other soft metal for the rivets.

7. Although the drawings show square corners, it is advisable to round all projections and edges and sand all surfaces, so there is no roughness anywhere.

8. Apply the chosen finish. Fit rope loops at the ends, with the knots between the uprights. Allow enough slack for comfortable gripping.

Materials List for Toy Box	
2 end panels	15 × 15 × 1/8 hardboard or 1/4 plywood
2 side panels	15 × 22 × 1/8 hardboard or 1/4 plywood
1 bottom	16 × 22 × 1/8 hardboard or 1/4 plywood
1 lid	16 × 22 × 1/2 plywood
8 end frames	3/4 × 3/4 × 14
4 end frames	3/4 × 3/4 × 15
4 side frames	3/4 × 3/4 × 22
2 bottom frames	3/4 × 3/4 × 17

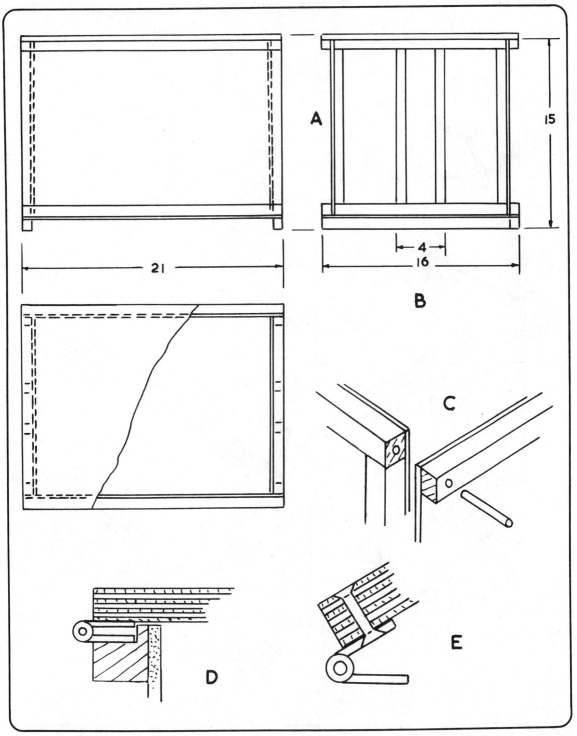

Fig. 11-21. Sizes and joint details of the toy box.

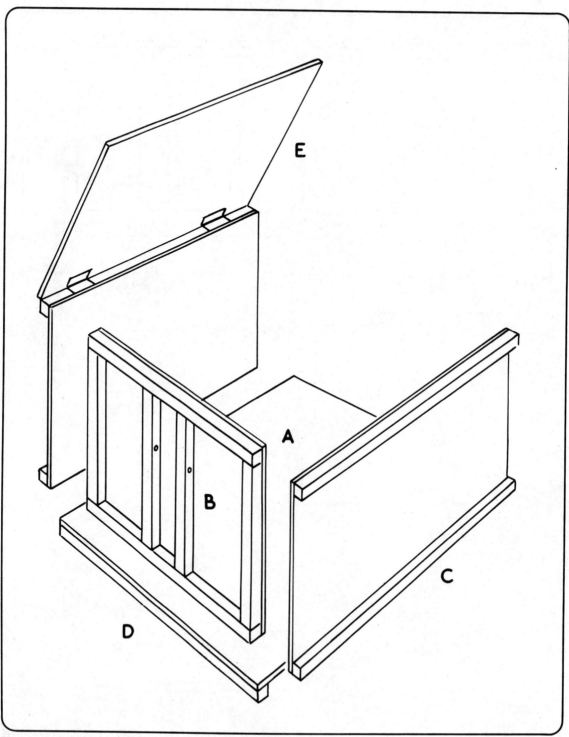

Fig. 11-22. How the parts of the toy box are assembled.

Chapter 12

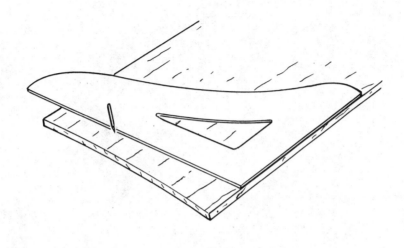

Tools

Being able to use the tools you have accumulated to make things is very satisfying. What is even more satisfying is making some of the tools to use in your hobby or occupation. Although it is possible to make some metal tools, this book is concerned with woodwork, so only wooden tools are described in this chapter.

Most wooden tools are concerned with holding or testing your work, so they have to be made accurately—but accuracy should be a major concern in your shop in any case. The truth of tools you make will be reflected in the accuracy of the things you make in your shop. Where appropriate, use close-grained hardwood that will stand up to wear. It is disappointing to put effort into making something of an inferior wood, then find it soon wears out of true.

DEPTH GAUGE

You can buy an engineering depth gauge. It will measure to any reasonable depth, but its stock is usually only a few inches long, so it will only span across a comparatively narrow opening—certainly much narrower than a woodworker will often use. This particularly applies to turning bowls and similar hollow things on a lathe. As you progress you need to know how deep below the rim level you have to cut, otherwise you might turn the wood so it is too thin for strength. You might also stop before you should. A depth gauge for checking bowls should be at least as far across as the largest bowl you expect to make and be able to adjust as deep as necessary.

A suitable depth gauge can be made of wood (Fig. 12-1). The sizes shown (Fig. 12-2A) should suit most woodworking requirements. An excessive length, just because you might need it one day, could be clumsy for general use. The depth probe is a piece of dowel rod, so if you ever need a longer one, a replacement is easily provided.

Any wood could be used, but polished hardwood for the stock looks good. The probe is hard-

Fig. 12-1. One use for a depth gauge is in checking the depth of a bowl being turned on a lathe.

wood dowelling. The wedge could be contrasting hardwood.

1. The stock and its hole must be accurate, so carefully square the wood and mark the position of the probe hole (Fig. 12-2B). It might be advisable to mark the hole position on top and bottom surfaces, then drill part way from both sides to ensure squareness. The hole should make a sliding fit on the dowel rod. If the first drilling does not satisfy you, start again on another piece of wood. This prevents wasted effort or wood that might have resulted had you shaped before drilling.

2. Make the wedge (Fig. 12-2C) 3/8 inch thick. The exact taper is not critical. Round the ends and a short distance back from each end, but leave the part that goes through the stock with square edges.

3. Mark the stock on both sides for the slot, which has its inner surfaces level with the hole. Use the wedge as a guide to the width and angle of the slot as you cut it. When the wedge is about halfway through the slot it should begin to emerge into the side of the hole, so when the tool is assembled the wedge will press against the side of the probe if it is pushed in. Leave final trimming of the sloping side of the slot until the other parts are completed and you can make a trial assembly.

4. Shape the stock, starting by thinning towards the ends and rounding them (Fig. 12-2D). This is not essential, but it improves appearance. The other way shape down to the ends (Fig. 12-2E).

Leave a short distance flat on the top. Leave the bottom flat and true.

5. The probe is shown 5 inches long (Fig. 12-2F), which should be enough for most turned bowls, but it could be any other length you require. The end that goes into the bowl can be tapered and the tip rounded. The other end could be rounded or left flat.

6. Try the parts together. Adjust the slot so the wedge secures the probe when slightly less than half the length of the wedge is through the stock. You might be able to lock the joint with

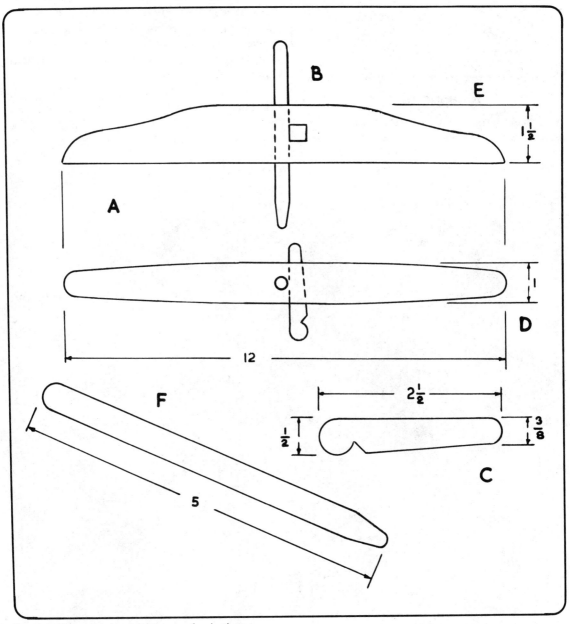

Fig. 12-2. Suggested sizes of the parts of a depth gauge.

hand pressure, or use a light tap with a hammer to tighten or loosen the wedge.

7. Wax on the probe will ease its adjustment. The stock could be varnished or polished.

Materials List for Depth Gauge	
1 stock	1 × 1 1/2 × 13
1 probe	6 × 3/8 dowel rod
1 wedge	3/8 × 1/2 × 3

MARKING GAUGE

You might already have a marking gauge in your woodworking tool kit, but an extra one is always useful. If a gauge is set to a size you will need again, a second one allows you to mark another width without having to reset the first. This reduces the risk of error. If you do not have even one marking gauge, it is a tool you can make, that should be as efficient as anything you might buy.

Purchased marking gauges use a screw to lock the stock to the stem. Although there are ways of arranging screw adjustments, most of us do not have the facilities for making them, so this marking gauge (Fig. 12-3) uses a wedge, which is a good traditional means of locking.

Use a close-grained hardwood. Some of the best traditional marking gauges were made of rosewood, but you are unlikely to find that. The tool looks good if the wedge is a different color hard-

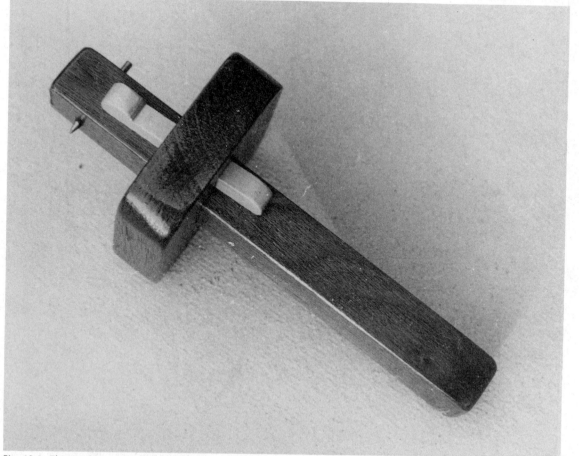

Fig. 12-3. This marking gauge has its stem locked with a wedge.

wood. The stem is usually made square, but it could be made of 3/4-inch hardwood dowel rod, which would simplify fitting because you only have to drill a hole in the stock. However, a round stem might turn in use unless wedged very tightly.

1. Prepare the wood for the stock and stem (Fig. 12-4A). Both can be left overlength until they have been fitted to each other. The stem is shown 7 inches long, which should be adequate for most settings and long enough to give a good grip.

2. Mark a square hole through the middle of the stock. It is advisable to do this on both sides, so you can cut the hole both ways and avoid the risk of the surface grain breaking out. Drill away most of the waste and cut the hole to shape. It should slide on the stem with minimum slackness, although some stiffness at first is acceptable. If a round stem is to be used, drill the stock for it (Fig. 12-4B).

3. The stock can be trimmed square and its corners rounded (Fig. 12-4C). Another shape is shown (Fig. 12-4D) with a curve to fit the hand. If the mortise gauge addition is to be used (see instruction 7) it will be better to make the stock square.

4. Make the wedge (Fig. 12-4E). It is 1/4 inch thick. Both ends are the same height. The exact taper is unimportant. The knob at the low end prevents the wedge from being pushed out of the stock, except when the stem has been removed.

5. Mark both sides of the stock for the slot for the wedge. At first, mark the low side to the wedge depth close to the knob and the other side to the depth 3/4 inch from that. Try the assembly and the action of the wedge. When at the low position the stem should slide freely, but when you push or knock in the wedge the assembly should lock tightly and squarely. If you have a round stem, the bottom of the wedge could be flat, but it will grip better if it is hollowed to match the rod used for the stem.

6. The marking pin (Fig. 12-4F) should be a drive fit in a hole in the stem. Ideally, it is a piece of tool steel wire under 1/16 inch in diameter, with a sharpened point. In practice, a nail (which is

made of the softer mild steel) will have a very long life and can be sharpened with a file.

7. If you mark out mortise and tenon joints frequently there are, almost certainly, some widths you use for many of them. Quite often these are 1/4 inch and 3/8 inch. It is possible to add marking pins for stock widths to your marking gauge. Make them by driving in fine nails at the correct distances apart on the faces square to the main marking pin (Fig. 12-4G). Cut each nail off about 1/8 inch above the wood and file a point on it. Try marking with the gauge. The widths between the marks can be adjusted to exactly what you want by filing the sides of the points. Make sure the points extend the same amounts.

8. The pins for marking mortises are shown at the same end of the stem as the main pin. You could put them at the other end and have up to four different widths, but if you do that you will not be able to take the gauge apart, except by removing the main pin and sliding the stock off that way. There is another advantage in having all the pins at one end. You can then use the other end as a pencil gauge, by setting the end of the stem at the correct distance from the stock and holding a pencil against it as it is pushed or pulled along the wood.

9. Varnish or hard polish would be inappropriate for this tool, but a rub with wax will improve appearance and lubricate the parts for adjusting and when they move against the wood being marked.

Materials List for Marking Gauge	
1 stem	5/8 × 5/8 × 8
1 stock	3/4 × 2 1/2 × 3
1 wedge	1/4 × 3/8 × 3

MORTISE GAUGE

The adaption of the ordinary marking gauge, as just described, allows you to mark certain standard widths of mortises and tenons, but if you need to mark other widths you have to adjust and gauge the lines with two settings of the single marking

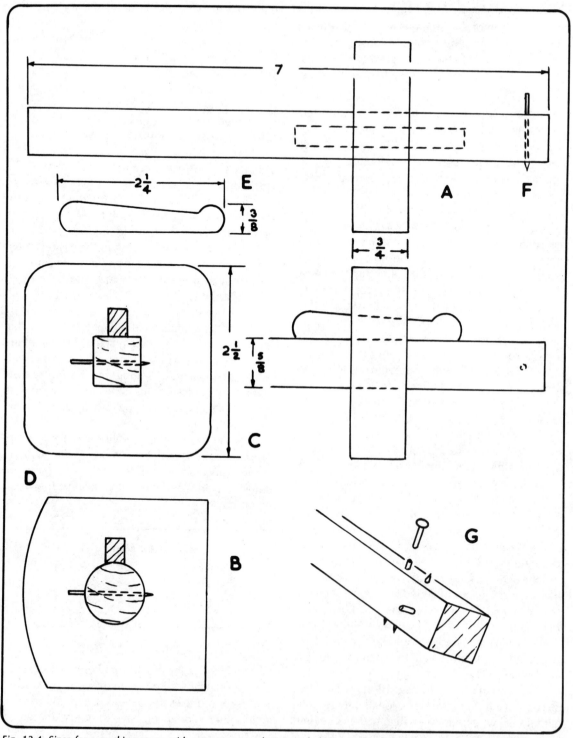

Fig. 12-4. Sizes for a marking gauge with square or round stem and alternative shapes of stock.

pin. It is better to have adjustable dual pins so you can mark both lines at the same time. There are screw-adjustment mortise gauges available, but you can make a mortise gauge in a similar way to the marking gauge, which can be used to mark lines at any distance apart—from 1/4 inch upwards.

Mortise and tenon joints do not usually have to be made very far from the edges of the wood, so the gauge could be shorter than the marking gauge (Fig. 12-5). The stem is divided and there is a separate wedge shown for each part (Fig. 12-6A). It would be possible to put one wedge on top of the stem, then tighten it after both parts have

been adjusted. With two wedges, however, it is easier to get each point at exactly the distance from the stock that is required, without affecting the adjustment of the other one. Read the instructions for the last project for more details of some processes of construction.

Similar hardwood to that described for the marking gauge can be used. Sizes could be altered, but those shown make a gauge that is comfortable to grip and easy to use.

1. Prepare the strips for the stem 3/8 inch thick and 5/8 inch wide. Glue on the piece at the

Fig. 12-5. A mortise gauge has two stems through the stock, with their own wedges so they can be adjusted separately.

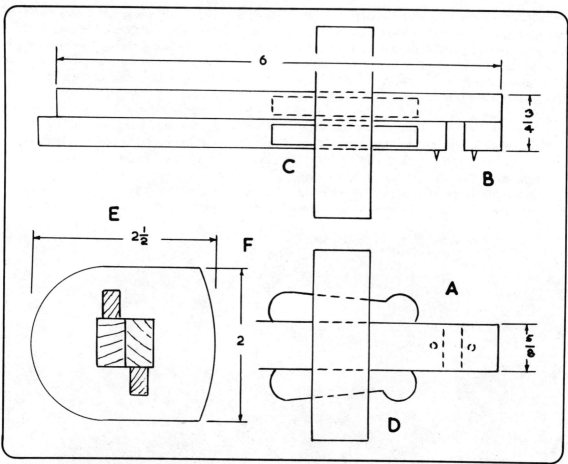

Fig. 12-6. Sizes of the mortise gauge.

end of the top part (Fig. 12-6B).

2. The pins are nails driven in and cut off, then filed to points as described for the mortise points on the marking gauge. Because they should be no more than 1/8 inch from the meeting ends of the wood, if you want to gauge lines 1/4 inch apart, it is advisable to drill slightly undersize holes for the nails and drive and file them before cutting the wood ends to size, to reduce the risk of splitting. If you start with the stem parts too long and anything goes wrong at this stage, you can cut off and try again.

3. Mark out and cut the hole in the stock, so the two parts of the stem will slide through (Fig. 12-6C).

4. Make the wedges similar to those for the

marking gauge, but they could be shortened to 2 inches (Fig. 12-6D). Cut their slots in the stock so they are on opposite sides and central over their own piece of stem (Fig. 12-6E). Try the action. Each part of stem should slide when its wedge is at the lower end, then be stopped when the wedge is pushed or knocked in.

5. A different outline of stock is shown (Fig.

Materials List for Mortise Gauge	
2 stems	3/8 × 5/8 × 7
1 stock	3/4 × 2 × 3
2 wedges	1/4 × 3/8 × 3

284

12-6F), but either of the shapes shown for the marking gauge could be used, or this shape used on that gauge.

6. Make a trial assembly and test gauging at various widths, then wax all parts before final assembly.

CENTER SQUARES

Some combination squares have a centering head. This is useful for finding the centers of comparatively small circular objects, but is not so much use if you want to draw lines square to very large curves, such as a patio border of 10 feet radius or the many irregular curves found in boat building. The type of center square used then is sometimes given the contradictory name of "round square."

A square for use on large curves has two pegs to press against the curved edge and a long blade with its edge square to a line between the pegs (Fig. 12-7). Two sizes are suggested. One is small with a simple outline (Fig. 12-8A). The other is larger with a slightly more complicated outline (Fig. 12-8B).

The squares could be made of solid wood or plywood. If considerable use is expected, a close-

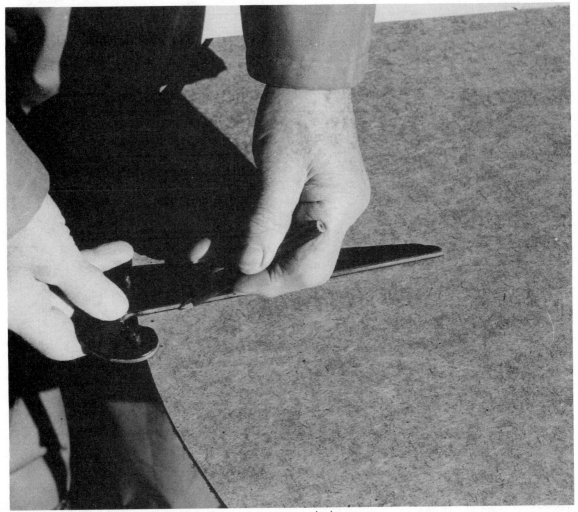

Fig. 12-7. A center square is used to draw lines square to a curved edge.

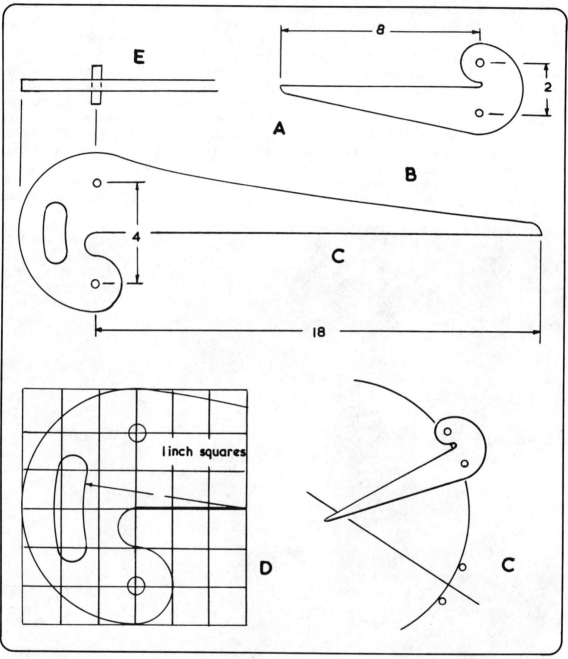

Fig. 12-8. Sizes for two center squares.

grained hardwood with a polished finish will be durable and good-looking. The pegs could be hardwood dowel rod or you could turn them from the same wood as the flat part.

The squares work on the geometric principle that if you draw a chord across the circumference of a circle (as represented by the pair of pegs), a line bisecting the chord (the edge of the blade) will point to the center of the circle and cross it if long enough (Fig. 12-8C). If a line is drawn along it and the process repeated at one or more other positions, the lines will cross at the center. Even when the circle is too big for the blade to reach the center, the line you draw will be square to the circumference. For all practical purposes this also applies to other curves, such as an ellipse or the curve of the gunwale of a boat. From this it will be seen that the important part of the construction is getting the blade edge straight and central and square to a line between the pegs. Other parts of the outline could affect appearance, but they will not affect accuracy. The pegs may project both sides, so the square can be used either side up.

1. Mark out the large square from a centerline which will be the edge of the blade (Fig. 12-8C). Mark out the positions of the peg centers (Fig. 12-8D) and the other parts around them. The slot is for convenience in handling and to lighten the end so the tool is unlikely to tip if left over the end of a piece of wood.

2. Cut the outline and drill for the pegs. The straight edge should be kept square, but the other edges can be rounded. Hollowing the back of the blade lightens the tool.

3. For most purposes the pegs may project 1/2 inch each side (Fig. 12-8E), but they could be longer if you expect to deal with edges rounded in their thickness. Make sure the holes are drilled squarely and the pegs are a tight fit, so they are perpendicular to the surface when glued in.

Materials List for Center Squares

Large square
1 piece	3/8 × 6 × 21
2 pegs	1 1/2 × 1/2 diameter

Small square
1 piece	1/4 × 4 × 11
2 pegs	1 1/2 × 3/8 diameter

---

4. The smaller square is made in the same way, but there is no need for the slot and the back of the blade could be straight.

5. The accuracy of your square can be tested on anything round, that is of greater diameter than the distance between the pegs, such as a paint can. Use the square with the pegs tight against the outside and draw along the blade in three or more positions. If the lines all cross at the same point, that is the center of the circle and your square will be accurate on any curve.

LARGE SQUARE

The common squares used in woodworking may reach 12 inches from an edge. Exceptionally they may reach 24 inches, but for a square line of greater length they are not much use. If you extend a line drawn with one of those squares the risk of error increases the further you go.

It is better to make a large square for use in the shop or when laying out shapes in the yard or elsewhere. Because most of us deal with standard sheets of plywood and other materials, a suitable size is 48 inches, or a little more, along one or both edges.

It is a geometric fact that if a triangle has sides in the proportion 3:4:5 the angle between the short sides will be 90 degrees, so if we draw such a triangle with at least one short side longer than we need, we will have made a square corner between lines that are long enough to bring our marking-out square to a convenient size. Of course, the square you make does not have to be in the proportion 3:4:5—that is merely the device for obtaining a 90 degree corner.

The square is most conveniently made of plywood. It could be a simple triangle or you can shape the long edge. Cutting away the center lightens the tool and makes it easier to pick up (Fig. 12-9A).

1. Plane a straight edge on your plywood so you can erect a line square to it. Decide on the units you will use. For a 48-inch length they could be 12 inches, so 3:4:5 becomes 36:48:60 inches.

2. From the point where you want the square

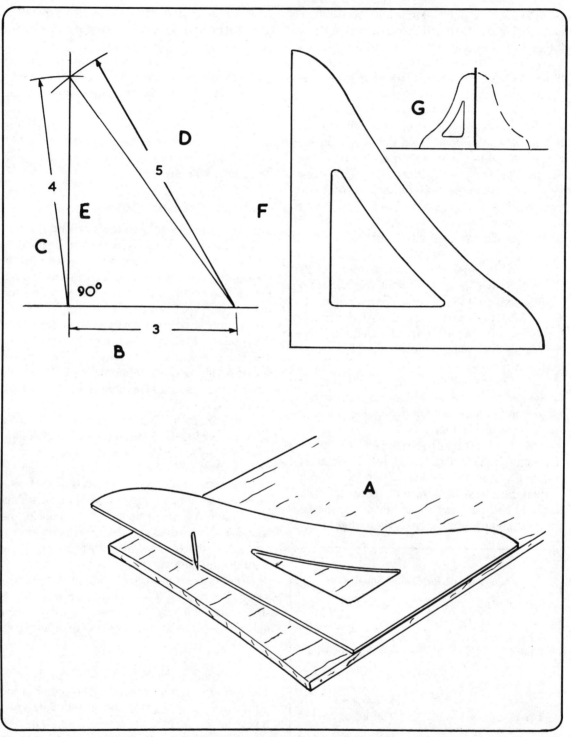

Fig. 12-9. A large square (A) can be marked out geometrically (B-E) and can be tested by turning over a straight edge (F,G).

line to be, measure three units (36 inches) to another point along the edge (Fig. 12-9B). From the first point, measure four units (48 inches) from the edge (Fig. 12-9C). You can swing a tape-rule, with a pencil against the 48-inch mark, to make a short arc that will obviously cross a squared line. From the other point, measure five units (60 inches) to a point on that arc (Fig. 12-9D). Draw a line from the first edge mark to pass through the marked point on the arc (Fig. 12-9E).

3. That line is square to the edge. Plane it and you can mark the rest of the tool to any shape or size you wish (Fig. 12-9F).

4. You can check the accuracy of your large square by putting it on a straight edge and drawing a line. Turn it over and the second position

should match the line drawn against the first (Fig. 12-9G).

5. It might be worthwhile staining or marking the square in some other distinctive way so you can easily find it among sheets of plywood, and are unlikely to mistake it for spare plywood and cut into it.

BENCH HOOK

Something to make and keep in the shop is one or a pair of bench hooks. The tool hooks over the edge of the bench and you press wood into it while sawing, but once you have it, you will find many other uses. If you have a pair, they can be used to support a long board you are working on.

Sizes are not critical, but you should consider

Fig. 12-10. A bench hook helps you hold wood for sawing on the bench.

the width of the bench top front board and not extend over it. Make the hook long enough to take the widest board you expect to saw.

The bench hook shown (Fig. 12-10) has one block cut back each side (Fig. 12-11A) so the saw drops through onto the hook instead of damaging the bench top. When the hook is turned over the block is full-width, which gives support when planing the end of a board. There can be saw guides cut in it (Fig. 12-11B) for sawing picture frame molding. The guide slots are not full-depth and molding being cut should be rested on scrap wood.

Assembly is accomplished with dowels. There could be counterbored screws, but do not have exposed screw heads that might blunt tools.

1. Make the main board (Fig. 12-11C) and check that it is flat so it will not rock, and that it has parallel edges.

2. Cut the two blocks. The full-width one

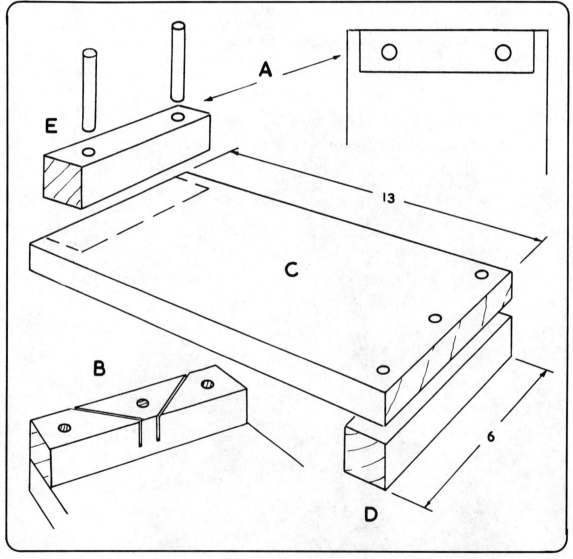

Fig. 12-11. The parts of a bench hook are dowelled together and may have guides cut for sawing miters.

(Fig. 12-11D) can be left too long to trim after fixing, but cut the ends of the other square (Fig. 12-11E).

3. Locate each block on the main board squarely and drill through for dowels—3/8-inch or 1/2-inch diameter should be satisfactory.

4. Glue the parts together, then trim off any surplus edges, ends, or dowels.

5. If the miter guide slots are wanted, mark them and cut them with the saw that will be used on molding (Fig. 12-11B).

Materials List for Bench Hook	
1 main board	× 6 × 13
2 blocks	1 1/4 × 1 1/4 × 6

THIN WOOD VISE

If you want to hand plane the edge of a long, thin piece of wood, it needs support underneath to prevent bending. If you grip it in a vise at the side of the bench, you cannot support the whole length and the finished planed edge will not be straight. The wood needs to rest on the top of the bench to keep it straight, but there has to be some way of holding it upright. That can be arranged with a special vise (Fig. 12-12). Two versions are shown on the drawing (Fig. 12-13). Both depend on the wedging action of acute tapers.

Any wood can be used, but the vises will be stronger and more durable if made from dense hardwood. Sizes are not critical. The height should reach more than halfway up the wood you expect to plane, if possible. A vise could be screwed to

Fig. 12-12. A block with dowels into holes in the bench top will act as a vise for holding thin wood on edge.

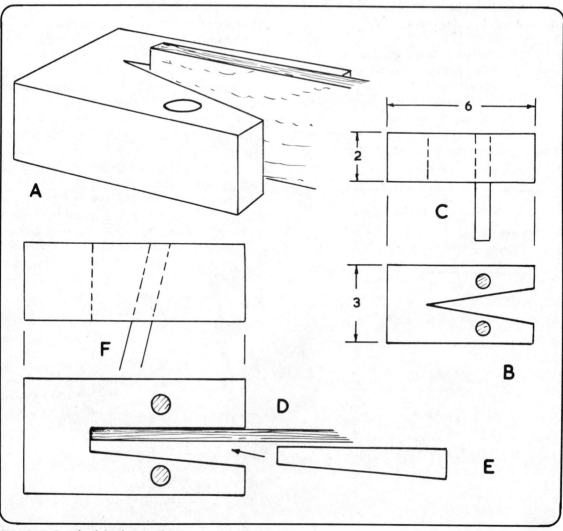

Fig. 12-13. Details of the thin wood vise.

the bench top, but that would leave it in the way of other work. A method of mounting with lift-out dowels is recommended.

1. In the simplest vise (Fig. 12-13A) the block of wood is cut with an acute V notch (Fig. 12-13B). The angle should be between 10 and 20 degrees. More important is that both sides of the cut are upright.

2. The block is shown with a pair of upright dowels, which could be 3/4-inch diameter (Fig. 12-13C). They are towards the open end, so the

planing action is unlikely to lift the vise. The dowels could slope (see paragraph 7).

3. Drill the bench top to take the dowels. This is most accurately done with the drill through the holes in the vise block before the dowels are glued into it.

4. For ease in fitting the dowels into the bench holes, taper their ends and reduce the size of the extended parts by sanding. Wax on the dowels can assist entry.

5. The other vise has one side of the V cut in line with the wood it is to hold (Fig. 12-13D).

Instead of relying on friction, the wood can be locked with a wedge (Fig. 12-13E). The block may be the same size as the first one. If the sloping side is at about 10 degrees, one wedge can cope with variations in thickness of wood of about 1/4 inch. If you want to be able to hold everything from veneer up to 1/2 inch, you will need a thick wedge for thin material and a thinner one for the stouter strips.

6. Cut the wedge to the same angle as the slot. Adjust its width at the thinner end so it is close to the end of the slot when it will take the thinnest wood you want it to grip. In use it can be pressed in by hand. A jerk backwards on the wood being held will free it.

7. The dowels could be upright, as described for the first vise, but they are shown sloping forward (Fig. 12-13F). A planing action then tightens them and there is no risk of the vise lifting, even if the dowels have worn loose in the bench holes.

Materials List for Thin Wood Vise	
1 block	2 × 3 × 6
2 pegs	5 × 3/4 diameter

Index

Edited by Cherie R. Blazer